What NRIs Are Not Told About India

A plain-English guide to the mind, money and law behind every cross-border decision

CA Sagar Soman

notionpress.com
INDIA · SINGAPORE · MALAYSIA

ISBN

Paperback 979-8-90540-871-7
Hardcase 979-8-90540-916-5

CONTENTS

AUTHOR'S NOTE

For more than two decades, the same few sentences have reached me from almost every corner of the world where Indians live and work.

"Sir, this maturity is tax-free, no?"

"Can I send this money back abroad?"

"My nominee will get everything, na?"

"I am returning to India next year. Anything I should check?"

The countries change. The time zones change. The accents change. The professional profiles change. The question often does not.

I have heard these questions from NRIs across more than twenty-five countries—from business owners in the Gulf, senior professionals in North America, doctors and consultants in the United Kingdom, technology leaders in Singapore, families in Australia, executives in Europe, seafarers, entrepreneurs, investors, returning Indians and Indian-origin families who have built impressive lives far away from home. Many of them hold positions of great responsibility. Many have created wealth, reputation and respect in competitive global environments. As an Indian, it is difficult not to feel proud when one sees how deeply and confidently Indians have entered the world—leading companies, building practices, running businesses, managing capital, serving institutions and creating a name for themselves in countries that were once only destinations on a passport.

And yet, after all that success, when the conversation turns to India, the uncertainty is often surprisingly similar.

Which account should I use? Will this money be taxed? Can I bring it back? Can I send it out again? What happens if I return? What happens after me? Is nomination enough? Will my foreign country ask questions? Is India seeing me as an NRI, a resident, or something in between?

That is the paradox of the NRI life. A person may understand the world very well and still feel uncertain about India. Not because he is careless. Not because he is financially immature. But because cross-border life does not fit into one simple answer.

This book begins in that gap.

Not in a statute.

Not in a product brochure.

Not in a sales meeting.

It begins in the distance between what the NRI asks and what the advisor thinks he has been asked.

I have seen this distance from both sides. For part of my own working life, I lived outside India. I know what it means to carry India from another country—not as an idea, but as a living file. Parents in India. Money in more than one currency. Bank accounts in more than one system. Tax questions in more than one jurisdiction. A return plan that keeps moving. A sense of belonging that does not obey geography.

Later, as a Chartered Accountant, I sat on the other side of the table—listening, explaining, questioning, teaching and often slowing down conversations that were moving faster than the facts allowed. Over 20-plus years of professional work, and through countless conversations with NRIs, returning Indians, Indian-origin families, advisors, relationship managers and institutional teams, one pattern became impossible to ignore: the NRI is often advised through fragments.

A product benefit here. A tax sentence there. A banking assumption somewhere else. A treaty reference used too casually. A nomination form treated as succession planning. A "tax-free" statement made without asking the most important follow-up question: tax-free where?

The issue is not always lack of sincerity. Most advisors I have worked with are sincere. Many are hardworking. Many genuinely want to serve the NRI client well. The issue is that sincerity is not a framework. Confidence is not a framework. Product knowledge is not a framework. In NRI advisory, a well-meaning answer can still become a wrong answer if the advisor does not know which legal system he is standing in.

That is why this book was written.

It was written because the NRI is not asking only about India. He is carrying India, his country of residence, his family, his bank accounts, his tax status, his future return, his documents and his legacy in the same file. That file cannot be handled by one-line comfort. It needs better questions.

This conviction was strengthened further through my work with NRI-facing professionals in the financial services industry. One important part of that journey was training more than 200 senior NRI sales professionals at HDFC Life. Standing in those training rooms confirmed what client conversations had already taught me: NRI business cannot be built only on enthusiasm, opportunity size or product training. It needs a common language. It needs structure. It needs the ability to separate Indian tax from FEMA, FEMA from banking, banking from repatriation, repatriation from foreign tax, nomination from succession, and client comfort from professional conclusion.

This book is my attempt to provide that structure.

Let me be precise about what it promises. This book will not turn every advisor into a tax lawyer, FEMA consultant, foreign-tax professional, succession lawyer, immigration advisor or compliance officer. It does not pretend to. Each of those disciplines deserves its own professional depth.

What this book will do is more practical and, in my view, more urgent. It will help the advisor become more alert before he speaks, more structured before he explains, more careful before he comforts, and more willing to say, "This needs to be checked," when the facts demand it. It will help him hear the second question hidden inside the first. It will help him know which question he is answering, which question he is not answering, and when the right professional must be brought into the room.

That is not hesitation. That is responsible advisory conduct.

A domestic client may ask one question and remain largely within one legal environment. An NRI client may ask one question and quietly open five doors. One door may belong to Indian income tax. One to FEMA. One to RBI banking routes. One to the law of the country where he lives. One to family and succession. The advisor's role is not to pretend that all five doors are the same. His role is to know which door has opened.

The detailed frameworks of this book will come immediately after this note. I will not unfold them here. For now, it is enough to say that the book is built on three disciplines: knowing where the advisor is standing, knowing when the law reads the client differently, and knowing how to advise with discipline before giving assurance.

I have written this book for individual life insurance advisors, NRI-facing financial professionals, relationship managers, training heads, insurance institutions, compliance teams and serious NRI readers who want to understand the real questions behind cross-border decisions. Some will use it to improve client conversations. Some will use it to train teams. Some will use it to reduce careless promises. Some NRIs will read it and finally understand why a sentence that sounded simple for years was never simple in law.

But the central figure of this book is still the NRI.

Not as a market. Not as a premium segment. Not as a remittance source. Not as a sales opportunity.

As a person living between countries, duties, memories, rules and unfinished decisions.

Before advising an NRI, one must first understand the NRI.

That is the emotional foundation of this book. The technical chapters stand on top of it.

A professional boundary must also be stated clearly. This book is educational in nature. It is not personal tax, legal, investment, insurance, FEMA, succession, immigration or foreign-law advice. Cross-border situations depend on facts, documents, dates, residential status, source of funds, account route, applicable law and the country involved. Where the facts require professional review, the right professional must be brought in.

I say this not as legal caution, but as professional respect—respect for the law, respect for the client, respect for the advisor's role, and respect for the damage that a casual sentence can cause when life is spread across borders.

If this book has one ambition, it is to shape a different kind of advisor. Not the loudest advisor. Not the fastest advisor. Not the advisor who answers every NRI question immediately. But the advisor who pauses; who listens beyond the sentence; who understands the person before the paperwork; who identifies the law before simplifying it; who separates the systems before joining the dots; who records the evidence before relying on memory; and who knows that trust is not built by saying "no issue," but by knowing which issue must first be checked.

An NRI does not merely cross a border. His money crosses. His family crosses. His tax position crosses. His identity crosses. His documents cross. His dreams cross.

The advisor who serves him well must learn to think across borders before he speaks across the table.

That is the discipline this book was written to teach.

CA Sagar Soman

Nagpur, India

June 2026

THE THREE FRAMEWORKS BEHIND THIS BOOK

This book is not a collection of NRI rules.

It is not a glossary of FEMA, tax, banking, insurance, repatriation and succession terms.

It is not a product manual dressed up as advisory education.

It is an attempt to do something I felt was missing for a long time: to give the NRI's financial journey one clear teaching architecture.

Over more than two decades of working with NRIs, returning Indians, Indian-origin families, advisors and institutional teams, I found plenty of information in the market. Rules were available. Articles were available. Tax notes were available. Product explanations were available. Bank processes were available. Individual answers were available.

What was missing was a framework.

A way to hold the entire NRI journey together.

From identity to banking.

From banking to taxation.

From taxation to investment.

From investment to return.

From return to legacy.

From legacy to documentation.

And from documentation to responsible advisory conduct.

That gap mattered to me personally, because I have not seen the NRI journey only from the outside. I have lived part of it myself. I know what it means to carry India while living outside India—the emotional pull, the practical confusion, the dependence on advisors, the half-understood rules, the delayed questions, the feeling that one is expected to know everything simply because one has moved abroad.

But an NRI does not automatically become a cross-border law expert because he earns in another country.

He still needs clarity.

He still needs structure.

He still needs someone to ask the right questions before giving him comfort.

That realisation stayed with me.

Later, when I began advising, teaching and training on NRI matters, the same pattern repeated itself again and again. The client's question was usually small. The life behind it was not. The advisor's intention was often good. The structure behind the answer was often missing.

That is where these three frameworks were born.

Not in one sitting.

Not as branding.

Not as clever terminology.

They were built slowly, over years of conversations, mistakes observed, questions repeated, training rooms handled, client anxieties heard, and advisory situations studied across countries.

The purpose was simple: if NRI life is cross-border, advisory thinking must also become cross-border.

A domestic financial journey usually travels through one primary legal environment. The NRI financial journey does not. It crosses identity, citizenship, residence, FEMA, RBI banking routes, Indian income tax, TDS, DTAA, foreign tax, reporting, investment access, return planning, succession and family documentation.

One client.

One question.

Many systems.

That is why ordinary product knowledge is not enough.

That is why enthusiasm is not enough.

That is why confidence is not enough.

The advisor needs a way to think.

This book is built on three such ways of thinking: **The Compliance Highway Rule™**, **The NRI Kaalchakra™**, and **The NRI INDIA Mantra™**.

They are not separate slogans. They are connected disciplines.

The Highway gives the map.

The Kaalchakra gives the timing lens.

INDIA gives the operating discipline.

Together, they create the backbone of this book.

The first discipline: know where you are standing

The first framework is **The Compliance Highway Rule™**.

Before an advisor answers an NRI, he must know which legal checkpoint he is standing at.

This sounds simple. In practice, it is where many mistakes begin.

A client asks about maturity. The advisor answers tax.

A client asks about sending money abroad. The advisor answers banking.

A client asks about nomination. The advisor answers claim process.

A client asks about return to India. The advisor answers emotionally.

But the real question may be sitting somewhere else.

The Compliance Highway Rule™ was designed to stop this confusion. It teaches the advisor to locate the issue before answering it. Is the conversation about the person and his papers? Is it about the route through which money moves? Is it about the tax, treaty, reporting or cost consequence?

The detailed structure will unfold in Chapter 2. For now, the reader should remember only this: in NRI advisory, the first responsibility is not to answer fast. The first responsibility is to know which counter you are standing at.

A right answer at the wrong counter is still a wrong advisory experience.

The second discipline: know when the law changes

The second framework is **The NRI Kaalchakra™**.

This framework came from one of the most common blind spots I have seen in NRI conversations: timing.

People think life changes when the flight lands.

Law does not always behave that neatly.

A person may leave India in one year, become resident abroad under another system, continue holding Indian accounts, visit India repeatedly, invest from abroad, file returns in two countries and still assume that one label—"NRI"—explains everything.

It does not.

Similarly, return to India is rarely just a homecoming. It is a change of clocks. The foreign country may read the person one way. FEMA may read him another way. Indian income tax may begin reading him differently from a particular date or year. The family may think he has "come back". The law may ask, "For what purpose, and from when?"

That is why this book uses the word **Kaalchakra** in its plain, professional and non-religious sense: the wheel of time.

It is a teaching metaphor for the NRI's legal timing.

The NRI Kaalchakra™ reminds the advisor that cross-border life creates legal jet lag. The body may cross the border in one day. The legal systems may not synchronise on the same day.

This framework will be introduced fully later in the book, especially when the return-to-India journey becomes central. At this stage, the reader only needs to carry one thought: in NRI advisory, timing is not a footnote. Timing can change the answer.

Before giving assurance, the advisor must learn to synchronise.

The third discipline: know how to advise

The third framework is **The NRI INDIA Mantra™**.

This is deliberately placed at the end of the book.

It is not introduced as the starting slogan because it is meant to be earned. The reader must first understand the NRI mind, the compliance map, the banking routes, the tax consequences, the investment realities, GIFT IFSC, return, legacy and documentation. Only then can advisory conduct be reduced into a practical operating standard.

That operating standard is INDIA.

Identify. Navigate. Define. Isolate. Anchor.

These five words are not meant to impress the reader. They are meant to steady the advisor.

Because the final test of advisory knowledge is not how much the advisor knows. It is what he does when the client asks a dangerous question in simple language.

"Tax-free, right?"

"Repatriable, right?"

"Nominee will get it, right?"

"Return to India is simple, right?"

At that moment, the advisor needs more than memory. He needs conduct.

He must identify the person. Navigate the route. Define the question. Isolate the systems. Anchor the answer.

Chapter 10 will unfold this fully. For now, the reader should know that INDIA is the final operating discipline of the book—the point where knowledge becomes professional behaviour.

Why these frameworks matter

The NRI world is large. The opportunity is large. But the responsibility is larger.

India now has one of the most significant global communities in the world. Indians are leading companies, building businesses, practising medicine, managing capital, serving institutions, running technology teams, sailing ships, building careers, supporting families and carrying India into every major financial centre.

That success deserves better advisory language.

An NRI should not be reduced to a premium segment.

He should not be treated only as a remittance source.

He should not be given casual comfort just because his question sounds simple.

And the advisor serving him should not be left to manage cross-border complexity with fragments, scripts and confidence alone.

This book was written because the NRI financial journey deserves a proper framework.

To the best of my study of the available material and my experience in this field, very little has attempted to hold the NRI's entire financial journey together in this manner—from the mind of the NRI to the movement of money, from tax to return, from legacy to advisory discipline.

That is the role these three frameworks play.

They do not replace the law.

They do not replace professional advice.

They do not make every advisor a tax lawyer, FEMA consultant, foreign-tax professional or succession lawyer.

They do something more practical.

They teach the advisor how to pause correctly.

How to locate the issue.

How to see timing.

How to avoid mixing systems.

How to ask better questions.

How to know when the matter must move to a qualified professional.

And how to serve the NRI with clarity, dignity and responsibility.

The reader should therefore carry these three frameworks throughout the book.

When the issue feels scattered, return to the Highway.

When the client's life is moving across borders, return to the Kaalchakra.

When the answer is forming too quickly, return to INDIA.

Because the future of NRI advisory will not belong merely to the advisor who knows more products.

It will belong to the advisor who can think across borders before he speaks across the table.

PROFESSIONAL NOTE

This book is written for educational and professional learning purposes.

Its purpose is to help readers understand the mind, money and law behind NRI decisions in plain English. It is not personal tax, legal, investment, insurance, FEMA, succession, immigration, foreign-law or foreign-tax advice for any specific person, family, transaction, advisor or institution.

NRI situations are fact-sensitive. A change in citizenship, residential status, country of residence, account route, source of funds, date of transaction, policy terms, asset location, family structure or documentation can change the answer. Readers should therefore verify the current legal, tax, regulatory and procedural position before acting or advising.

The law and regulatory references in this book have been reviewed for publication in June 2026, including relevant transition from the Income-tax Act, 1961 to the Income-tax Act, 2025 wherever applicable. However, tax laws, FEMA regulations, RBI directions, IRDAI regulations, IFSCA rules, forms, banking procedures, treaty positions and foreign-country laws may change from time to time. Readers must consult the relevant statute, rule, notification, circular, regulator, bank, insurer, tax authority or qualified professional before relying on any position in a live case.

This book deliberately separates Indian income tax, FEMA, RBI banking rules, insurance regulation, IFSCA/GIFT IFSC, DTAA, foreign tax and succession law. These systems should not be mixed. DTAA is not automatic exemption. Nomination is not succession. NRE does not mean every issue is tax-free. GIFT IFSC is not a tax-free escape. A product feature is not a legal conclusion.

All examples, names, characters, locations and situations used in this book are illustrative. Some may be fictional, some may be composite, and some may be simplified for teaching. They are not intended to identify any particular client, advisor, institution, insurer, bank, family or real transaction. Any resemblance to an actual person, family, institution or situation is purely coincidental. No confidential client information has been used.

Where the book refers to well-known public figures, publicly reported situations or widely discussed citizenship, residence, tax, succession or cross-border examples, such references are used only as educational illustrations of a legal or advisory principle. They are based on information available in the public domain and are not intended as comment, criticism, endorsement, investigation or conclusion about any individual, family, institution or decision.

Any reference to an institution, product category, jurisdiction, regulator, bank, insurer, intermediary or professional role is made only for educational context. It should not be read as endorsement, criticism, recommendation, guarantee or professional opinion on any specific product, institution, structure or course of action.

Advisors and financial professionals should use this book to improve diagnosis, questioning, documentation, escalation and responsible conduct. It should not be used to make promises, bypass compliance processes, give guarantees, or offer conclusions beyond one's role, licence, training or professional competence.

The spirit of this book is simple: understand the NRI, separate the systems, verify the facts, document the trail, and advise with responsibility.

PART I

THE NRI MIND AND THE COMPLIANCE MAP

CHAPTER 1

UNDERSTANDING THE NRI

The Life Behind the Label

1.1 WHAT DOES "NRI" REALLY MEAN?

Say the word *home* to ten NRIs and you will not hear the same answer twice.

For one, home is the flat in Borivali where his parents still keep his school trophies in a cupboard.

For another, home is a rented apartment in Dubai, where the children speak better English than Malayalam and know India mostly through summer holidays.

For a third, home is not a place at all. It is a recurring question: *Where will we finally settle?*

The word is the same. The coordinates are not.

That is the first mistake many advisors make with NRIs. They treat the word as a category. In reality, it is a condition—of distance, duty, belonging, obligation and unfinished decisions.

An NRI may be a twenty-eight-year-old software engineer in Dublin, sending money home for a sister's wedding. He may be a fifty-eight-year-old plumber in Muscat, sharing a room with five other men and counting the years left before return. She may be a nurse in Manchester, a ship officer from Kochi, a boutique owner in Nairobi, a consultant in Singapore, or a second-generation Indian-origin teenager in Toronto who has never lived in India but still calls India "back home" because everyone around the dinner table does.

Same word. Different lives.

Different passports. Different bank accounts. Different tax outcomes. Different emotional maps.

And that is why the advisor who begins with product has already arrived late. The advisor must first understand the person behind the word.

The financial industry often imagines the NRI as one person: a globally earning professional in Dubai, Singapore, London or New York, financially comfortable and ready for a large-ticket policy conversation.

That image is convenient. It is also incomplete.

NRIs are not a luxury segment. They are a life segment.

They are sons, daughters, spouses, parents, workers, founders, nurses, seafarers, consultants, technicians and retirees. Some left India to build wealth. Some left because there was no other choice. Some send money home out of love. Some do it out of duty. Most do it out of both.

Before an advisor explains a policy, a tax position or a repatriation rule, he must understand this: the NRI does not merely live outside India. He lives between India and somewhere else.

For the advisor, this emotional map is not decorative. It is practical.

A client who sends money to India every month may be telling you something about responsibility. A client who maintains an NRE account for years may be telling you something about return, family liquidity or unfinished India plans. A client who buys property in his hometown may be telling you something about belonging. A client who delays estate planning is often telling you something about discomfort, not ignorance.

The advisor who reads only the proposal form will miss these signals. The advisor who reads the life behind the form will ask better questions.

A word on the word itself. Through this chapter, *NRI* is used the way families use it at the dinner table—a warm shorthand for Indians and people of Indian origin living abroad. The law is less romantic. *Non-resident, NRI, OCI, PIO* and *foreign citizen of Indian origin* do not mean the same thing, and the difference can decide how a person is taxed, how he may bank and what he is allowed to own. Chapter 2 draws those lines precisely. This chapter has the quieter task that must come first—understanding the life before the label is ever tested.

1.2 THE SACRIFICE FEW SEE

Behind every NRI is a journey. And behind every journey is a quiet, often invisible, sacrifice.

Not all NRIs leave India chasing dreams of Silicon Valley or the Wall Street glow. Sometimes it is a career posting—a deputation to London, a promotion to lead a project in Frankfurt, a management transfer to Singapore. The offer comes with better pay, global exposure and a new title. Hidden in the fine print is a clause no one discusses: you will miss home in ways you never imagined.

Leaving India is not just about geography. It is a transition of identity.

What gets left behind is not just a house—it is home.

> Home, where the TV volume was always a little too loud. Where chai came without a clock and guests came without a plan. Where the neighbour's child called your mother aunty and knew your birthday better than your cousin in Canada. You trade that for the efficiency of systems and the silence of loneliness.

At first, it is manageable. New job, new country, new routines. The fridge is stocked with ready-to-eat biryani and frozen packets. You try to cook your mother's aloo sabzi, following each step from an online video recipe site. But no matter how precisely you follow the method, something is missing—the aroma, the warmth, the feeling that the food was made for you.

Then the emotional tax begins to show up quietly.

You finish work early one evening and walk into an apartment that is efficient, clean and completely silent—not the silence of peace, but the silence of emptiness. You video-call your parents and notice that your father now takes longer to get up from the sofa. You miss your sister's baby shower. You send gifts, but the moment is already gone.

You hear that the small shop next to your childhood home has been replaced by a four-storey commercial building. The aunties you once waved to from your balcony have moved. The new neighbours speak a different language. Even your gully has changed — narrower, louder, unrecognisable.

You return after four years for a wedding and struggle to navigate your own neighbourhood.

But what hits you hardest isn't just the skyline—it's the loss of the small joys.

Your old weekend routine of buying groceries and filling up the fridge feels important where you live now. But back in India? It's an afterthought. People press a button and tea gets delivered with the biscuits. Your friends don't worry about stocking up.

But this convenience hides something else—the loss of the familiar. That uncle's kirana store, where you once handed over a handwritten grocery list and came back after two hours to pick up the packet... it's gone. Replaced by a dark store or a glass-fronted supermarket.

Your son—born and raised in the UK—sits beside you during a cricket match. You cheer when India scores. He cheers when England takes a wicket. You look at him, and for a brief second, you smile and ache at the same time. You wonder whether you have passed on your passport, but not your identity.

Later, you scroll through your Diwali timeline. Everyone's arguing about pollution and why firecrackers should be banned. And you get it. You agree.

But you also remember how loud those same people are on the roads the next morning—honking through traffic, refusing to carpool, revving engines in silent zones. The contradiction stings.

Because festivals were one of the few ways you could still feel Indian. And now, even that feels debated.

Your sacrifices were never only economic. They were cultural, emotional, and invisible.

Your parents don't remind you of this. Your friends don't mention it.

But you know it. You live it.

If you are an advisor hoping to truly serve NRIs, you need to see this side of the story. Because behind every remittance, every investment, and every policy purchased—is a longing. A longing to stay connected. To protect from a distance. To belong, even when you no longer fully live there.

That is the real cost of leaving home.

1.3 THE CULTURAL SHIFT: FROM JOINT DECISIONS TO SOLO RESPONSIBILITY

In India, money is never just money.

It is a shared language. A family affair. A slow-burning conversation that unfolds over dinner, during power cuts, or while reading the Sunday newspaper.

When someone receives a first salary, an elder says: *Start a savings plan, do not waste it.* When someone gets married, the chorus is almost predictable: *Buy gold. Gold is security.* When a new job is announced, a relative chimes in: *Now is the time to think long-term—maybe take a good life insurance plan.*

In most Indian households there is always someone who becomes the financial compass. A financially wise parent. An elder sibling who has handled the family's taxes for years. An aunt who knows which bank gives the best deposit rate. Or the family elder, whose word becomes the final say on where the family invests, what it saves and how it protects.

This ecosystem of inherited wisdom is comforting—even when it arrives unsolicited. You do not always have to figure things out. You simply follow the rhythm of the family.

Until one day, you leave.

You board a flight to the Gulf, the United States or Australia—chasing opportunity, growth and a better future. And the chorus fades.

Now you earn more than ever. But the questions get heavier.

> Should I save here or in India? Do I need insurance there or here? What about my parents? My child? My retirement?

And now, the person answering those questions is you.

For the first time, you are not just the breadwinner. You are the planner. The executor. The final word.

It is liberating. And it is lonely.

And then comes the classic dilemma: spend or save?

You walk through a mall in California, or Dubai, or Birmingham. The discounts are tempting. The lifestyle is seductive. A smartwatch, a designer wallet, a spontaneous holiday?

And just as you are about to swipe the card, your inner desi voice whispers: *Did you save first? What about Papa's health cover? Did you buy that term plan you were planning last year?*

It is a daily tug-of-war between indulgence and instinct. Between freedom and responsibility. Between living abroad and staying rooted within.

This is the invisible emotional weight every NRI carries. And that is where the advisor's role becomes more serious than product explanation. He steps into a vacuum—not to replace the family, but to become the missing voice of financial wisdom.

To serve an NRI is to understand his dual life—his ambitions and his guilt, his shopping cart and his sleepless nights.

If the advisor can become a calm sounding board in that loneliness, the conversation changes. The client no longer feels he is being sold to. He feels someone has understood the responsibility he is carrying.

That is where trust begins.

1.4 THE COMFORT OF THE KNOWN

When an NRI has an investable surplus in hand, the mind does not immediately go global.

It goes local. Not current-local—but emotionally local.

Most NRIs instinctively weigh only two or three geographies: the country they live in now, the country they came from, and perhaps one or two where they once worked. Those become the only places that count when money is on the table. The reason is simple—people do not trust PDFs. They trust lived experience.

You can show an NRI a glossy brochure, charts and projections. But if he has not seen someone he knows earn from it—or if he has heard one cautionary story—he will politely nod and pass. *Paper pe sab sahi hota hai*—on paper, everything looks right. What actually builds confidence in an Indian mind is the friend who made money in property back home, the uncle whose policy matured and paid exactly what was promised, the former colleague in Dubai who now owns two flats in Nagpur. That is what makes him think: *even I can do this.*

The reverse is equally true. A country he has never lived in—however stable or advanced—feels too foreign to trust with money. This is not irrationality. When you are living thousands of miles from your parents, juggling two time zones and filing compliance declarations on a Friday night, the last thing you want is to decode unfamiliar rules in a place you do not even visit.

So when an NRI evaluates an Indian financial product, he is rarely asking only what the return is. He is asking whether the money can come back when it is needed, whether the account used to pay for it will matter later, whether the maturity will be credited smoothly, whether the proceeds will be taxable in India, abroad or both, whether his spouse will understand the paperwork if something happens to him, and whether his children—who may never live in India—will be able to claim what he intended for them.

A resident Indian may evaluate a product as an investment. An NRI evaluates it as a cross-border arrangement, even when he does not use that phrase. This is where many advisory conversations fail: they answer the product question but miss the life question.

And even when the NRI has surrendered his Indian passport, India stays on the shortlist. Not as one option among many—as home base. The streets may have changed and the skyline may be new, but the language, the family and the roots remain. With them comes a quiet belief: *at least in India, someone will help me if things go wrong.*

This is the comfort of the known—not the comfort of systems, but the comfort of people. It is also why an NRI will overtrust the familiar even when it is inefficient: money left idle in fixed deposits because a cousin said they were safe; gold bought every year because that is what the elders advised at every wedding. The instinct underneath is control—and for the NRI, control comes from familiarity, not from sophistication.

This is where an NRI advisor plays a larger role than he may realise.

He is not merely explaining a product. He is bridging the emotional gap between decision and doubt.

If he can speak the language of home and the logic of finance, if he can explain structures without jargon, and if he can help the NRI feel clear rather than cornered, he becomes a familiar point of clarity in a cross-border life.

The advisor's job is not to pitch India. India is already in the client's heart.

The advisor's job is to help the client examine India with affection and discipline together.

Because behind many NRI decisions is a quiet wish:

I hope my money can grow where I once grew up.

1.5 THE PRIDE THAT DISTANCE SHARPENS

Pride, for an NRI, does not always erupt on national holidays or in viral reels. More often it grows quietly—with every milestone India reaches while he watches from far away. A space mission.

A global summit hosted with precision. A new metro line connecting cities he once left behind.

It begins slowly. You are in Toronto, scrolling through the evening news, when a headline makes you pause—"India overtakes Japan to become the world's fourth-largest economy." Your eyes stop. Not out of surprise, but out of a quiet, measured pride: *we are getting there.*

This is no longer a sleeping giant. It is a country on the move, and you are watching it from a distance. In that moment, something shifts inside. The country you left for "better prospects" is now building some of the world's most talked-about success stories—and even while living abroad, you feel connected to that rise.

It is a view only NRIs have. Like watching from thirty-five thousand feet—a perspective shaped not by daily traffic jams or unplanned city layouts, but by progress reports, global headlines and comparisons.

You start noticing India differently.

Digital payments are no longer a convenience story; they are part of everyday national infrastructure. Indian companies are no longer asking only for global approval; many are competing for global relevance. Space missions, highways, metros, manufacturing corridors, startup stories and policy ambitions begin to appear in conversations abroad. Some headlines are exaggerated. Some figures are still debated. But the larger signal is hard to miss: India is no longer only the country the NRI remembers. It is also a country in motion.

These are signals to the diaspora that India is no longer only emotional. It is also economically relevant, institutionally ambitious and increasingly central to global conversations.

When NRIs see this transformation—when they watch a country they once left for "better prospects" now stand taller in the world—they feel a different kind of pull. The country they left is not standing still. The place that shaped them is still shaping itself.

This is pride not born only of sentiment, but of substance. For an advisor working with NRIs, this awareness is essential.

When you speak to NRIs, speak of the India they miss, but also recognise the India they are trying to understand from a distance. Bring this India into the conversation not as a pitch, but as perspective.

The India in their memory and the India in the headlines are not always the same. A good advisor helps them hold both with maturity.

1.6 REMITTING WITH LOVE: THE DIASPORA'S SILENT CONTRIBUTION

India's economic narrative today is not just one of resilience—it is one of reinvention. In FY 2023–24, India's GDP grew by 8.2%, making it the fastest-growing major economy in the world, despite global headwinds (Source: Ministry of Statistics and Programme Implementation, Press Release, May 2024). This growth is not a one-off. It reflects deep structural momentum, driven by public infrastructure investments, renewed manufacturing output, and rapid digital adoption across sectors.

Even more compelling is India's consumer base. With a projected 580 million middle-class consumers by 2030, the domestic market offers a scale few nations can match (Source: World Economic Forum & Bain & Company, "The Rise of India's Middle Class," 2022). This middle-income population is the engine behind a consumption economy—accounting for nearly 70% of GDP—that fuels sustained demand for goods, services, housing, healthcare, and insurance (Source: World Bank India Overview, 2023).

For NRI investors evaluating long-term opportunities, India represents not just a sentiment-driven bet on one's homeland—but a data-driven, demographically backed case for serious long-term evaluation.

The Global Indian – NRI Demographics & Client Profiling

With over 35 million Non-Resident Indians (NRIs) and Persons of Indian Origin (PIOs) worldwide, India's diaspora is not only the largest but also among the most economically influential globally (Source: Ministry of External Affairs; World Bank Blogs, Dec 2024). But the real insight lies in where these Indians reside—because geography shapes financial behaviour.

The Gulf region is home to 17% of this diaspora, with the UAE (10%) and Saudi Arabia (7%) being dominant hubs. These NRIs are often income earners focused on remittances, family responsibilities, and secure financial instruments. The United States (15%) and Canada (8%) follow closely, representing a more compliance-driven, legacy-planning-focused segment.

Other major clusters include Malaysia (8%) and the United Kingdom (5%), with Australia also emerging as a key destination, though specific figures vary. Together, these six countries account for over half of India's global diaspora—a concentrated opportunity for Indian financial advisors.

Client profiling begins with geography. An NRI's country of residence influences everything: from the regulatory restrictions they face to their emotional connect with Indian financial products. For an insurance professional, this is not data—it's direction.

India's ₹11 Lakh Crore Signal – The Emotional and Economic Power of Remittances

India's leadership as the world's largest recipient of remittances—crossing $129.1 billion (₹11 lakh crore approx) in 2024—isn't just a statistic. It's a deeply human story. These inflows aren't driven by investment motives alone. They are powered by memory, responsibility, and silent gratitude (Source: World Bank Blogs, Dec 2024).

In countless Indian households, parents have spent their entire lives living not for themselves, but for their children—sacrificing comforts, postponing dreams, and often taking on loans just to educate their son or daughter, hoping they'd find success abroad. Many lived in rented apartments their entire lives, never buying a house because "the child's future comes first." They skipped vacations, ignored retirement savings, and quietly bore hardships. That's the emotional reality behind every degree earned overseas, every work visa stamped, every flight that took a young Indian out of the country.

And when those children begin to earn—whether in Dubai or Dallas, Doha or Dublin—they don't just send money home. They send dignity back. They buy the first house their parents can truly call their own. They upgrade hospital treatments. They pay off those old loans that once bought them a plane ticket. And in doing so, they turn remittances into acts of fulfilment.

That's why nearly 59.2% of India's remittance inflow is used for family maintenance—not just survival, but emotional security. Roughly 20% is placed into Indian bank deposits, not for high returns but as standby capital, quietly converted into rupees and kept ready for future needs. Only 8% goes directly into investments like real estate or equity markets (Source: RBI & World Bank).

Now consider this: while the Gulf region hosts only 17% of Indian migrants, it contributes nearly 30% of remittance inflows. The UAE alone sends over $23 billion, followed by the US ($17 billion), Saudi Arabia ($11 billion), and Qatar ($6.5 billion). This disproportionality tells us something vital—the remittance mindset is driven not just by earning power, but by emotional intent. A blue-collar worker in the Gulf may earn less than an executive in New York, but his sense of duty to support ageing parents is often stronger, more immediate, and more consistent.

And what about the 20% that sits in Indian bank deposits? This is one of the most overlooked financial pools in the NRI advisory conversation. Already converted into INR, resting in NRO savings accounts or term deposits, this money is not chasing returns—it's waiting. Waiting for guidance. Waiting for someone to say, "You could convert this into a monthly pension for your parents" or "Let us understand what this money is meant to protect." That is where the NRI advisor earns relevance.

Because in India, sending money home isn't a transaction. It's closure. It's pride. It's the moment a child becomes a provider, not just a success story.

And that's why our ₹11 lakh crore isn't just the largest remittance volume in the world—it's also the most meaningful.

1.7 BEFORE THE LAW READS THE FILE

This chapter has stayed close to the person on purpose.

The NRI is not a dollar earner, a remitter, a passport holder or a premium opportunity. He is a person living between distance and duty, freedom and responsibility, memory and movement. An advisor who does not understand that life will find that every technical answer he gives later rests on sand.

But understanding is only the first half of the work.

The same client who feels Indian may not be Indian in law. The same person who calls India home may be a foreign citizen, an OCI cardholder, a non-resident under FEMA and, in that very same year, a resident under the Income-tax Act. One word—*NRI*—can carry affection in a family conversation and something far more exacting in a legal file.

So before the advisor arranges a single rupee, he needs a way to tell which person is actually sitting across the desk, and which laws are watching the conversation. Chapter 2 gives him that discipline. It is called the Compliance Highway Rule™, and it begins where every cross-border relationship must begin—with Papers.

First, understand the life behind the label.

Then test the label.

Because the advisor's first product, long before any policy, is understanding.

Notes

[1] Ministry of Statistics and Programme Implementation, Press Note on Provisional Estimates of Annual GDP for 2023–24, 31 May 2024.

[2] World Economic Forum and Bain & Company, future consumption / middle-class consumer projections for India.

[3] World Bank India Overview / relevant World Bank consumption or GDP overview source used by author.

[4] Ministry of External Affairs, Population of Overseas Indians, latest available country-wise NRI/PIO table.

[5] World Bank Blogs / KNOMAD, Migration and Development Brief, December 2024, India inward remittance estimate for calendar year 2024.

[6] Reserve Bank of India / World Bank remittance utilisation data relied upon by the author. The proportions cited are based on available survey data and may vary by survey year, sample and methodology.

End of Chapter 1

CHAPTER 2

SELLING ACROSS BORDERS

The Compliance Highway Rule™
Every Advisor Must Know

There are over 35 million Overseas Indians living outside India. [1]

Let us translate that into a number that actually lands.

Three and a half crore.

Three and a half crore people. Earning in dollars, dirhams, pounds, and ringgits. Sending money home. Buying flats in their parents' cities. Taking care of ageing parents from six time zones away. Building lives in countries their children will grow up calling home—while keeping a corner of the heart permanently reserved for India.

That is not a niche segment. That is a population larger than many countries on this planet. Larger than Australia. Larger than the Netherlands, Chile, and Romania.[2]

For an NRI advisor who genuinely understands this world, it is a staggering opportunity.

For one who doesn't—it is an even more staggering headache.

And the headache, almost always, starts with three letters.

N. R. I.

Before we go any further into statutes and residential status, I want to take you somewhere more familiar.

A matrimonial proposal.

You know exactly the scene I am describing.

It is a perfectly ordinary Tuesday evening. Nothing is happening. The TV is on. Someone is eating something they probably shouldn't be eating this late. Then the phone rings—and it is *that* aunty. Every Indian family has one. She has been running an unofficial matrimonial operation from her drawing room since approximately 1998, she is on seventeen family WhatsApp groups, and she treats the task of finding matches with the kind of dedication that would make a Swiss watchmaker feel slightly inadequate.

Her voice on the phone carries the specific energy of someone who has found something good and cannot wait another second to tell you.

"Hello? Suno—ek proposal aaya hai. Very good family. And—the boy is a DOCTOR.*"*

That last word. She says it the way a news anchor announces a breaking news. With weight. With significance. With the quiet implication that the correct response is gratitude.

And in that moment—admit it—the entire family's temperature changes.

Papa puts the remote down. Not on the side table. *Down.* With both hands. Like he is now available for serious conversation.

Dadi, whose hearing has been selectively unavailable for the past forty years, suddenly catches every syllable from the next room.

Someone leans out of the kitchen—still holding the ladle—just to confirm they heard correctly.

Doctor.

The image assembles itself without being invited. White coat. Stethoscope draped just so. The calm, reassuring voice that says *everything is under control.* A steady income. Security. The kind of son-in-law you describe to other people with a particular expression—not quite smiling, but not *not* smiling either.

The aunty is still talking but nobody is fully listening because the family has already started planning the wedding in their heads.

Then—and this is the moment that matters—one sensible person in the room asks the question.

"Doctor? Which field?"

The aunty pauses.

Because she does not entirely know.

And this is where the proposal—and your entire understanding of the NRI market—either gets better or falls completely apart.

Because "doctor" is one of those words that sounds perfectly clear until the moment you actually need one.

Let us test this with Bollywood, because Bollywood has—without meaning to—given us the most comprehensive study of how dangerously misleading one word can be.

The aunty, when she said *"DOCTOR,"* had a very specific image in her mind.

She was imagining **Shah Rukh Khan**.

Not just any Shah Rukh Khan. Specifically, the arms-wide-open, wind-in-the-hair, I-have-arrived-to-solve-your-every-problem Shah Rukh Khan. The one who shows up at the right moment, says exactly the right thing, and makes the whole family feel that everything will be fine.

What the family might actually get is a completely different Shah Rukh.

They might get **Dr. Jahangir Khan** from *Dear Zindagi*. Same actor. Same face. Completely different room. Walk in with a fever and he will, very warmly, ask you when the heaviness in your body first started—and whether you have considered what it might be trying to tell you.

They might get **Dr. Asthana** from *Munna Bhai M.B.B.S.*—Boman Irani, dean of a medical college, runs his institution with great precision.

Or they might get **Dr. Mohan Bhargava** from *Swades*—NASA scientist, idealist, builder of village power systems.

Same word. *Doctor.* Three completely different rooms. Not one of them wrong.

The label was not lying. It was simply never enough information.

And until the family asked *which kind*—they did not know who was actually about to walk through their door.

Now replace the word "doctor" with "NRI."

Client walks in. Sits down. Smiles.

"Sir, I am NRI."

And the matrimonial-style excitement begins quietly in the advisor's head.

Foreign income. India connection. Dollar earnings. Family here. Good premium potential. This is a good proposal.

But which NRI?

Because right now, without asking a single follow-up question, you could be sitting across from completely different people—each of whom will require a completely different room.

The 26-year-old software engineer in Austin on an H-1B visa, who left India fourteen months ago. His FEMA residential status changed the day he boarded the flight—FEMA does not wait for the financial year to end. His Income Tax residential status for this year may still read *Resident*—because the Income Tax Act runs on day-count, and fourteen months ago was mid-year. Two different answers to the question *"is he resident?"*—and both of them are correct, under their respective laws.

The merchant navy officer from Kochi, eight months a year at sea on a vessel registered in a foreign country. His Section 6 residential status calculation as per Income Tax Act, 2025 requires a reading that most advisors get wrong. Miss it, and the advice you give him is built on the wrong foundation.

The retired couple in Dubai. Twenty years of NRE accounts, a comfortable life, annual winter visits to India. They mention, almost as an aside, that they are thinking of coming back permanently. The moment they return with that intention, a clock starts under FEMA—not at the end of the financial year, not after six months, but from that day. And most of what they have assumed about their finances for two decades will begin to shift in ways nobody warned them about.

The second-generation Gujarati entrepreneur in Nairobi. Grandfather from Rajkot. Never held an Indian passport. His family has always called him NRI—it feels natural, it feels correct, it feels like an identity. Under every statute this book will walk you through, he is something else entirely.

In conversation, all four say the same three letters.

Under the law, they are four different people, in four different rooms, with four different sets of rights, restrictions, obligations, and exposures.

The immigration law classifies them one way. FEMA examines them by a different standard. The Income Tax Act arrives at its own conclusion. None of these three is obliged to agree with the others—because each law has a different job, a different clock, and a different question it is trying to answer.

Your job—before the product, before the plan, before you say a single word about premium or sum assured—is to figure out which room you are standing in.

Because the advisor who hears *"I am NRI"* and starts building the file is exactly like the family that books the banquet hall the moment the aunty says *"doctor hai."*

The label sounded like information. It was only the beginning of the investigation.

So ask the question that cross-border advisory actually starts with:

"When you say NRI—under which law, for which purpose, and as of which date?"

That question is not the end of the conversation.

It is the start of the only conversation worth having.

This chapter is built around one discipline: never let one law answer another law's question.

Immigration and citizenship law decide whether the person has the legal doorway to India. FEMA decides whether the cross border transaction is permitted on the date it is undertaken. The Income Tax Act decides how income is taxed after applying its own residential status tests.

The same human being can look different under each of these laws. That is not a defect in the system. That is the design of the system.

The advisor who understands this becomes useful.

The advisor who does not understand this becomes dangerous.

2.1 THE CHAPTER'S CORE RULE

If you remember only one line from this chapter, remember this:

Immigration is not FEMA. FEMA is not Income Tax. Income Tax is not Immigration.

They may all be looking at the same person, but they are not asking the same question.

A cardiologist, a neurologist, and an orthopaedic surgeon may all examine the same patient. The cardiologist does not read the knee scan. The neurologist does not certify the heart valve. The orthopaedic surgeon does not comment on brain chemistry. Each specialist has a boundary.

The law works in the same way.

Immigration law asks, "Who are you to India, and may you enter or stay?"

FEMA asks, "Can this money, asset, account, investment, or transfer move today?"

Income Tax asks, "For the year gone by, what income can India tax, and in which lane does the person fall?"

The advisor's role is not to impress the client by using legal terms. The advisor's role is to keep the terms in their correct lane.

Because in NRI advisory, most mistakes are not made because the advisor knows nothing. Many mistakes are made because the advisor knows one law and uses it everywhere.

A PAN card does not answer a FEMA question.

An OCI card does not automatically answer a tax question.

A tax exemption does not authorise a prohibited transaction.

A green light under one law does not remove a red light under another.

This is where the Compliance Highway Rule™ enters.

2.2 THE COMPLIANCE HIGHWAY RULE™

A client calls. Indian citizen, eleven years in Sharjah, wants to sell his ancestral land in Coimbatore and route the proceeds into a guaranteed-return policy in India. He says, *"Sir, I am NRI. I can do this, no?"*

That single sentence carries three different questions hidden inside it. Most advisors hear it as one question and answer it as one. That is where the mistakes begin.

Over years of NRI advisory work—across taxation, FEMA permissibility, repatriation, banking architecture, and the strange intersections that arise when a client is simultaneously a citizen of one country and a tax resident of another—I have found that every cross-border financial decision, without exception, can be tested against a single rule. I have named that rule the **Compliance Highway Rule™**.

Here is the rule, stated formally.

Every cross-border financial decision must clear three checkpoints—Papers, Signal, and Toll—in that order. Each is governed by a separate statute. Each runs on its own clock. Each answers a different question. None can substitute for another. A green light at one checkpoint is not a green light at the next.

That is the theorem. The rest of this section explains why it is constructed the way it is, what each checkpoint does, and what the rule rules out.

Why a highway?

The metaphor of the highway is not decoration. India's cross-border regulatory architecture *is* a road system. It has separate regulators responsible for separate functions, each operating from its own statute, each with its own form of enforcement. The Ministry of External Affairs and the Ministry of Home Affairs handle entry, identity, and citizenship. The Reserve Bank of India and the Ministry of Finance handle transaction permissibility under FEMA. The Central Board of Direct Taxes handles tax under the Income-tax Act. Three different rule-keepers. Three different rule-books. Three different checkpoints.

A road system has another feature that matters for our purpose—*the checkpoints come in a fixed order*. You do not approach a tollbooth before your vehicle is licensed to be on the road. You do not negotiate a traffic signal before you have been admitted to the road in the first place. The sequence is built into the architecture. The same is true of India's cross-border regime. The moment an advisor tries to skip a checkpoint or reorder them, he produces advice that is either unsafe for the client or indefensible for himself.

That is why the metaphor is not "three laws to consider" or "three angles to check," but a *highway*—because the order is not optional, and the checkpoints do not negotiate with one another.

Papers—the checkpoint that asks whether you are on the road at all

Papers is the first checkpoint, and it is the most underestimated of the three. Papers means citizenship, passport, visa category, OCI card, immigration registration, and the validity of those documents as on today. It is governed by the *Citizenship Act, 1955* (Sections 7A–7D for OCI), the *Immigration and Foreigners Act, 2025,* and the orders and notifications of the Ministry of Home Affairs and the Bureau of Immigration.

The question Papers asks is the most basic question of all: *does this person have legal standing on India's road for the action proposed?*

If a person does not have valid papers, he is not on the road. He is in the parking lot at the edge of the road, looking in. Whether the traffic signal further down is green or red is a question that does not yet arise for him. Whether the tollbooth would charge him five thousand rupees or fifty thousand is a question that does not yet arise for him. The signal and the toll *presume* that the vehicle is legitimately on the road. If the vehicle is not on the road, the other two checkpoints have no work to do.

Think of it the way you think of driving a car. Without a licence, without registration, without insurance, the question of which lane to take or how fast to drive does not arise—you are not permitted to start the engine. India's cross-border road works the same way. Without standing, there is no transaction to permit and no tax to compute.

This is why a foreign national of Indian origin without an OCI card cannot simply walk into the general NRI/OCI purchase lane for immovable property in India, regardless of how much tax he is willing to pay. If he is outside that lane, the advisor must test a specific permission, inheritance or approval route. The purchase lane for residential and commercial property is open to NRIs and OCI cardholders—Papers grants standing in that lane. Without standing in the lane, the FEMA question and the tax question never open.

Most advisors reach for FEMA first, because FEMA feels like the more financial, more technical, more advisor-flavoured question. That instinct is wrong. *Identity precedes permission. Standing precedes transaction.* Papers is the foundation; the other two checkpoints are built on top of it.

Signal—the checkpoint that asks whether this transaction is permitted today

Signal is the second checkpoint, and Signal means FEMA. The *Foreign Exchange Management Act, 1999*—together with the rules, regulations, master directions, and notifications issued under it—forms the signal at the intersection of India's cross-border money movement.

The choice of a *signal* as the metaphor is precise, and it carries the entire theoretical weight of how FEMA actually works.

A traffic signal has three features that distinguish it from every other kind of regulatory mechanism. First, *a signal decides in the present tense.* It is green or red or amber at the moment the vehicle approaches the intersection—not at the moment the vehicle started its journey, and not at the moment the vehicle reaches its destination.

Second, *a signal decides transaction by transaction*. Each crossing of the intersection is a separate event. The fact that the light was green for the previous car does not mean it is green for this one. Third, *a signal sits at the point of action*. It is not at the start of the road and not at the end. It is at the exact place and time the decision must be made.

FEMA mirrors all three features. FEMA asks what the person's *FEMA residential status* is today, on the date of this transaction. It asks what the source of the funds is today, what the account being used is today, what the nature of the asset is today, and what the rulebook in force is today. It does not look back over the financial year. It does not look forward to where the money will eventually end up. It looks at *now*.

Green means the transaction may proceed without further condition. Amber means it may proceed within a limit or a condition—the *Liberalised Remittance Scheme* corridor of USD 250,000 a year for residents, the USD 1 million annual repatriation corridor for non-residents, the *current-account versus capital-account* distinction that determines whether the door is open by default or shut by default. Red means stop.

And here is the part of the Signal checkpoint that advisors most often miss: *a red signal cannot be cured by offering to pay tax*. The signal and the toll are not negotiating with each other. They are at different points of the road, governed by different statutes, administered by different ministries. The Income-tax Act has no power to give a green light to a FEMA-prohibited transaction. Tax compliance is not FEMA permission. The two are independent—and that independence is the heart of the theory.

Toll—the checkpoint that asks what is owed for the journey already travelled

Toll is the third checkpoint, and Toll means India's income-tax law—the *Income-tax Act, 2025* for tax years beginning on or after 1 April 2026, and the *Income-tax Act, 1961* for the years that closed before it.

The choice of a *tollbooth*—not a second signal, not another barrier—is again precise.

A tollbooth has three features that distinguish it from a signal. First, *it sits at the end of a stretch of road.* You meet it after you have travelled the road, not before. Second, *it calculates retrospectively.* It does not ask where you are going; it asks where you have been and how much road you have covered. Third, *it has a camera, and the camera looks backward.* It records the journey already completed and bills accordingly.

The Income-tax Act mirrors all three features. *Section 6*—the residence provision under both the *Income-tax Act, 1961* and the *Income-tax Act, 2025*—does not ask what the person intends to do in the coming year. It looks back over the tax year that has closed and counts the days the person spent in India. Based on that day-count, it classifies him into one of three lanes—*Resident and Ordinarily Resident, Resident but Not Ordinarily Resident,* or *Non-Resident.* The lane determines the scope of income that India can tax, the rate at which TDS applies, and the treaty relief that may be claimed under the relevant DTAA article, supported by a *Tax Residency Certificate* and the prescribed treaty-particulars declaration—historically *Form 10F,* and *Form 41* for tax years beginning on or after 1 April 2026.[3]

The tollbooth does not ask whether the transactions during the year were permitted under FEMA. It does not ask whether the visa was valid. It is not a permission gate. It is a measurement-and-collection point for the year already completed.

This is why FEMA residential status and Income-tax residential status can—and routinely do—diverge for the same person in the same year. A software engineer who moves to Dubai in October becomes a *Person Resident Outside India* under FEMA from the day he leaves with the intention of indefinite stay; under section 2(v) read with section 2(w) of FEMA, his status changes from that day. Under the Income-tax Act, however, his residential status for that financial year is determined by his total day-count in India over the year—and because he was physically in India until October, he may well remain a *Resident* for tax that year, while being a non-resident under FEMA. Two different statuses, simultaneously, in the same person, in the same year—and both legally correct.

The signal looks at the moment of crossing. The booth looks back over the road already travelled. *That is the difference, and it is the entire point of the theory.*

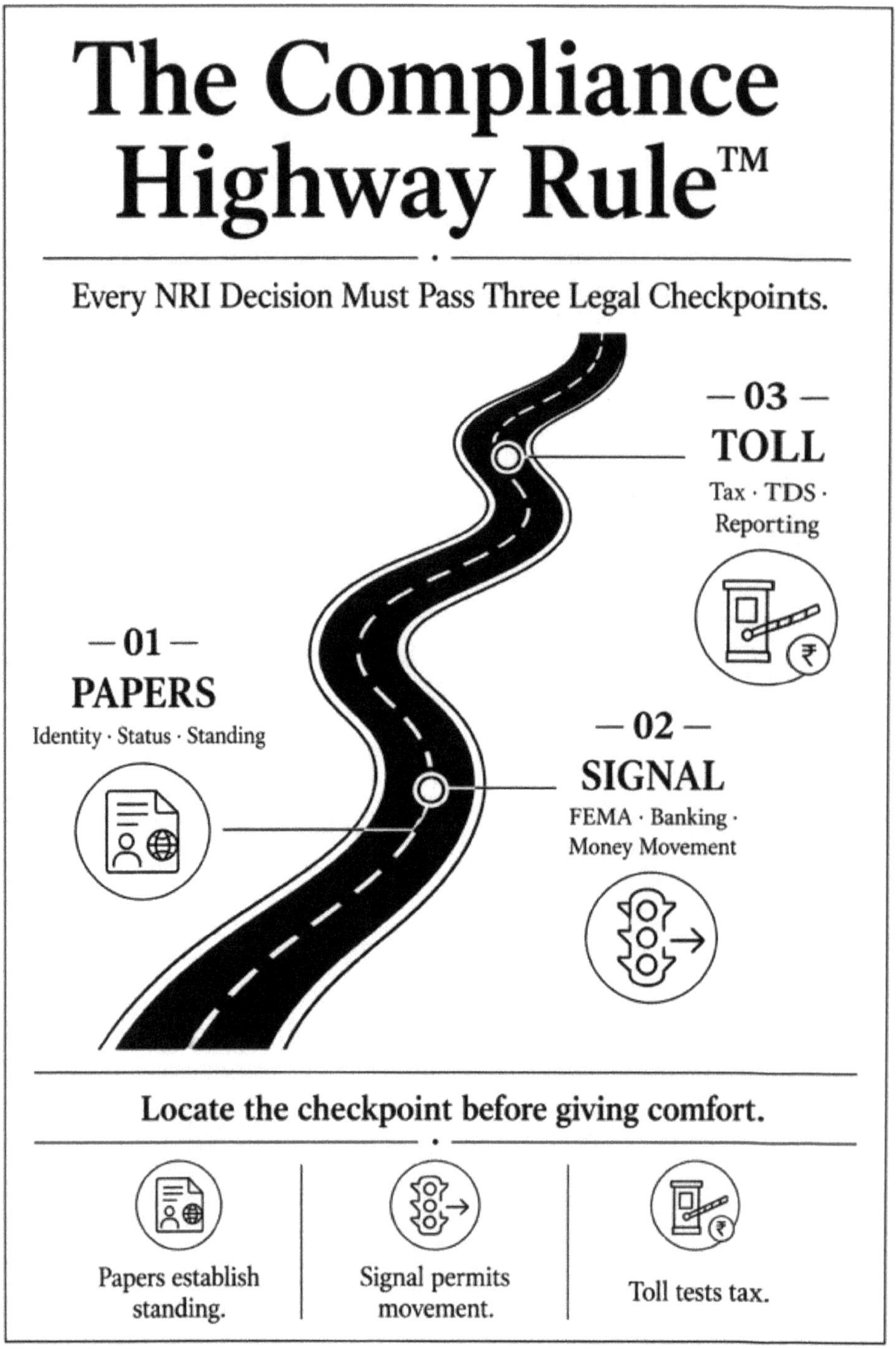
The Compliance Highway Rule™
Every NRI Decision Must Pass Three Legal Checkpoints.
— 03 —
TOLL
Tax · TDS · Reporting
— 01 —
PAPERS
Identity · Status · Standing
— 02 —
SIGNAL
FEMA · Banking · Money Movement
Locate the checkpoint before giving comfort.
Papers establish standing.
Signal permits movement.
Toll tests tax.

Why three checkpoints, and why in this order

The Compliance Highway Rule™ rests on three claims that distinguish it from the way most advisors think about cross-border compliance.

The first claim is *separation*. Each checkpoint is governed by a separate statute, administered by a separate regulator, and operated on a separate clock. They were not designed to mirror each other; they were designed to do different jobs.

The second claim is *independence*. A green at one checkpoint does not imply a green at another. A red at one cannot be cured by a green at another. The checkpoints do not negotiate. They do not trade. The advisor who tries to settle a FEMA problem with a tax payment, or a Papers problem with a DTAA article, is not applying the rule—he is misunderstanding it.

The third claim is *sequence*. Papers comes first because standing precedes everything. Signal comes second because permission must be tested at the moment of action. Toll comes third because tax consequences crystallise after the year is over. Reverse the order and you produce wrong advice, because each checkpoint logically presupposes the one before it.

Separation. Independence. Sequence. These three claims together are what give the rule its predictive power. Run any cross-border question through them honestly and you will reach an answer that is defensible at every stage.

There is one thing this map does not yet show. For a single decision in a settled year, the Highway is enough: it tells the advisor which checkpoint owns the question—Papers, Signal or Toll. But the Highway answers *where* a question belongs. It does not yet answer *when* each checkpoint begins reading the same client differently. In the years when life itself is moving—the year a client leaves India, the year he returns, sometimes the year he shifts between two foreign countries—the three checkpoints can fall out of step with one another, each on its own date. That second question—about timing, not place—is the work of a later chapter.

What the rule rules out

Like any well-formed theory, the Compliance Highway Rule™ does not only tell you what to do; it also tells you what is not allowed.

It rules out *tax-first thinking*—"I am willing to pay the tax, so let me do the transaction." Tax payment is not FEMA permission.

It rules out *treaty-first thinking*—"My DTAA article allows this." A DTAA article governs the taxability of income; it does not authorise a transaction that FEMA prohibits.

It rules out *visa-first thinking*—"I have a valid OCI." An OCI card grants standing on the road; it does not by itself decide whether today's transaction is permitted or what tax is owed for the year.

It rules out *status-conflation thinking*—"I am NRI, so I can do everything an NRI can do." NRI is a label that means different things under different laws. The question is always *which checkpoint is using the label, and for what purpose*.

A valid visa does not make a prohibited FEMA transaction valid. A favourable DTAA article does not authorise a transaction that FEMA does not permit. An Indian tax exemption does not make the receipt tax-free in the country where the NRI lives. The sequence is the protection—for the client, and for you.

The advisor's drill

The advisor who internalises the Compliance Highway Rule™ runs every cross-border conversation through these three checkpoints, in this order, without exception. He does not promise. He does not guess. He pauses, separates the client's single question into three statutory questions, and answers each from its own home—citizenship from the Citizenship Act, permissibility from FEMA, taxability from the Income-tax Act.

That pause—the half-second between the client's question and the advisor's answer—is the quiet credibility that clients can feel within ten minutes of the first call. It is also what they remember six months later, when they are recommending you to a cousin in Sharjah.

So when the next call comes—when the client says, *"Sir, I am NRI. Can I do this?"*—do not answer immediately.

Say instead: *"Let us first see which checkpoint is asking the question."*

That is the beginning of good NRI advice. Everything that follows in this book is the application of this one rule across the ground where it actually decides outcomes—money routes, taxation, return, and legacy among them. Master the rule first. The chapters will then walk you, checkpoint by checkpoint, through the cases.

2.3 WHY "NRI" CANNOT BE USED AS A UNIVERSAL LEGAL WORD

Now that the highway is clear, we can return to the word NRI.

In common speech, NRI means an Indian living abroad or a person of Indian origin living abroad.

In legal work, that is not enough.

Under FEMA, NRI is generally used as a transaction category linked to a person resident outside India who is an Indian citizen, while many FEMA permissions separately refer to OCI or person of Indian origin depending on the regulation.

Under the Income Tax Act, people often use NRI to mean Non Resident, but the Act actually determines residential status through Section 6. It is a year wise tax result, not a passport identity.

Under citizenship and immigration law, the question is different again. The person may be an Indian citizen, a foreign citizen, an OCI cardholder, or a foreign national requiring visa permission.

That is why the advisor must stop asking only, "Are you NRI?"

The better question is:

"NRI under which law, for which purpose, on which date, and for which transaction?"

This one question changes the quality of the entire advisory conversation.

2.4 THE SINGER WHO MET THREE CHECKPOINTS

A good framework proves itself when the facts become messy. Not when the client is a neat Indian passport holder in Dubai with an NRE account and a simple premium payment. That case is too easy. The real test comes when the person has music in India, presence in India, property in India, visa issues in India, and eventually citizenship in India—but each event belongs to a different law.

The publicly reported FEMA proceedings involving singer Adnan Sami are useful for exactly that limited reason.[4] The purpose of discussing the matter here is not to comment on the individual, his music, his intentions, or his personal journey. It is only to show how the same person can move through three separate legal lanes—Papers, Signal and Toll—and why an advisor must not allow one lane to answer another lane's question.

Public memory remembers the singer first. In the early 2000s, *Kabhi To Nazar Milao* with Asha Bhosle, followed by songs such as *Lift Kara De and Tera Chehra,* placed him firmly inside Indian popular culture. To the listener, he had already become familiar. To the law, familiarity meant nothing.

The law does not hum along.

It classifies.

It dates.

It separates.

That is why his story is a near-perfect Compliance Highway Rule™ case.

The first checkpoint was **Papers**.

On 13 March 2001, he arrived in Mumbai on a one-year visitor visa issued by the Indian High Commission in Islamabad. As his work in India expanded, the visa was extended from time to time.

That is all this fact proves.

It proves entry. It proves stay. It proves an immigration track. It does not prove FEMA eligibility. It does not prove tax residence. It does not convert a visitor into a person permitted to undertake every financial act in India.

This is where advisors often make their first mistake. They see a person living in India and assume the legal system sees one continuous status. It does not. Immigration law may allow a person to be present in India. FEMA may still restrict what that person can acquire in India. The Income-tax Act may still compute residence by its own annual day-count test.

Same person. Three separate readings.

The second checkpoint was Signal.

The Appellate Tribunal record and public reporting refer to the acquisition, in December 2003, of eight flats and five parking spaces at Oberoi Sky Garden, Lokhandwala, Mumbai, for approximately ₹2.53 crore. The proceedings treated the purchaser's nationality at the time of acquisition as material because Regulation 7 of the then applicable FEMA immovable-property regulations restricted acquisition of immovable property in India by citizens of specified countries, including Pakistan, without prior RBI permission.

That date matters.

Under the FEMA rules then applicable, citizens of Pakistan were not permitted to acquire immovable property in India, other than a lease not exceeding five years, without prior permission of the Reserve Bank of India. RBI's published guidance under FEMA 21/2000-RB put the restriction plainly: a citizen of Pakistan, Bangladesh, Sri Lanka, Afghanistan, China, Iran, Nepal or Bhutan could not acquire or transfer immovable property in India, other than a lease not exceeding five years, without prior RBI permission.

This was not a music question.

It was not a popularity question.

It was not even a "how long has he been living in India" question.

It was a Signal question: on the date of acquisition, was the transaction permitted under FEMA for a person of that status?

If the permission was absent, the light was red.

In December 2010, the Enforcement Directorate passed an order directing confiscation of the properties and imposing a ₹20 lakh penalty. That order was later tested in appeal before the Appellate Tribunal for Foreign Exchange.

Then, years later, the Papers lane moved again.

In October 2013, Mumbai Police issued an overstay notice after a visa lapse. Reports recorded the last visa as valid from 26-09-2012 to 06-10-2013 and referred to regularisation steps under immigration law.

But notice the discipline of the highway.

The 2013 overstay issue did not decide the 2003 FEMA acquisition.

It did not become an income-tax ruling.

It did not retroactively approve the property purchase.

It remained what it was: a Papers issue.

The Papers lane deepened further in 2015 and 2016. His Pakistani passport expired on 26-05-2015 and was not renewed. In 2015, India allowed him to stay indefinitely on humanitarian grounds. On 1 January 2016, the Ministry of Home Affairs granted him Indian citizenship by naturalisation.

These were important immigration and citizenship events. But they still belonged to Papers.

They did not travel backward in time and turn the 2003 Signal green.

This is the part every advisor must absorb. Later citizenship can change future identity. It does not automatically sanitise a past FEMA transaction. The Signal tests the status and permission on the date the transaction was undertaken. A later passport cannot be used as a remote control for an earlier acquisition.

The final Signal outcome came in September 2019.

On appeal, the FEMA Appellate Tribunal set aside the confiscation, noting, among other things, that no foreign exchange was involved. But it enhanced the penalty to ₹50 lakh. Since ₹10 lakh had already been deposited, ₹40 lakh was directed to be paid within the prescribed period.

That result is the teaching point.

The flats were not ultimately confiscated. But the contravention did not vanish. The consequence changed. The principle did not.

The 2003 transaction remained tied to the 2003 Signal.

Only after Papers and Signal are separated should the advisor approach **Toll**.

The Income-tax Act is not interested in whether a visa was extended. It is not interested in whether FEMA permission was required for a property purchase. It does not decide residence by nationality, by cultural belonging, by public familiarity, or by later citizenship.

It counts days.

Under section 6, residential status is determined financial year by financial year. If the individual satisfies the statutory day-count test for a particular financial year, he may be resident for that year. If he does not, he remains non-resident for that year. Once residence is triggered, the next question is whether the person is ROR or RNOR, which depends on the statutory look-back tests.

That is Toll.

It is backward-looking. It is annual. It is mechanical. It does not borrow sympathy from Papers or permission from Signal.

So the correct reading of this case is not: he came to India, became famous, bought property, had visa issues, and later became Indian.

That is the newspaper version.

The advisor's version is sharper:

Papers allowed entry, extensions, regularisation, humanitarian stay, and eventually citizenship.

Signal tested the 2003 property acquisition against the FEMA rule applicable on that date to a Pakistani national.

Toll would separately test each financial year under section 6 by counting days of presence in India and then applying the resident, RNOR and ROR rules.

One person.

Three checkpoints.

Three different legal consequences.

This is why the Compliance Highway Rule™ is not a memory trick. It is a professional discipline. It stops the advisor from saying, "He was living in India, so it must have been fine." It stops the advisor from saying, "He later became a citizen, so the earlier issue disappears." It stops the advisor from saying, "If immigration allowed him to stay, tax and FEMA must follow."

They do not follow.

They run parallel.

The safest advisor is not the one who knows the most labels. It is the one who refuses to let one label do another law's work.

2.5 THE POSSESSION TRAP—AND THE ADVISOR'S SHORTCUT

The Adnan Sami case is a public example of the Compliance Highway Rule™. But the same mistake can happen in a much quieter way in an ordinary advisor's file.

Consider a person of Indian origin living in the United States. He was once an Indian citizen. He booked an apartment in Mumbai while he still held an Indian passport. He paid instalments over two years. The builder issued receipts. The family discussed possession. Everyone spoke as if the flat was already his.

Then, before registration, he became a U.S. citizen and surrendered his Indian passport. He did not obtain an OCI card before the date on which the flat was to be transferred in his name.

To the family, nothing has changed. He is still "our Indian son abroad."

To the builder, the file may still look workable. PAN is available. Aadhaar is available. Old Indian address is available. Payment history is available.

But FEMA does not look at the file through family memory.

It looks at the person's legal status on the date of the transaction.

That is the possession trap. Booking a flat, paying instalments, or holding Indian identity documents does not by itself decide whether title can validly pass on the date of registration. If, on that date, the buyer is a foreign citizen of Indian origin without the required Indian-side status or permission, the transaction must be tested again under FEMA.

This is where many people take comfort in the wrong documents.

They say, "Aadhaar is there."

They say, "PAN is there."

They say, "The bank account is old."

They say, "The builder will not ask."

But Aadhaar and PAN are identification documents. They are not FEMA permissions. They may help establish who the person is. They do not decide whether the person, as a non-resident foreign citizen, is permitted to acquire that property in India.

This distinction is not technical hair-splitting. It is the difference between a transaction that is merely processed and a transaction that is legally defensible.

A registration may go through because the system saw documents. That does not mean the transaction was compliant. If the facts are later examined—through banking records, passport history, citizenship records, repatriation requests, family disputes, or regulatory review—the inconsistency can surface. At that point, the explanation "but PAN and Aadhaar were available" will not solve the problem.

It may make the problem worse.

The same temptation exists in life insurance.

An advisor meets a client abroad or speaks to him on video call. The client has Aadhaar. He has PAN. He has an Indian mobile number. His parents live in India. The premium may even be paid from an Indian account. So the advisor thinks, "Why complicate the proposal? Let us issue it as a resident case."

The file moves faster.

The policy gets issued.

The advisor feels the matter is closed.

But in insurance, issuance is not the final test. The real test comes later—when the claim has to be settled, when maturity proceeds must be credited, when money has to move across borders, when the nominee is outside India, when bank account classification matters, when tax declarations are reviewed, or when FATCA/CRS information does not match the original proposal.

A wrong declaration at inception can sit quietly inside the file for years. It may not object when the policy is issued. It may not object when the premium is collected. It may not object when renewal notices are sent.

But it can object when the family needs the money.

That is why the advisor must be very careful at the beginning. If the client is non-resident, disclose him as non-resident. If he is a foreign citizen, disclose that. If he is an OCI, record that correctly. If he is a PIO without OCI, do not treat him casually as if he were an Indian resident merely because he has Indian documents. If premium source, bank account, nominee, tax residence, or claim-credit route has a cross-border angle, bring that fact into the file.

The advisor's duty is not to make the proposal look simple.

The advisor's duty is to make the policy stand clean when tested.

This is exactly why the Compliance Highway Rule™ matters. **Papers** tells you who the person is in immigration, citizenship, and identity terms. **Signal** tells you whether the transaction and money movement are permitted under FEMA on that date. **Toll** tells you how the Income-tax Act will treat the income, receipt, or reporting obligation for the relevant financial year. These three checkpoints may use the same documents, but they do not ask the same question.

Aadhaar may help identify.

PAN may help tax reporting.

Passport and OCI may affect legal status.

Bank account type may affect premium route and claim credit.

None of them should be used to hide the others.

A good advisor does not use available documents to avoid difficult facts. He uses the correct documents to prove the correct facts. That is the difference between a shortcut and a defensible file.

And in cross-border insurance, that difference matters most on the day the client is no longer available to explain what the advisor should have disclosed.

2.6 THE FAMILY DRAMA THAT DECODES NRI, OCI AND PIO

The possession trap usually begins with one innocent-looking mistake: bad vocabulary.

A client says, "I am NRI."

The advisor hears, "Indian client abroad."

The builder hears, "Indian-origin buyer."

The bank sees Aadhaar and PAN.

The family says, "Arre, he is our own only."

But the law does not work with emotional labels. It asks a sharper question: **who is this person under the law that is being applied today?**

Across two decades of working in NRI taxation and FEMA, I have seen smart people stumble on surprisingly simple questions.

Can I buy a flat?

Do I need a visa?

Can I vote?

Can I open an NRE account?

Can I receive inheritance?

Can my policy proceeds move abroad?

The statutes were available. The answers existed. But the conversation kept breaking down because the words were not memorable. Advisors were trying to remember sections, rules and exceptions before they had understood the character standing at the door.

So I built a teaching device that has anchored my trainings, and now anchors this book.

It is my own analogy, refined over years of client work:

NRI is India's son.

OCI is India's son-in-law.

PIO—used in this book to mean a foreign national of Indian origin who has not taken OCI—is the divorced son-in-law.

If you need a visual, borrow the familiar *Kabhi Khushi Kabhie Gham* frame: the mother at the door, aarti thali ready, the house lit up for the son's return.

That is the NRI.

The son may be living abroad, earning abroad, raising children abroad, and returning only during holidays. But he remains India's citizen. His room may not be used every day, but it still has his nameplate. The door opens differently for him.

Now shift the frame.

Think of the red-carpet culture every Indian family recognises around the son-in-law. He is welcomed. He is respected. Sometimes he is pampered more than the son. He may get enormous practical freedom inside the house. But he does not decide family policy.

That is the OCI.

The OCI is not an Indian citizen. He does not vote. He does not hold constitutional rights reserved for citizens. But for many practical purposes—travel, residence, economic participation, education, banking and property, subject to restrictions—India gives him a privileged doorway. OCI cardholders do not have voting rights, but receive parity with NRIs in economic, financial and educational fields, except in matters such as acquisition of agricultural or plantation properties.

Finally, imagine the divorced son-in-law.

There is history. There is familiarity. Everyone knows the connection. The family may remain courteous. But the protocols change. Entry is not automatic. Privileges are not assumed. Past relationship does not become present authority.

That is the PIO without OCI, as the term is used in this book.

This is not wordplay. It is a practical way to separate three things that advisors often mix: **identity and entry, economic participation, and political rights**. The analogy holds attention. The law then supplies the boundaries.

The Son—NRI under FEMA

Think of Arjun, an Indian citizen who moves to Dubai for employment.

In family terms, his room in Mumbai still has his nameplate. In compliance terms, he is outside India for FEMA because he has gone abroad for employment or a similar purpose indicating stay outside India. He still holds an Indian passport. He does not need a visa to enter India. He can vote in India, subject to the applicable electoral procedure. He can purchase residential or commercial property in India, subject to the usual FEMA restriction that agricultural land, plantation property and farmhouse are not in the general purchase lane.

He also uses the standard non-resident banking architecture: NRE, NRO and FCNR(B), depending on the source, currency character and repatriability of the funds.

A quiet but important aside: overseas students also fit this "son" frame in practice. When an Indian citizen leaves for higher studies—say, a student in Boston—the student may be treated as resident outside India for FEMA and banking purposes. In other words, the student abroad is still the son in this analogy: Indian citizen, living outside India, using non-resident banking and investment rules.

The son is outside the house. But he is still the son.

The Son-in-Law—OCI

Now picture Devika, a Swiss citizen who holds an OCI card.

In the family drama, the red carpet is out. She has a lifelong, multiple-entry doorway into India. She is not treated like a tourist who must knock every time. The OCI framework gives her substantial practical freedom: she can visit, stay, study, work, run a business within the ordinary framework, open eligible non-resident accounts, and own residential or commercial property in India, subject to the restriction on agricultural land, plantation property and farmhouse.

That is the son-in-law position.

Welcomed. Empowered. Comfortable.

But not a decision-maker in family policy.

In one sentence: **permanent VIP guest, financially empowered, not political.**

This distinction matters because many clients assume OCI is "almost citizenship." It is not. It is a privileged status. It gives a strong practical bridge to India, but it does not restore political rights that belong only to citizens.

For an advisor, that is the line to remember. OCI is powerful. OCI is useful. OCI is often the cleanest documentation route for a foreign citizen of Indian origin. But OCI is not Indian citizenship.

The Divorced Son-in-Law—PIO without OCI

Now consider Mr Iyer in Toronto.

He was born into an Indian-origin family. His parents were Indian. His surname, culture, food, language and family property all connect him to India. But he is now a foreign citizen and has not taken OCI.

Everyone knows the history.

The law still asks for the document.

In this book, when I use the word PIO in this context, I mean a foreign national of Indian origin who has not taken OCI.

Under FEMA, PIO is a lineage concept. It generally refers to a person resident outside India who is a foreign citizen, other than of specified restricted countries such as Pakistan or Bangladesh, and who traces the required Indian connection through former Indian citizenship, parentage, grandparentage, great-grandparentage, or qualifying spouse relationship. In that sense, PIO was never merely a visa label. It was a way for FEMA and RBI frameworks to decide whether a foreign citizen of Indian origin could access certain India-facing financial routes—banking, investment, remittance, inheritance, and other permitted transactions.

Separately, India also had a PIO Card scheme, introduced as an immigration convenience for persons of Indian origin. That card gave long-term India-entry benefits, but it did not make the holder an Indian citizen. The PIO Card scheme was merged into the OCI framework in 2015. No new PIO cards are issued now. More importantly, the old PIO-card travel window has expired. Indian missions had advised that PIO cards would be accepted as valid travel documents only up to 31 December 2025, and that thereafter a former PIO cardholder must either hold OCI or obtain the appropriate visa for travel to India.

Therefore, when this book says "PIO without OCI", do not read it as a comfortable travel status. Read it as a foreign citizen of Indian origin whose lineage may be relevant under FEMA, but who has not yet obtained the OCI doorway. That person may have Indian roots, Indian family, Indian documents, and Indian assets—but he must still be tested under the correct law for the correct transaction.

That is why the divorced son-in-law image is useful.

He may be welcomed. He may have family history. He may have emotional rights in the living room. But his entry is by protocol, and his permissions are not the same as the son or the son-in-law.

He needs a visa unless another applicable facility exists. He does not vote. He is not in the same general purchase lane as an NRI or OCI for Indian residential or commercial property merely because he is of Indian origin. Inheritance may be a different doorway.

Specific RBI approval may be another. But do not confuse those doorways with a clean NRI/OCI purchase lane.

This is exactly where the possession trap begins.

A PIO without OCI may still have Aadhaar. He may still have PAN. He may still have a family address in India. But Aadhaar is proof of identity; UIDAI expressly states that Aadhaar does not confer citizenship or domicile. PAN is a tax-identification instrument; it does not decide citizenship, FEMA status, or property eligibility. Therefore, neither Aadhaar nor PAN should be used to dress up a cross-border file as a domestic one.

The divorced son-in-law may be known to the family.

But if he wants the son-in-law doorway, he must become OCI.

The "Who Can Do What" Table

For field use, reduce the family drama into a simple working table. This is not a substitute for checking the latest law, but it is a powerful first filter.

Question clients ask	NRI—Indian citizen living abroad	OCI—Foreign citizen with OCI card	PIO (without OCI)—Foreign national of Indian origin
Enter India without visa?	Yes—enters as an Indian citizen on an Indian passport.	Yes—OCI gives a lifelong multiple-entry facility, subject to current immigration rules.	No general PIO-based visa-free right. Needs OCI or an appropriate visa/e-Visa, unless an independent nationality/passport-category exemption applies.
Vote in Indian elections?	Yes	No	No

Question clients ask	NRI—Indian citizen living abroad	OCI—Foreign citizen with OCI card	PIO (without OCI)—Foreign national of Indian origin
Buy residential/ commercial property?	Yes	Yes	Should not assume purchase rights exist; each transaction must be checked under applicable FEMA permission or approval route / Inheritance allowed.
Buy agricultural/ plantation/ farmhouse?	No	No	No
Open NRE / FCNR(B) accounts?	Yes	Yes	Yes
Open NRO account?	Yes	Yes	Yes

This table is designed for advisors, not academics. Its job is to stop the wrong first answer.

The deeper answer may still depend on documents, citizenship history, country of residence, account source, inheritance route, marriage, nomination, tax residence, treaty position, or local foreign law. But the first filter must be clean.

Is he the son?

Is he the son-in-law?

Or is he the divorced son-in-law?

Once the role is clear, the transaction can be tested.

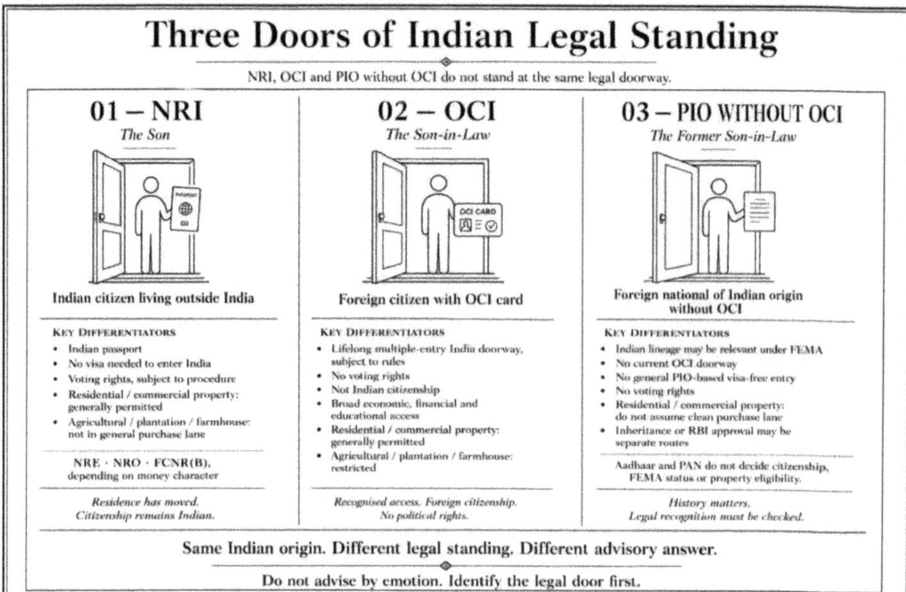

Three Doors of Indian Legal Standing: NRI, OCI and PIO Without OCI
The analogy helps memory, but the advisory lesson is legal: Indian citizenship, OCI recognition and Indian-origin lineage do not create the same entry, rights or transaction permissions.

2.7 THE RELATIVE TRAP—SAME FAMILY, DIFFERENT LAW

There is one more word advisors must handle carefully before applying the Compliance Highway Rule™: **relative**.

In ordinary life, relative is an emotional word. It includes the cousin who attends every wedding, the uncle who helped in difficult times, the niece who feels like a daughter, and the family friend everyone calls *mama*.

Law is not so generous.

Under the **Companies Act**, "relative" is a tight statutory list. It includes specified relationships such as spouse, parents, son, daughter, brother, sister, and the prescribed step-relations. It does not expand merely because the person is close to the family.

Under the **Income-tax Act**, especially for gift taxation, the list is different and wider in its own way. It includes spouse, siblings, siblings of spouse, siblings of parents, lineal ascendants and descendants of the individual or spouse, and the spouses of such persons.

This distinction matters because the same gift, loan, credit, transfer or family arrangement may face two separate tests.

For tax, the question is: **does the recipient qualify as a relative under the Income-tax Act so that gift is not taxable?**

For FEMA, the question is different: **does the transaction fit the relationship and permission route prescribed under the relevant FEMA/RBI framework?**

The answers need not be the same.

A person may be close enough to be treated favourably under one law and still not fit the route required under another. That is why an advisor must never say, "He is family, so it is allowed."

Family is not the test.

The statute is.

This is the Compliance Highway Rule™ at work again. **Toll** may say the gift is not taxable. **Signal** may still ask whether the cross-border transaction is permitted. One green light does not turn the other green.

The field rule is simple:

When a client says "relative", ask: relative under which Act?

2.8 WHY PIOs SHOULD TAKE OCI—AND TIME STATUS CHANGES CAREFULLY

The practical rule for advisors is simple: **if a foreign citizen of Indian origin is eligible for OCI, the client should be guided to obtain it early, not at the last minute.**

This is not because OCI makes the client an Indian citizen. It does not. But OCI gives one thing that matters enormously in real life: a cleaner doorway to India.

Imagine someone who exchanged Indian citizenship for a U.S. passport. She knows she should apply for OCI. The form is available.

The appointment can be taken. The documents can be assembled. But life keeps postponing it.

Work trips.

School pickups.

Tax season.

"Next month for sure."

So she remains a foreign citizen of Indian origin without OCI.

Then, one night at 2:07 a.m., the call comes from Mumbai. Her mother is in the ICU and asking for her.

In that moment, the distinction between PIO and OCI stops being technical.

She reaches for her passport and laptop in the same motion, only to hit the wall she created by delay: visa forms, photograph specifications, appointment slots, processing timelines, uncertainty. The airline website keeps refreshing. Her cousin keeps asking, "When do you land?"

She can only answer, "As soon as they let me."

That is the difference OCI makes in real life.

When love calls, the client should not be standing in a queue.

She should be boarding.

This is why the old comfort around PIO status must not be allowed to continue in advisor conversations. For travel, stay and long-term India-facing planning, OCI or the appropriate visa route must be dealt with properly.

That same discipline matters in financial planning.

If the client is planning to change citizenship, do not treat it as a private passport decision with no financial consequences. It may affect the way future India-facing transactions are documented.

The advisor's role is not to create fear. It is to create sequence.

If citizenship is changing, ask what India-facing transactions are pending.

If OCI is needed, build the timeline around it.

An advisor who understands this will not ask only, "Does the client have Aadhaar and PAN?"

He will ask the better question:

Which family role does the law recognise today?

Because once that answer is clear, the rest of the highway becomes easier to drive.

But identity is only the first checkpoint. Once you know who is standing in front of you, the money still has to travel—through an account, a currency, a route, and a rule about whether it may leave India at all. The next mistake is rarely in the label. It is in the rail.

That is where cross-border advice stops being a word and becomes a route—and where the next part of this book begins.

Notes

[1] Overseas Indian population: approximately 35.42 million (about 15.85 million Non-Resident Indians and 19.57 million Persons of Indian Origin), per the Ministry of External Affairs (stated in Parliament, 2024). The diaspora is the largest in the world. Figures are periodically revised.

[2] Country comparisons use latest available national population estimates (United Nations / national statistics). The Indian diaspora figure exceeds the individual populations of Australia, the Netherlands, Chile and Romania on current estimates.

[3] Form 10F applies for the financial year 2025–26 and earlier; Form 41 applies for tax years beginning on or after 1 April 2026 under the Income-tax Rules, 2026. See the Technical Source Note below.

[4] This discussion is based only on publicly available judicial and media records concerning the FEMA proceedings titled Shri Adnan Sami Khan v. The Special Director, Directorate of Enforcement, Mumbai, decided by the Appellate Tribunal for Foreign Exchange on 12 September 2019, together with contemporaneous public reporting of the Enforcement Directorate order and the appellate outcome. The example is used strictly for educational purposes to explain the separation between immigration/citizenship status, FEMA transaction permissibility and income-tax residence. It should not be read as any comment on the individual's personal character, intentions, professional work, citizenship journey or private life. The Tribunal set aside confiscation while keeping the section 13(1) finding intact and enhancing the monetary penalty; readers should refer to the official/public case record for the full factual and procedural context.

Technical Source Note

This chapter should be read with the Citizenship Act, 1955 (including the OCI provisions in sections 7A to 7D), the Immigration and Foreigners Act, 2025, and the orders of the Ministry of Home Affairs and the Bureau of Immigration for questions of identity and entry; the Foreign Exchange Management Act, 1999, together with the rules, regulations and Reserve Bank of India directions issued under it, for questions of transaction permissibility; and India's income-tax law for questions of taxability—the Income-tax Act, 2025 and the Income-tax Rules, 2026 for tax years beginning on or after 1 April 2026, and the Income-tax Act, 1961 and the earlier rules for years that closed before that date. Residential status is tested under section 6, which carries the same number under both Acts; the dividing line between them is the commencement date of the tax year. For cross-border remittances, the declaration and certificate framework moves from Form 15CA and Form 15CB (Rule 37BB, for payments up to 31 March 2026) to Form 145 and Form 146 (Income-tax Rules, 2026) for remittances on or after 1 April 2026; the treaty-particulars declaration moves from Form 10F to Form 41 for tax years beginning on or after 1 April 2026. The PIO card scheme was merged into OCI in 2015, and PIO cards ceased to be accepted as travel documents after 31 December 2025. Foreign tax, succession, immigration, insurer underwriting and banking outcomes must be checked separately for the facts and the jurisdiction involved. Statutory positions should be confirmed against the bare Act, the Rules and current notifications before reliance.

End of Chapter 2

PART II

MONEY ROUTES AND TAX CONSEQUENCES

CHAPTER 3

BANKING FOR NRIs & CLAIM CREDIT RULES

NRE, NRO, FCNR(B) and the Legal Rail of Money

In NRI advisory work, banking is not the wrapper around the transaction. It is the transaction's legal nervous system. The premium does not travel in theory. The maturity value does not arrive in theory. A claim does not get settled in theory. Every one of these events moves through an account, a currency, a status classification, a repatriation rule, and a documentary trail. That is why the real question is never merely whether a policy can be purchased. The real question is whether the money, when it returns, will still have the same legal character the client assumed it had when it left his hands. Under FEMA and the RBI deposit framework, NRO, NRE and FCNR(B) are not three names on a form. They are three different rails, and different rails produce different exits.

In the language of the **Compliance Highway Rule™**, Chapter 3 belongs mainly to the **Signal**. Chapter 2 answered the first question: who is the client in law? Indian citizen, OCI, PIO, resident, non-resident—those were the Papers. Chapter 3 asks the next question: once the client is legally identified, which account may receive, hold, pay, or release the money?

FEMA does not look at bank accounts as mere containers. It looks at them as routes. NRE, NRO, FCNR(B), resident savings, foreign account—each route carries a different legal character. The same policy can produce a different exit depending on the account through which the money entered and the account into which the proceeds are later credited.

A useful way to think about NRI banking is to stop imagining bank accounts as containers and start imagining them as railway tracks.

The client may stand in the same branch, sign the same proposal form, and buy the same insurance product. Yet if the money boards a different track, it may not reach the same destination later.

One track is designed for India-sourced rupee money. One is designed for foreign earnings converted into rupees with repatriable character. One is designed for foreign currency deposits. The policy may look identical. The exit will not. That is why the advisor who treats the bank account as clerical paperwork usually discovers, too late, that it was the first strategic decision in the case.

3.1 REMITTANCE AND REPATRIATION ARE NOT THE SAME LEGAL DOOR

In Chapter 1, we saw remittance as an emotional act.

A son in Dubai sends money for his father's treatment. A daughter in Toronto transfers funds for the renovation of the family home. A seafarer from Kochi keeps money moving into India because that is how he remains present in a house where he physically cannot be.

To the family, all of this is simply "money sent home".

To the law, it is not that simple.

The same word that carries love at the dining table may carry a completely different meaning at the bank counter. In cross-border work, loose language produces loose advice. And few words are used more loosely than *remittance* and *repatriation*.

They are not the same conversation.

Remittance usually belongs to the resident-side outward movement framework. It asks whether a person resident in India may send money outside India for a permitted purpose. The money is starting from the Indian resident side and moving abroad through a permitted foreign exchange route.

Repatriation asks a different question. It asks whether money already sitting in India is sitting there in a form, account, and legal character that allows it to move out of India. The issue is not merely whether the client wants to send it abroad. The issue is whether the money is eligible to leave, through which route, subject to which conditions, and supported by which documents.

The same bank counter may process both. They do not answer the same legal question. That distinction is not academic. It changes the limit. It changes the paperwork. It changes the bank's operating lens. And in an insurance conversation, it can change the client's expectation at maturity or claim stage.

A resident individual using the Liberalised Remittance Scheme is generally dealing with the USD 250,000 annual framework for permitted current and capital account transactions. An NRI or PIO seeking to move eligible NRO balances, sale proceeds, inherited assets, legacy amounts, or certain India-held proceeds abroad is usually dealing with the remittance-of-assets or NRO repatriation framework, where the familiar benchmark is USD 1 million per financial year, subject to prescribed conditions, documentation, and tax compliance.

Both routes may involve money leaving India.

But they do not answer the same legal question.

One asks:

"May I send this money abroad?"

The other asks:

"What kind of money is this, and does it retain the right to go abroad?"

That is the difference the advisor must hold clearly before discussing NRE, NRO, FCNR(B), maturity credit, or claim proceeds.

Exhibit 3.1: Remittance and Repatriation—Two Different Legal Questions

Point	Remittance	Repatriation
Core question	May a resident individual send money outside India for a permitted purpose?	May money already in India be taken outside India because it is eligible to move out?

Point	Remittance	Repatriation
Usual person	Person Resident in India	Person Resident Outside India / NRI / OCI / PIO / eligible non-resident claimant
Common framework	Liberalised Remittance Scheme or other permitted outward-remittance route	FEMA remittance-of-assets route, NRO repatriation route, or specific permission under the relevant regulation
Typical source	Resident-side income, savings, or assets	NRO balances, sale proceeds, inheritance, legacy, maturity proceeds, claim proceeds, or eligible repatriable funds
Common limit	USD 250,000 per financial year under LRS for resident individuals, subject to permitted purposes	USD 1 million per financial year for eligible NRO balances/assets under the remittance-of-assets framework, subject to conditions
Legal lens	"May I send?"	"What kind of money is this, and does it retain repatriable character?"
Documentation	Purpose code, bank declarations, PAN, Form A2, LRS documentation, and tax/TCS checks where applicable	Form 145/146 where applicable, tax-paid proof, source documents, inheritance/sale/maturity papers, bank scrutiny, and FEMA declarations
Common advisor mistake	Treating every outward transfer as if it belongs to LRS	Treating every NRO or policy maturity credit as freely repatriable

The practical rule is simple.

Do not begin with the amount.

Begin with the character of the money.

If the client is a resident Indian sending money abroad, ask which outward-remittance route permits the transfer. If the client is an NRI seeking to move India-held money abroad, ask how the money came into India, where it is parked, whether tax has been dealt with, and whether the account or asset retains repatriable character.

In NRI banking, money does not merely move.

It carries a history.

And once we understand that history, the three rails—NRE, NRO, and FCNR(B)—begin to make sense.

3.2 THE THREE BANKING RAILS

The three main NRI banking rails perform different jobs.

The NRE account is a rupee account for foreign earnings brought into India through permitted banking channels. Its core character is repatriability. The money has entered India from outside, and FEMA generally allows it to move back out.

The NRO account is the India-side rupee account. Rent, dividends, pension, refunds, Indian sale proceeds, and other India-linked credits typically belong here. The account is useful, but it does not carry the same free repatriability as NRE. Current income may generally be remitted subject to documentation, and other eligible balances or asset proceeds move under the prescribed framework, subject to taxes, limits, and conditions.

The FCNR(B) deposit is different again. It is a foreign-currency deposit maintained with an Indian bank. Its value lies in preserving foreign-currency denomination while giving the client the comfort of holding money with an Indian bank. For many NRIs, that comfort matters. The money remains in foreign currency, but it is not floating in an unfamiliar offshore arrangement. It sits within the Indian banking system, with the confidence, familiarity, and institutional comfort that many families associate with Indian banks.

At first glance, all three may appear to be "NRI banking options." But that is exactly where the misunderstanding begins.

They are not three versions of the same account.

They are three different rails.

One rail is for India-linked rupee money.

One rail is for foreign earnings converted into rupees with repatriable character.

One rail is for foreign currency held through an Indian bank.

The policy may be the same.

The premium amount may be the same.

The insurer may be the same.

But the banking rail can change the exit.

NRO—The India-Side Account

The NRO account is where many NRI misunderstandings begin. Clients often see their NRO balance on internet banking and assume that visibility equals mobility. It does not.

To understand NRO correctly, the advisor must first understand how it usually comes into existence.

In many cases, an NRO account is not a fresh account opened after a dramatic banking event. It begins as the client's ordinary resident rupee account.

The client leaves India for employment, business, vocation, or another purpose indicating an intention to stay outside India for an uncertain period. Later, during KYC updation or banking compliance, the client informs the bank that he is now a non-resident. Once that status is updated, the existing resident rupee account is required to be redesignated as an NRO account.

RBI explains the principle in simple words:

> *"When a resident becomes an NRI, his existing Rupee accounts are designated as NRO."*

That is the key.

For the client, the account may look almost unchanged. The account number may remain the same. The IFSC may remain the same. The internet banking screen may look familiar. The relationship manager may be the same person.

But legally, the account has changed character.

It is no longer an ordinary resident savings account. It has become the NRO rail because the person behind the account has become non-resident under FEMA.

This is why advisors must be careful when a client says, "This is just my old Indian savings account."

Operationally, the client may be describing what he sees.

Legally, the advisor must understand what it has become.

Once redesignated, the NRO account has its own FEMA character. It is designed for India-linked rupee money. Rent, pension, dividends, refunds, Indian sale proceeds, and domestic payments belong naturally here. But the account is not a free outward highway.

NRO money may legally belong to the client, but that does not mean it is freely exportable in the way NRE money generally is. India-sourced funds carry an Indian tax and documentation trail. Before money moves out, the bank must satisfy itself about the nature of the credit, the applicable taxes, the supporting documents, and the FEMA route.

Documentation Caution: Form 145 and Form 146

Form 145 and Form 146 should not be described as automatic requirements for every outward movement of money. The correct question is narrower: what is the character of the money, is the remittance chargeable to tax in India, does Rule 220 require reporting, does any exemption category apply, and what documentation does the authorised dealer bank require for its FEMA and tax-compliance file? In NRO repatriation, the documentation trail is often as important as the account balance itself.

The familiar USD 1 million per financial year framework is not a casual convenience. It is a regulated route for eligible balances and eligible asset proceeds, subject to prescribed conditions, payment of applicable taxes, and documentary comfort. Where the amount exceeds the permitted framework, or where the source documents are weak, the transaction can become slower, more expensive, and in some cases approval-dependent.

Not all NRO credits are alike.

Current income such as rent, dividend, pension, or interest may follow one documentation route. Capital receipts such as sale proceeds, inherited assets, or legacy balances may require a heavier file. The bank will not look only at the account name. It will look at the nature of the credit.

That is why advisors must stop speaking of NRO as though it were merely "the NRI account."

It is not.

It is the India-linked operating account. It is excellent for receiving India-source money and handling India-side obligations. It is far less elegant where the client's real objective is to preserve a clean repatriable trail for funds originally earned abroad.

The money is not stuck in NRO in the literal sense.

But it is controlled.

And in cross-border planning, controlled is not the same thing as flexible.

NRE—The Repatriable Bridge

The NRE account serves a fundamentally different purpose.

It is the repatriable rupee bridge for funds coming from outside India or otherwise carrying repatriable character. It allows overseas money to be brought into India, held in rupees, used in India, invested from India, and still remain on a cleaner repatriable track.

That is why the intelligent question is not:

"Is NRE better than NRO?"

The intelligent question is:

"Do you even need an NRE account for this client's use case?"

If the client's India life is mainly rent collection, family maintenance, and domestic payments, NRO may be the real base account. But if the client is bringing foreign earnings into India and wants those balances to remain legally mobile later, NRE becomes strategically relevant.

This distinction matters sharply in insurance.

When a premium is paid merely because one account was convenient, the advisor may unintentionally decide the client's future exit route. A maturity value or claim amount does not float in the air when it is paid. It must land somewhere. It must be credited through a banking channel. It must carry a history.

The NRE account helps preserve that history where the funds are eligible.

FCNR(B)—The Foreign-Currency Deposit

FCNR(B) belongs to a third category.

It is not an everyday operating account at all. It is a foreign-currency term-deposit structure maintained with an Indian bank.

This distinction matters because many clients casually speak of "NRE, NRO and FCNR" as though all three were comparable current-use accounts. They are not.

NRO and NRE are rupee account categories. FCNR(B) is a deposit category designed for the client who does not merely want repatriation, but wants to preserve foreign-currency denomination itself during the deposit period.

Some clients want India exposure. Others want India access without converting their earnings into rupees for the entire holding period.

NRE helps the first category.

FCNR(B) often helps the second.

For a cautious NRI family, FCNR(B) offers a particular comfort. The funds are maintained in foreign currency, reducing rupee-conversion risk during the deposit period. At the same time, the deposit is with an Indian bank, which gives many clients the psychological and institutional comfort of keeping money within the Indian banking system rather than in an unfamiliar offshore structure.

There is also a more advanced use case, which advisors should at least be aware of.

FCNR(B) can become relevant for non-residents who are planning to relocate back to India. The reason is not only currency. It is also tax timing. In broad terms, interest on qualifying FCNR(B) deposits may continue to enjoy exemption while the returning individual remains RNOR, subject to the conditions of the Income-tax Act. The same continuing privilege does not apply in the same way to NRE fixed deposits once the person's FEMA residential status changes.

This is not a point every advisor needs to explain in detail at the first meeting.

But it is exactly the kind of point that separates a form-filling advisor from a cross-border advisor.

The client may ask about an account.

The specialist hears a return-to-India plan.

That is the difference.

The three banking rails may sit inside the same branch.

They do not perform the same legal function.

Exhibit 3.2: Choosing the Right Banking Rail for an NRI Client

Feature	NRO Account	NRE Account	FCNR(B) Account
Full Form	Non-Resident Ordinary Rupee Account	Non-Resident External Rupee Account	Foreign Currency Non-Resident (Bank) Account
Governing Regulation	Regulation 5(1)(iii) read with Schedule 3, FEMA (Deposit) Regulations, 2016	Regulation 5(1)(i) read with Schedule 1, FEMA (Deposit) Regulations, 2016	Regulation 5(1)(ii) read with Schedule 2, FEMA (Deposit) Regulations, 2016
Currency	Indian Rupees	Indian Rupees	Permitted foreign currencies
Account Type	Savings / Current / Fixed Deposit / Recurring Deposit	Savings / Current / Fixed Deposit / Recurring Deposit	Term deposit only

Feature	NRO Account	NRE Account	FCNR(B) Account
Core Purpose	To receive and use India-linked rupee income and payments	To hold foreign earnings in rupees with repatriable character	To hold foreign earnings in foreign currency through an Indian bank deposit
Typical Use Case	India-sourced income, legitimate dues, local payments, domestic expenses, and proceeds that do not clearly retain repatriable character	Foreign remittances and repatriable India-linked income/ proceeds that have not lost repatriable character	Foreign-currency term deposits where immediate INR conversion is not desired
Repatriation	Current income is repatriable; balances/eligible assets generally up to USD 1 million per financial year, subject to tax and documentation	Principal and interest generally repatriable	Principal and interest generally repatriable
Interest Taxability in India	Taxable in India; TDS may apply, subject to applicable law and treaty position	Exempt under Section 11 read with Schedule IV, Sl. No. 1 of the Income-tax Act, 2025, subject to conditions	Exempt under Section 11 read with Schedule IV, Sl. No. 14 of the Income-tax Act, 2025, read with the relevant conditions inherited from section 10(15)(iv)(fa) of the Income-tax Act, 1961
Exchange Rate Risk	INR exposure; conversion risk arises if funds are repatriated or evaluated in foreign currency	INR exposure after foreign currency is converted into INR	Lower INR risk during deposit tenure, since funds remain in permitted foreign currency

Feature	NRO Account	NRE Account	FCNR(B) Account
Joint Holding with Resident Relative	Permitted with resident on former-or-survivor basis, subject to FEMA/ bank conditions	Permitted with resident relative on former-or-survivor basis; resident operation only within permitted/POA framework	Permitted with resident relative on former-or-survivor basis; resident operation only within permitted/ POA framework
Nomination Facility	Available	Available	Available
Advisor's Lens	Good for India-side money; less elegant for clean repatriability	Good for preserving repatriable rupee trail	Good for preserving foreign-currency denomination and useful in select return-to-India planning cases

The advisor should read this exhibit as a decision tool, not as a substitute for the operative conditions governing the specific transaction.

Once that architecture is understood, the advisor's real job becomes clearer.

You do not choose the account by looking at today's premium convenience.

You choose it by looking at tomorrow's maturity or claim problem.

Where is this money expected to end up? In India for retirement? Abroad for liquidity? In the hands of a resident spouse? In the hands of a non-resident child? In foreign currency for a returning resident who does not want to lose continuity?

The wrong way to structure an NRI case is to begin with:

"Which account do you already have?"

The right way is to begin with:

"What must this money be capable of doing when the policy pays out?"

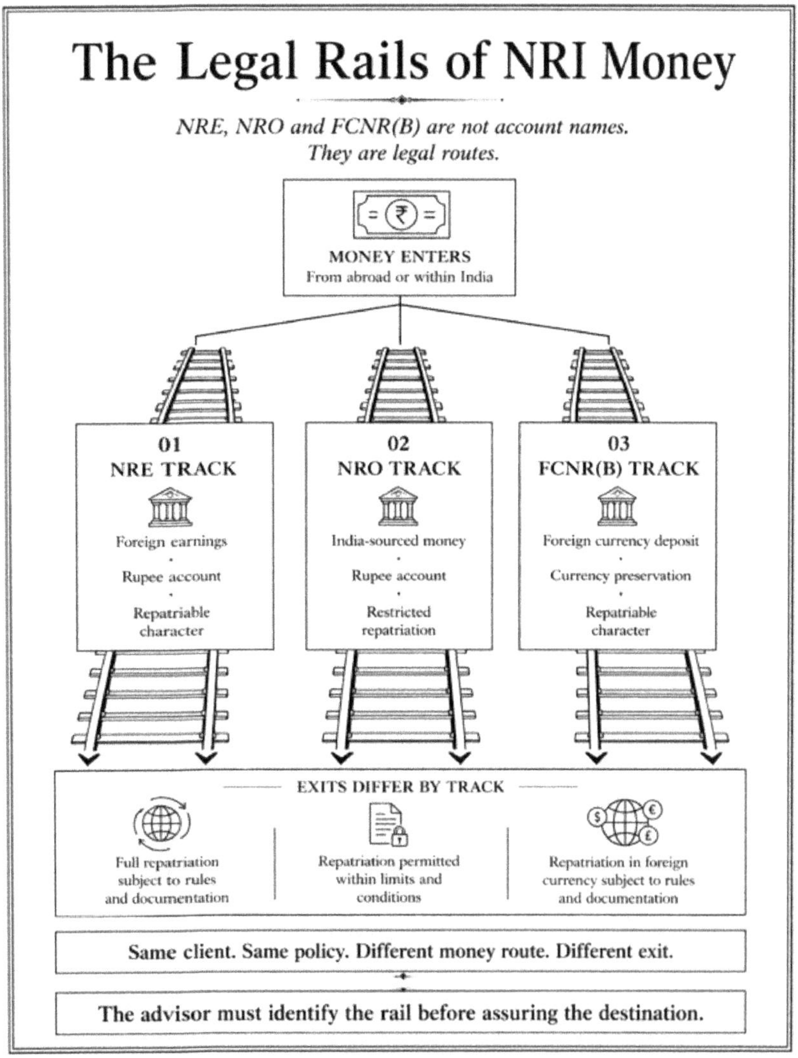

3.3 WHAT YOU SOW IS WHAT YOU REAP

That brings us to the core principle of this chapter.

In FEMA, banking works a little like farming.

The premium is the seed.

The account is the soil.

The claim is the harvest.

What you sow is what you reap.

If the premium is sown through a repatriable rail, the proceeds may generally preserve repatriable character to that extent, subject to policy terms, documentation, and applicable FEMA conditions. If the premium is sown through non-repatriable rupees, the proceeds may carry that restriction to that extent.

This is where many NRI cases go wrong.

The client sees one policy number.

The insurer sees one contract.

The advisor remembers one sale.

But FEMA looks at the funding trail.

Think of a farmer who owns two plots of land. He sows part of his seed in the first plot and part in the second. At harvest, he cannot insist that the entire crop must come from the first plot merely because that plot is more convenient. Each plot produces the harvest that belongs to the soil in which the seed was planted.

NRI insurance works in much the same way.

If part of the premium history belongs to NRE, FCNR(B), or eligible foreign remittance, that part may support repatriable treatment where the rules and documents permit it. If another part belongs to NRO or another non-repatriable rupee trail, that part cannot be casually converted into an NRE-style outcome at maturity.

The rail remembers.

The funding trail remembers.

The law remembers.

This is not merely a useful analogy. It is how the insurance and exchange-control architecture must be read.

An NRI policy is not only an insurance contract. It is also a movement-of-money arrangement. The premium does not merely buy cover or build value. It creates a history. At maturity, surrender, or claim stage, that history does not disappear.

The insurer and the bank may still need to ask: where did the money come from, in what currency was the policy issued, through which account were premiums paid, who is receiving the proceeds, and where are the proceeds expected to land?

That is why the exit does not suddenly become independent of the entry.

A rupee policy funded from a rupee account may follow one path. A policy funded through NRE, FCNR(B), or eligible foreign remittance may preserve a different FEMA character, where the governing rules and documents support it. A policy funded through NRO or another non-repatriable rupee trail may narrow the exit route.

The policy may still pay.

The claim may still be valid.

The proceeds may still belong to the client or beneficiary.

But the route by which those proceeds travel may not be the route the client imagined.

One clarification is important before proceeding.

The premium-paying account does not, by itself, decide the taxability of the policy proceeds. That is a Toll question, and it belongs to Chapter 4. Whether a receipt is exempt, taxable, withheld, treaty-protected, or reportable must be tested under the Income-tax Act and, where relevant, the country-of-residence tax law.

Chapter 3 is asking a different question.

It is asking how the proceeds may move.

That is why the advisor must not reduce the advice to a casual sentence such as:

"Pay from NRE and everything is solved."

That is too broad.

The better sequence is this:

What is the policy currency?

Who is the policyholder?

Who is the beneficiary or claimant?

What was the premium source?

Where must the proceeds finally land?

Those five questions give the FEMA analysis its structure.

3.4 THE CLAIM-CREDIT DECISION TREE

Before advising on where maturity, surrender, or death-claim proceeds may be credited, ask the five questions in sequence.

The claim-credit answer is not found in the policy brochure alone. It is found at the intersection of policy currency, premium source, beneficiary status, RBI insurance instructions, bank documentation, and tax compliance.

Exhibit 3.3: Claim Credit Decision Tree

Step	Question to Ask	Why It Matters
1	What is the residential status of the beneficiary or claimant under FEMA on the date of payment?	FEMA status determines which receiving account is legally available. A non-resident claimant and a resident claimant may access different receiving rails.
2	Was the policy issued in rupees or foreign currency?	Policy currency affects the denomination and settlement architecture of the claim. A rupee policy and a foreign-currency policy do not travel through identical rails.
3	Were premiums paid from foreign currency / repatriable funds or from non-repatriable rupee funds?	The premium source influences the FEMA character of the proceeds. Repatriable premium history may support repatriable treatment to that extent. Non-repatriable history may narrow the exit.
4	Is the payment being settled in rupees or foreign currency?	Settlement currency interacts with account eligibility. Rupee claims and foreign-currency claims do not necessarily land in the same type of account.
5	Does the beneficiary want use in India, credit to NRO, credit to NRE / FCNR(B), or overseas remittance?	The intended destination must be checked against FEMA eligibility. Wanting overseas remittance is not the same as being entitled to it. Eligibility depends on the answers to Steps 1 to 4.

Only after these five questions are answered can the claim-credit route be advised with confidence.

The advisor who skips straight to Step 5—"Where do you want the money?"—is advising on the destination without checking whether the road exists.

Claim Credit Decision Tree

Before deciding where the claim money goes, trace the legal character of the money.

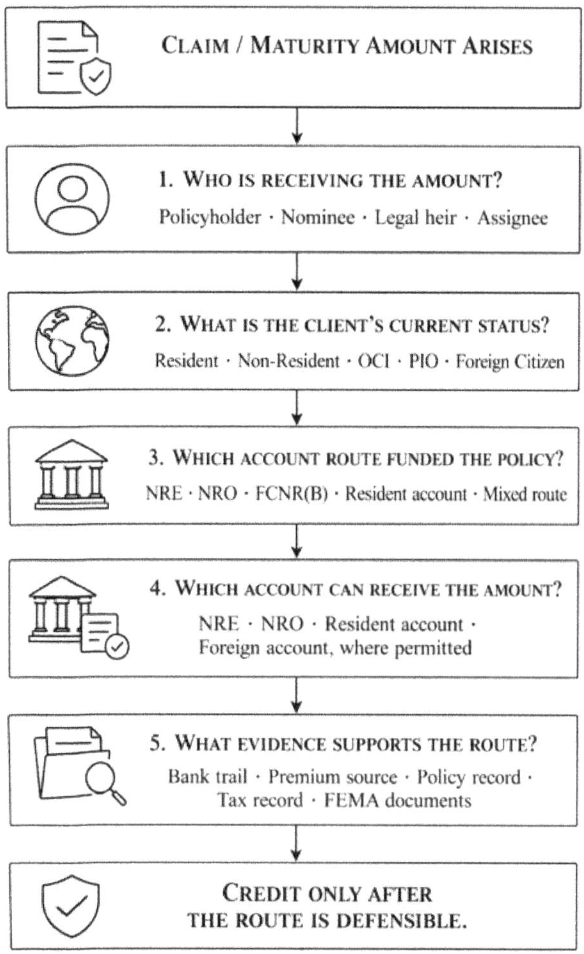

A claim is not only a payment event. It is a money-route event.

3.5 THE RIGHT POLICY, WRONG RAIL

Meera lives in Singapore and buys an Indian life insurance policy.

Her advisor focuses on the product illustration, the projected maturity value, and the expected benefit for her family. The policy is suitable. The insurer is sound. The premium is affordable.

For the first few years, Meera pays the premium from her NRE account because the money is coming from her Singapore salary. Later, life becomes busy. The relationship manager changes. One year, for convenience, the premium is paid from her NRO account, where rent from her Hyderabad flat has accumulated. A few more premiums follow the same route.

Nobody objects.

The insurer accepts the premium.

The receipts are generated.

The policy continues.

Fifteen years later, the policy matures.

Meera now wants the entire maturity value credited to her NRE account and remitted to Singapore. The bank asks for premium-source history, tax documents, and confirmation of the eligible credit route. What looked like a simple maturity now becomes a file-reconstruction exercise.

The mistake was not the policy.

The mistake was treating the bank account as an administrative detail.

In NRI cases, the account is part of the advice.

One wrong premium payment may not destroy the structure entirely. But it can divide the character of the proceeds. One part may retain a repatriable trail. Another part may carry a non-repatriable rupee character. By maturity, the client is no longer arguing with the insurer. She is arguing with her own banking history.

This is precisely why two clients can hold the same policy and still reach two very different outcomes.

The insurer did not change.

The policy did not change.

The banking character changed.

In cross-border insurance, repatriability is not hidden in the brochure.

It is hidden in the premium trail.

3.6 HOW PREMIUM SOURCE SHAPES THE CLAIM ROUTE

Once the premium-source logic is understood, the claim-credit rules begin to make practical sense.

If the beneficiary is non-resident and the premium history supports repatriable treatment, the proceeds may remain within the repatriable non-resident framework, including NRE, FCNR(B), overseas remittance, or another permitted route, depending on policy currency, settlement framework, and documentation.

If the premium history is non-repatriable, the claim may still be payable, but the correct landing rail may be NRO. The client may then have to use the permitted NRO repatriation route, with the necessary tax and banking documents, if money is to move abroad.

This is the point at which many clients discover that they were never buying only a policy.

They were building a claim route.

Credit to NRE or FCNR(B) is not a matter of preference alone. It depends on whether the proceeds are eligible to retain repatriable or foreign-currency character under the applicable insurance, banking, and FEMA framework. Where the proceeds arise from non-repatriable rupee funding, the correct landing account may be NRO.

Exhibit 3.4: How Premium Source Influences the Claim Route

Beneficiary/ Claimant	Premium Paid From	Likely Claim-Credit Mode	Likely FEMA Outcome
NRI / non-resident claimant	Foreign remittance / NRE / FCNR(B)	Overseas remittance / NRE / FCNR(B), where eligible	Repatriable or foreign-currency trail may be preserved to the extent supported by premium source, policy currency, settlement framework, insurer process and AD-bank documentation
NRI / non-resident claimant	NRO / non-repatriable rupee source	NRO	Rupee settlement to NRO; not eligible for NRE / FCNR(B) credit at initial settlement
NRI / non-resident claimant	Mixed premium trail	Split treatment based on premium trail	Foreign-currency / repatriable settlement only to the eligible proportion
NRI / non-resident claimant	Resident rupee funding before later becoming non-resident	Usually NRO	Later NRI status does not automatically convert old resident-rupee funding into repatriable character
Resident claimant	NRE / FCNR(B) / foreign remittance trail	Resident account / RFC, where eligible	Resident claimant cannot receive into NRE / FCNR(B); foreign-currency settlement, if any, follows resident account rules
Resident claimant	NRO / resident rupee / non-repatriable rupee trail	Resident savings / current account	Resident rupee receipt; premium trail remains relevant for character analysis

Note: This table applies to life insurance policies issued by Indian insurers. For rupee life insurance policies where the claimant is resident outside India, foreign-currency settlement is permitted only in the proportion in which premium has been paid in foreign currency against the total premium payable. Non-resident beneficiaries may credit eligible foreign-currency-settled proceeds to NRE / FCNR accounts. Policies funded from non-repatriable rupees are generally settled in rupees to NRO.

A caution is necessary here.

Do not confuse a genuine legacy transition case with a resident savings account that was wrongly continued after the person became non-resident. The first concerns historic resident funding followed by a later change in residential status. The second is a KYC and redesignation defect and must be analysed separately.

The beneficiary's residence changes the receiving rail.

It does not rewrite the funding history.

The mixed-funding rule is where this chapter becomes brutally practical.

Advisors often think in absolutes. Either the claim is repatriable, or it is not. Mixed funding destroys that simplicity. If part of the premium history comes from repatriable or foreign-currency sources and part comes from non-repatriable rupees, the outcome may have to be split.

The repatriable portion remains repatriable only to the extent the funding history and rules support it. The non-repatriable portion remains where it legally belongs.

In other words, one incorrect premium payment may not destroy an otherwise clean structure.

But it can divide it.

That is why premium-source records are not administrative trivia.

They are evidence of legal character.

3.7 THE SAVINGS-ACCOUNT ILLUSION

This is where one of the most expensive shortcuts in NRI banking must be named plainly: the old resident savings account that was never redesignated after the client became a person resident outside India.

The mistake rarely looks dramatic.

The client moves to Canada, Dubai, Singapore, or London. His Indian savings account continues to operate. The account number remains the same. Internet banking works. Premiums get paid. Family members deposit and withdraw money. The relationship manager does not call. Nothing appears broken.

But legally, something has changed.

Once a resident Indian becomes a person resident outside India, the resident rupee account is required to move into the non-resident banking architecture, usually by redesignation as an NRO account. That redesignation is not a cosmetic banking label. It is the legal relabelling of the route on which the money is travelling.

Hasnain's case is typical.

He moves to Canada but does not update his Indian bank. His old resident savings account continues. He tells himself it is simpler this way. If he converts it into NRO, there may be TDS, paperwork, declarations, and questions. So he avoids the update and continues as before.

Years later, a maturity amount is received. Hasnain now wants to move money abroad and assumes he can use the familiar NRO repatriation route.

That is when the shortcut becomes expensive.

The bank does not look only at Hasnain's intention. It looks at the account classification, KYC status, source of funds, tax trail, and FEMA route. A resident savings account wrongly continued after the client became non-resident does not become a clean non-resident repatriation rail merely because the client now needs one.

This is the deeper advisory lesson:

Never design a FEMA position to save TDS.

TDS is withholding.

FEMA is permissibility.

One affects cash flow.

The other decides whether the road exists.

In NRI banking, today's convenience can become tomorrow's route defect. The advisor's job is not to help the client avoid paperwork. The advisor's job is to ensure that the client's status, account, money, and documents are speaking the same legal language.

3.8 CLAIM CREDIT IS NOT SUCCESSION OWNERSHIP

One final distinction is necessary before this chapter closes.

Where life insurance is involved, the words nominee, beneficiary, claimant, and legal heir are often used loosely. They should not be.

For this chapter, the question is narrow:

Where may the claim proceeds be credited?

That is a banking and FEMA question.

It is different from the succession question:

Who is ultimately entitled to own the money?

A nominee may help the insurer process the claim. A claimant may submit documents. A beneficiary may be named in the policy structure. A legal heir may have a separate ownership claim under succession law. Chapter 8 deals with that larger inheritance question.

Here, the point is simpler.

Even if the insurer knows whom to pay, the bank must still know where the money may lawfully land.

If the recipient is resident in India, one receiving architecture may apply. If the recipient is non-resident, another may apply. If the premium trail is repatriable, one route may be available. If the premium trail is non-repatriable, the proceeds may have to land differently.

Nomination does not erase the premium trail.

Family intention does not override account character.

Convenience does not replace FEMA.

The insurer may settle the claim.

The bank must still read the route.

3.9 WHEN THE CLIENT LEAVES OR RETURNS, THE RAIL MUST BE REVIEWED

The banking rail can also change when the client's residential status changes—when he leaves India, and again when he returns. The fuller treatment of return to India belongs to Chapter 7; the warning belongs here too. An account that was correct during one phase may not remain correct once FEMA begins reading the person differently. NRE accounts, NRO accounts, FCNR(B) deposits, resident accounts, RFC possibilities, future credits and future remittances all deserve review at each transition.

The full timing framework arrives in Chapter 7 as **The NRI Kaalchakra™**—the three legal time zones of cross-border transition. Chapter 3 needs only its domestic seed: the client experiences one movement, but FEMA and Indian income tax may not read that movement at the same moment.

FEMA reads residential status for exchange control, banking routes, account redesignation, remittance and repatriation. The Income-tax Act reads residential status through its own annual tax-year tests. The two clocks may move differently. A client may trigger a FEMA banking review on return while his income-tax residential status for that financial year is still being tested separately. So the advisor's first question is not where the client feels he belongs. It is: **which clock is reading this client as what, and from when?** In banking terms, that means asking which status applies, which account is being used, and whether the money is still on the correct route.

The practical rule is simple. When the client leaves India, review the banking rail. When the client returns to India, review it again. **Synchronise before you assure.**

3.10 THE SIGNAL HAS BEEN READ. NOW COMES THE TOLL.

The deeper lesson of this chapter is larger than NRO, NRE, and FCNR(B).

Banking, in NRI life, is biography written in legal form.

It records where the money came from.

It records whether India was the source, the destination, or the corridor.

It records whether the client wanted India-side utility, clean repatriability, foreign-currency preservation, family access, or return-to-India continuity.

The advisor who understands this does not begin with:

"Which account do you have?"

He begins with:

"What must this money be capable of doing later?"

That is the real banking question in NRI insurance.

By the end of this chapter, one principle should be clear: NRE, NRO, FCNR(B), resident accounts, and foreign accounts are not interchangeable containers. They are legal rails. The rail chosen at premium stage can affect the rail available at maturity, surrender, or claim stage.

The claim-credit answer depends on status, source, currency, claimant, account character, documentation, and the FEMA route available on the date of payment.

But once the money lands, another question begins.

Is the receipt taxable in India?

If it is exempt, on what conditions—and under which provision of the Income-tax Act in force for that year?

Is TDS applicable?

Can a DTAA reduce, reallocate, or support the tax position?

And what happens in the country where the NRI actually lives?

Banking answers the route question.

Tax answers the consequence question.

Chapter 3 followed the Signal. Chapter 4 moves to the Toll.

Technical Source Note

This chapter should be read with the Foreign Exchange Management Act, 1999, together with the Foreign Exchange Management (Deposit) Regulations, 2016, the applicable Reserve Bank of India Master Directions and FAQs, and authorised dealer bank processes, for questions of account character, NRE, NRO and FCNR(B) classification, redesignation, remittance, repatriation and claim-credit routing. Income-tax questions should be read under India's income-tax law for the relevant year—the Income-tax Act, 2025 and the Income-tax Rules, 2026 for tax years beginning on or after 1 April 2026, and the Income-tax Act, 1961 and the earlier rules for years that closed before that date; the dividing line is the commencement date of the tax year. For remittances to non-residents, the declaration and certificate framework moves from Form 15CA and Form 15CB (Rule 37BB, for payments up to 31 March 2026) to Form 145 and Form 146 (Income-tax Rules, 2026) for remittances on or after 1 April 2026. The USD 250,000 Liberalised Remittance Scheme benchmark for resident individuals and the USD 1 million per financial year remittance-of-assets benchmark for eligible NRO balances and assets operate subject to prescribed conditions, applicable taxes and documentation, and should be confirmed against the current Reserve Bank of India Master Direction. The taxability of life-insurance maturity, surrender and death proceeds is a separate question addressed in Chapter 4; succession and ownership are addressed in Chapter 8; and foreign tax, insurer underwriting and banking outcomes must be checked separately for the facts and the jurisdiction involved. Statutory positions should be confirmed against the bare Act, the Rules and current notifications before reliance.

End of Chapter 3

CHAPTER 4

INSURANCE TAXATION FOR NRIs

What They Don't Tell You

The phone call came on a Saturday morning.

Aditya Sharma was sitting on his deck in San Jose, coffee cooling beside him, watching the eucalyptus shadows move across his lawn. His brother in Pune had called to congratulate him.

> "Twenty-five years, my friend. You stayed disciplined the whole time. The maturity is tax-free, just like the agent promised when you signed up in Mumbai."

Aditya smiled.

He had bought the policy the year he moved to California. Every year, the premium had gone out from his NRE account like clockwork. The maturity had landed two weeks ago—neat, large, exactly as projected on the brochure his agent had handed him in 2001. The brochure had said tax-free. The agent had said tax-free. Now his brother was saying tax-free.

Three reassuring voices.

One continuous sentence.

Twenty-five years long.

That was Saturday.

On Tuesday, his US tax preparer sent him a one-line email with an attachment.

Subject: *Indian life insurance policy—US reporting and tax review required.*

The worksheet did not say India had taxed him wrongly. It said something more uncomfortable: the United States was asking questions India had never needed to ask.

> *Was the policy a foreign financial asset?*
>
> *Did it have a cash surrender value?*
>
> *Had it crossed any reporting threshold?*
>
> *Did the contract qualify as life insurance under US tax rules?*
>
> *If it was investment-linked, did it create any additional classification or reporting issue?*

The number at the bottom was not small—not because every Indian policy is taxable in America, but because nobody had asked the American question for twenty-five years.

Somewhere between Mumbai and California, between the brochure and the maturity, between tax-free in India and reportable abroad, an entire conversation had gone missing.

This chapter is that conversation.

4.1 THE THREE BLIND SPOTS

Most NRI clients leave the policy purchase meeting with a single sentence ringing in their ears:

"It's all tax-free under Section 10(10D)."

They take that sentence with them to Dubai, to Toronto, to London, to San Jose, to Singapore and to Auckland. For years, they repeat it to spouses, parents, friends and sometimes even to tax preparers abroad.

Then maturity arrives.

That is when three blind spots become visible.

The first blind spot is that the Indian exemption has structure. What advisors have long known as Section 10(10D) of the Income-tax Act, 1961 is now housed, under the Income-tax Act, 2025, in Section 11 read with Schedule II, Sl. No. 2. It is not a blanket exemption for every insurance receipt in every situation. It is a conditional exclusion from total income, subject to statutory tests such as issue-date rules, premium-to-sum-assured ratios, aggregate premium thresholds, product classification and specific exclusions.

The second blind spot is that the client's country of residence has its own tax law. India can exempt a receipt under Indian law. That exemption travels exactly as far as India's borders. It does not automatically bind the United States, Canada, the United Kingdom, New Zealand, Australia, France, Germany, the Netherlands, or any other jurisdiction.

The third blind spot is the DTAA. Most advisors invoke it as if it were a magic eraser. It is not. A Double Taxation Avoidance Agreement is not an amnesty. It is a rulebook. It decides which country may tax, how much it may tax, and how double taxation will be relieved where both countries remain in the picture.

These three blind spots decide whether the policy ends in the celebration Aditya's brother imagined, or in the email he received from his preparer.

The question is no longer only:

> *Will I pay tax in India on this policy?*

The better question is:

> *How will this policy be treated in India, what will be withheld in India, and what will the country of residence do with the same receipt?*

CHAPTER 4 IS A TOLL CHAPTER

By now, the *Compliance Highway Rule*™ is familiar.

Papers. Signal. Toll.

Chapter 2 identified the person. That was the Papers checkpoint. Is the client an Indian citizen, OCI, PIO, resident, non-resident, or something else in law?

Chapter 3 followed the money. That was the Signal checkpoint. Which bank account may receive, hold, pay, or repatriate the money—NRE, NRO, FCNR(B), resident savings, or a foreign account?

Chapter 4 reaches the Toll.

The Toll does not ask whether the client is emotionally attached to India. It does not ask whether the premium was paid from NRE or NRO. That was largely Chapter 3's question.

The Toll asks a different question:

> *Is this receipt taxable, exempt, withheld, treaty-protected, creditable, or reportable?*

For an NRI, there may be two tollbooths.

India has one.

The country of residence may have another.

India may say: exempt. The country of residence may say: taxable. India may say: no TDS. The country of residence may say: report it anyway. India may collect tax at source. The foreign country may still ask whether credit is available.

The advisor's job is not to collapse these answers into one comforting sentence. The advisor's job is to keep the tollbooths separate.

India may close its tollbooth one way; the country of residence keeps its own clock. So the advisor asks not only *what does India say?* but *which country is reading this client as tax-resident in the year this receipt arises?* This is the quiet timing problem behind the law—the one Chapter 7 takes up in full.

4.2 THE CENTRAL RULE OF THIS CHAPTER

The central rule is simple:

For Indian tax purposes, life insurance taxability is usually policy-driven, not NRI-driven.

A maturity receipt does not become taxable merely because the policyholder is an NRI. A death claim does not lose its Indian exemption merely because the nominee lives abroad. A surrender does not change its basic Indian character only because the recipient's passport has foreign stamps.

First, India tests the policy.

What kind of policy is it? When was it issued? In which tax year is the receipt arising? What is the annual premium, aggregate premium and actual capital sum assured? Is it a ULIP or a non-ULIP? Is the event a death claim, maturity, survival benefit, surrender, partial withdrawal, annuity instalment, assignment, or Keyman-linked receipt?

Then ask the core Indian tax question:

Does the familiar Section 10(10D) exemption, now housed in Section 11 read with Schedule II, Table: Sl. No. 2 of the Income-tax Act, 2025, apply?

If it does not, the next question is not merely "is it taxable?" The advisor must identify the correct tax character: ordinary non-exempt life-insurance income, non-exempt ULIP capital gains, annuity or pension income, salary-linked benefit, business receipt, or Keyman insurance income.

That test is broadly the same for residents and non-residents.

The NRI difference usually begins after the policy test is complete.

It begins with withholding.

It begins with documentation.

It begins with the old Section 195 conversation, now to be read through Section 393(2) of the Income-tax Act, 2025, particularly the non-resident payments table where the receipt is chargeable to tax in India.

It begins with DTAA eligibility and treaty documentation.

It begins with the possibility of foreign tax credit where the same income is taxed in more than one country.

Most importantly, it begins with the country where the client is actually tax-resident when the receipt arises.

That is the crux of NRI insurance taxation.

The first question is an Indian policy question: **is this receipt exempt or taxable in India?**

Do not overcomplicate it.

The second question is an NRI handling question: **once India has answered, what happens to TDS, documentation, DTAA, credit and the country where the client actually lives?**

Do not oversimplify it.

Many mistakes happen because advisors reverse the two. They make the Indian exemption sound complicated, and the NRI consequences sound casual. The order must be the opposite: keep India's policy test clean, and keep the cross-border consequences separate.

4.3 THE FOUR-STEP FRAMEWORK

For advisors, the sequence should be remembered in four steps.

Exhibit 4.1 The Four-Step NRI Insurance-Tax Framework

Step	Question	Why it matters
1	Test the policy	Determines Indian exemption or taxability
2	Test the withholding	Determines whether tax is deducted in India
3	Test the treaty	Determines whether DTAA relief, rate cap, exemption, refund or credit may apply
4	Test the country of residence	Determines foreign taxation, reporting, estate, inheritance, credit or disclosure consequences in the year the receipt, surrender, claim or reportable event arises

This is the clean working order. The advisor does not need to become a tax counsel. But the advisor must know the order of thinking. Most mistakes happen because the order is reversed.

The client asks, "Is it tax-free?"

The advisor answers, "Yes."

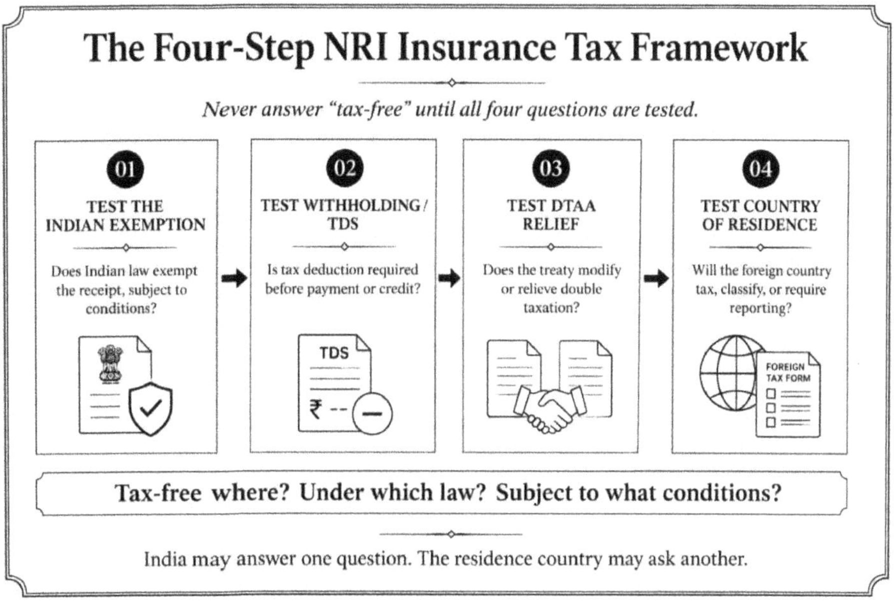

The safer answer begins differently:

"First, we test whether it is exempt in India. Then we check whether any TDS applies because of your NRI status. Then we check whether the DTAA changes the withholding or credit position. Finally, your country of residence must confirm its own tax treatment."

That is not a long answer.

It is a safe answer.

4.4 READY RECKONER, NOT A LEGAL OPINION

Before we enter the table, one clarification is necessary.

This chapter is not a legal opinion. It is a professional warning light.

It does not attempt to cover every assignment, employer arrangement, legacy product feature, policy variation or foreign tax classification. That would defeat the purpose of this book.

The purpose is to teach the advisor a discipline: answer the Indian tax question cleanly, but do not mistake that answer for the full NRI answer.

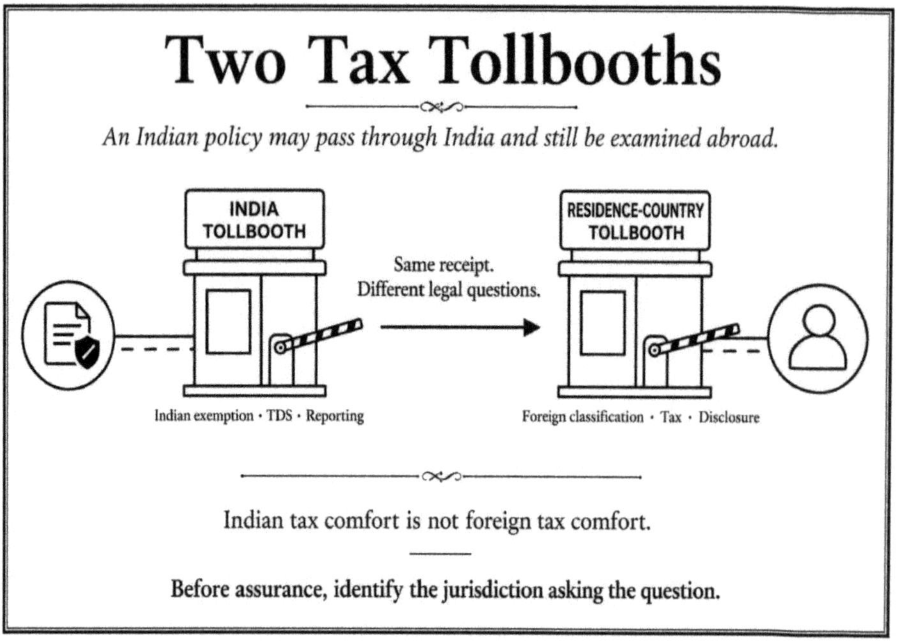

Most life insurance policies sold in India are structured to remain tax-efficient under Indian law, provided the statutory conditions are satisfied. Many ordinary maturity receipts and death claims will still sit comfortably within what advisors have historically known as the Section 10(10D) exemption, now placed under Section 11 read with Schedule II, Table: Sl. No. 2 of the Income-tax Act, 2025.

The danger does not lie in every case being complex.

The danger lies in the advisor using one sentence—"tax-free"—without knowing where that sentence stops.

The reckoner below is built for practical use. It gives the general treatment; the short notes after the table carry only the essential cautions.

Exhibit 4.2 · Life Insurance Taxation Ready Reckoner

Resident vs NRI—general Indian treatment under the Income-tax Act, 2025

Product/ receipt	Premium deduction	Maturity/survival /surrender—general Indian tax treatment	Death benefit	Resident TDS	NRI TDS without DTAA
Pure term insurance	Section 123 read with Schedule XV, subject to ₹1.5 lakh overall ceiling and applicable tax regime.	No maturity value	Generally excluded from total income under Section 11 read with Schedule II, Table: Sl. No. 2, unless a statutory carve-out applies.	No withholding where the receipt is excluded from total income.	No withholding where the receipt is excluded from total income.
Term with return of premium/ TROP	Section 123 read with Schedule XV, subject to ₹1.5 lakh overall ceiling, actual capital sum assured limits and applicable tax regime.	Generally excluded from total income if Section 11 read with Schedule II, Table: Sl. No. 2 conditions are satisfied. If not excluded, taxable income is generally the income component, subject to the prescribed computation mechanism.	Generally excluded from total income, unless a statutory carve-out applies.	If taxable: Section 393(1), Table: Sl. No. 8(i)—2% on income comprised in the sum, subject to ₹1 lakh threshold.	If chargeable: Section 393(2), Table: Sl. No. 17—tax is generally deducted at the rates in force applicable to the NRI. In practice, this could be 30% plus applicable surcharge and cess for income taxable under "Income from Other Sources", unless a lower rate applies because of the nature of income, a lower / nil deduction certificate is obtained, or treaty relief is claimed.

Product/ receipt	Premium deduction	Maturity/survival /surrender—general Indian tax treatment	Death benefit	Resident TDS	NRI TDS without DTAA
Endowment /money-back/ whole life	Section 123 read with Schedule XV, subject to ₹1.5 lakh overall ceiling, actual capital sum assured limits and applicable tax regime.	Generally excluded from total income if Section 11 read with Schedule II, Table: Sl. No. 2 conditions are satisfied. If not excluded, taxable under Section 92(2)(*l*) on the income component, as computed in the prescribed manner.	Generally excluded from total income, unless a statutory carve-out applies.	If taxable: Section 393(1), Table: Sl. No. 8(i)—2% on income comprised in the sum, subject to ₹1 lakh threshold.	If chargeable: Section 393(2), Table: Sl. No. 17—rates in force on the taxable income component, subject to surcharge, cess and lower / nil deduction route

Product/ receipt	Premium deduction	Maturity/survival /surrender—general Indian tax treatment	Death benefit	Resident TDS	NRI TDS without DTAA
Guaranteed-return / non-par non-linked policy	Section 123 read with Schedule XV, subject to ₹1.5 lakh overall ceiling, actual capital sum assured limits and applicable tax regime.	Generally excluded from total income if Section 11 read with Schedule II, Table: Sl. No. 2 conditions are satisfied. For policies issued on or after 1 April 2023, the ₹5 lakh aggregate annual premium threshold must be checked. If not excluded, taxable under Section 92(2)(l) on the income component	Generally excluded from total income, unless a statutory carve-out applies	If taxable: Section 393(1), Table: Sl. No. 8(i)—2% on income comprised in the sum, subject to ₹1 lakh threshold	If chargeable: Section 393(2), Table: Sl. No. 17—rates in force on the taxable income component, subject to surcharge, cess and lower / nil deduction route.

Product/ receipt	Premium deduction	Maturity/survival /surrender—general Indian tax treatment	Death benefit	Resident TDS	NRI TDS without DTAA
Single-premium non-linked policy	Section 123 read with Schedule XV, but deduction may be restricted by the actual capital sum assured rule.	Needs careful testing. Single-premium structures often require closer review of premium-to-sum-assured conditions and aggregate premium thresholds. If Schedule II exclusion fails, taxable under Section 92(2)(l) on the income component	Generally excluded from total income, unless a statutory carve-out applies	If taxable: Section 393(1), Table: Sl. No. 8(i)—2% on income comprised in the sum, subject to 1 lakh threshold	If chargeable: Section 393(2), Table: Sl. No. 17—rates in force on the taxable income component, subject to surcharge, cess and lower / nil deduction route.

Product/ receipt	Premium deduction	Maturity/survival /surrender—general Indian tax treatment	Death benefit	Resident TDS	NRI TDS without DTAA
ULIP—within ₹2.5 lakh threshold	Section 123 read with Schedule XV, subject to ₹1.5 lakh overall ceiling, actual capital sum assured limits and applicable tax regime.	Generally excluded from total income if Section 11 read with Schedule II, Table: Sl. No. 2 conditions are satisfied, including the ₹2.5 lakh aggregate annual premium threshold for relevant ULIPs	Generally excluded from total income, unless a statutory carve-out applies.	No withholding where the receipt is excluded from total income	No withholding where the receipt is excluded from total income.

Product/ receipt	Premium deduction	Maturity/survival /surrender—general Indian tax treatment	Death benefit	Resident TDS	NRI TDS without DTAA
ULIP—high premium / non-exempt	Section 123 read with Schedule XV, subject to restrictions; premium deduction and payout exclusion must be tested separately	If Section 11 read with Schedule II, Table: Sl. No. 2 exclusion fails, profits or gains from receipt of any amount, including bonus, under the ULIP are taxable under the head "Capital gains" under Section 67(5), computed in the prescribed manner.	Generally excluded from total income, unless a statutory carve-out applies.	If taxable: Section 393(1), Table: Sl. No. 8(i)—2% on the income comprised in such sum, subject to the ₹1 lakh threshold. This is the resident withholding route for taxable life-insurance policy sums; the final tax character of the gain remains capital gains under Section 67(5).	If chargeable: Section 393(2), Table: Sl. No. 17—tax to be deducted at "rates in force" on the taxable capital gains. In ordinary maturity / surrender cases involving a non-exempt ULIP treated as a unit of an equity-oriented fund, the gain would generally be long-term capital gain taxable under Section 198 at 12.5% on such long-term capital gains exceeding ₹1,25,000, with applicable surcharge and cess. DTAA relief, documentation and lower / nil deduction certificate may modify the withholding position.

Product/ receipt	Premium deduction	Maturity/survival /surrender—general Indian tax treatment	Death benefit	Resident TDS	NRI TDS without DTAA
Child plan	Section 123 read with Schedule XV, subject to ₹1.5 lakh overall ceiling, actual capital sum assured limits and applicable tax regime.	Follows the underlying policy. Do not treat "child plan" as a separate tax class. Test whether it is traditional, ULIP, annuity-linked or otherwise structured.	Generally follows the underlying policy terms and Schedule II treatment	As per underlying policy.	As per underlying policy
Immediate annuity	Section 123 read with Schedule XV only where the payment qualifies under the relevant annuity / pension item and the applicable tax regime.	Annuity instalments are generally taxable when received. Do not treat annuity instalments like ordinary life-insurance maturity proceeds.	Death-related benefit depends on the structure of the annuity contract and must be checked separately.	Section 393(1), Table: Sl. No. 8(i)—2% on the income comprised in the sum, subject to the ₹1 lakh threshold. Since annuity instalments are generally fully taxable when received, the taxable component will ordinarily be the annuity instalment itself.	Section 393(2), Table: Sl. No. 17—tax to be deducted at rates in force on taxable annuity / pension income. For ordinary insurer-paid annuity income payable to a non-resident, the practical non-treaty withholding position is generally 30% plus applicable surcharge and cess. Lower / nil deduction certificate or treaty relief may modify the final withholding.

Product/ receipt	Premium deduction	Maturity/survival /surrender—general Indian tax treatment	Death benefit	Resident TDS	NRI TDS without DTAA
Deferred annuity / insurer pension plan	Section 123 read with Schedule XV only where the payment qualifies under the relevant deferred annuity / pension item and the applicable tax regime.	Pension / annuity receipts are generally taxable when received. Where deduction was claimed earlier, the amount received, withdrawn, or received as pension may be taxable in the year of withdrawal or receipt under Schedule XV. Surrender, commutation, return of purchase price and death-linked payouts must be checked against the contract terms.	Death-related benefit depends on the structure of the contract and must be checked separately.	Section 393(1), Table: Sl. No. 8(i)—2% on the income comprised in the sum, subject to the ₹1 lakh threshold. Since annuity instalments are generally taxable when received, the taxable component will ordinarily be the annuity instalment itself.	Section 393(2), Table: Sl. No. 17—tax to be deducted at rates in force on taxable annuity / pension income. For ordinary insurer-paid annuity income payable to a non-resident, the practical non-treaty withholding position is generally 30% plus applicable surcharge and cess. Lower / nil deduction certificate or treaty relief may modify the final withholding.

Product/ receipt	Premium deduction	Maturity/survival /surrender—general Indian tax treatment	Death benefit	Resident TDS	NRI TDS without DTAA
NPS exit + annuity purchase	Section 124 for NPS contribution deduction, including the additional ₹50,000 deduction; Section 123 / Schedule XV interaction to be checked	On normal exit, up to 60% lump-sum payment is generally excluded under Section 11 read with Schedule II, Sl. No. 6. Amount used for annuity purchase is not treated as received at that stage; annuity income is taxable when received.	As per NPS / annuity terms.	No TDS on the exempt lump-sum exit component where the statutory conditions are satisfied. Taxable annuity income is subject to withholding based on the payer and character of payment. For ordinary insurer-paid taxable annuity, Section 393(1), Table: Sl. No. 8(i) should be considered. Salary-linked pension cases require separate review under Section 392.	If chargeable to a non-resident: Section 393(2), Table: Sl. No. 17—rates in force on taxable annuity / pension income, subject to treaty and lower / nil deduction route.

Product/ receipt	Premium deduction	Maturity/survival /surrender—general Indian tax treatment	Death benefit	Resident TDS	NRI TDS without DTAA
MWPA-endorsed policy	Same as underlying policy. MWPA endorsement does not create a separate premium deduction code.	Same as underlying policy. MWPA affects beneficial protection and entitlement; it does not by itself change the Indian tax character of the policy proceeds.	Same as underlying policy.	Same as underlying policy	Same as underlying policy
Keyman insurance policy	Not a personal Section 123 deduction for the insured. Business deduction, if any, depends on the payer's facts and business nexus.	Not eligible for ordinary Schedule II life-insurance exclusion. Taxable depending on character—salary, business income or income from other sources. Section 92(2)(d) specifically covers Keyman receipts where not taxable as salary or business income.	Not protected like an ordinary exempt life-insurance death claim.	Insurer payout to resident: Section 393(1), Table: Sl. No. 8(i)—2% on the income component, subject to the ₹1 lakh threshold. Salary / perquisite character: Section 392. Business-receipt	Insurer payout to non-resident: Section 393(2), Table: Sl. No. 17—tax at rates in force on the sum chargeable to tax. Salary / perquisite character: Section 392. Business-receipt character: rates in force, subject to DTAA, documentation and lower / nil deduction certificate.

Product/ receipt	Premium deduction	Maturity/survival /surrender—general Indian tax treatment	Death benefit	Resident TDS	NRI TDS without DTAA
				character: regular business tax treatment; withholding depends on payer facts.	
Employer–employee / group life	Depends on who pays, who owns, who benefits and whether there is any perquisite element.	Ordinary group term cover may be simple. Assignment, surrender value, employer-funded benefit or perquisite element may trigger tax review.	Generally excluded where it is an ordinary group life death benefit and not a Keyman or taxable employer-linked arrangement.	Ordinary exempt group life death benefit: no TDS. Taxable salary / perquisite benefit: Section 392. Taxable insurer payout not treated as salary: Section 393(1), Table: Sl. No. 8(i)—2% on the income component, subject to the ₹1 lakh threshold.	Exempt group life death benefit: no TDS. Taxable salary / perquisite benefit: Section 392. Taxable non-salary insurer payout to non-resident: Section 393(2), Table: Sl. No. 17—tax at rates in force on the sum chargeable to tax, subject to DTAA, documentation and lower / nil deduction certificate.

Product/ receipt	Premium deduction	Maturity/survival /surrender—general Indian tax treatment	Death benefit	Resident TDS	NRI TDS without DTAA
Surrender / early exit	Earlier Section 123 / Schedule XV deduction reversal may arise if policy continuity conditions are breached.	Excluded only if Section 11 read with Schedule II, Table: Sl. No. 2 conditions are satisfied. If not excluded, non-ULIP receipts are generally taxable under Section 92(2)(l) on the income component; non-excluded ULIPs are taxable as capital gains under Section 67(5).	Not applicable	If taxable: Section 393(1), Table: Sl. No. 8(i)—2% on income comprised in the sum, subject to ₹1 lakh threshold	Section 393(2), Table: Sl. No. 17—rates in force on the taxable income component. For non-ULIP policy surrender, the taxable component is generally the income component. For non-exempt ULIP surrender, the capital-gains character under Section 67(5) must be preserved. DTAA relief, documentation and lower / nil deduction certificate may modify the withholding.

Notes to the Reckoner

- **Practical guide, not legal opinion.** This table gives the general Indian tax and withholding treatment for advisor education. Old policies, high-premium policies, assignments, employer-funded structures, Keyman policies, annuity contracts, NPS-linked structures, unusual product features and foreign tax positions require separate review.

- **1961 Act to 2025 Act bridge.** What advisors earlier knew as Section 10(10D) is now dealt with through Section 11 read with Schedule II, Table: Sl. No. 2 of the Income-tax Act, 2025. The old Section 80C / 80CCC / 80CCD deduction framework is now principally reflected through Section 123 / Section 124 read with Schedule XV. The old resident life-insurance TDS conversation under Section 194DA is now to be read through Section 393(1), Table: Sl. No. 8(i). The old NRI withholding conversation under Section 195 is now to be read through Section 393(2), especially Table: Sl. No. 17 for non-salary chargeable sums.
- **Deduction and payout exclusion are different.** Premium deduction is tested separately from the tax treatment of maturity, surrender, survival benefit, death claim or annuity receipt. A policy may receive deduction at the premium stage and still need separate testing at the payout stage.
- **Policy conditions must be tested.** The Schedule II exclusion depends on the policy terms, issue date, premium-to-actual-capital-sum-assured ratio, aggregate premium thresholds, product classification and statutory carve-outs. Ordinary death claims are generally protected, but Keyman policies and specified exclusions must be separately checked.
- **ULIP and non-ULIP thresholds.** For relevant ULIPs, the ₹2.5 lakh aggregate annual premium threshold must be checked. For relevant non-ULIP policies issued on or after 1 April 2023, the ₹5 lakh aggregate annual premium threshold must be checked. Aggregation rules and product-specific conditions matter.
- **Withholding is not final tax.** Resident TDS, NRI TDS, DTAA relief, lower / nil deduction certificates, PAN, TRC, Form 41, computation support and refund claims can change the practical outcome. The table states the broad non-treaty domestic-law position.

- **Foreign tax is separate.** This table deals with Indian tax and withholding. It does not decide taxability, reporting, estate tax, inheritance tax, PFIC / FIF / chargeable-event treatment or similar consequences in the country where the client is tax-resident.

4.5 WHAT ACTUALLY CHANGES FOR NRIs

This is the point to hold firmly.

The Indian taxability test is broadly similar for residents and NRIs because the law first tests the policy, not the passport. If the policy is exempt for a resident, it will usually be exempt for an NRI as well, on the same policy conditions. If the policy is taxable for a resident, it is usually taxable for an NRI too, subject to the exact charging provision and the treaty position.

The difference is not usually the first tax question.

The difference is the handling.

For residents, a taxable payout may move through the resident withholding route now reflected in Section 393(1), Table: Sl. No. 8(i), where applicable. For NRIs, the payer generally has to examine Section 393(2), particularly the non-resident payments table, where the sum is chargeable to tax in India. That is where the conversation changes.

Can a DTAA reduce the withholding? Should the client apply for a lower or nil deduction certificate? Will the client file an Indian return and claim refund? If India taxes the income, will the country of residence give credit? If India exempts the income, will the foreign country still tax or report it?

These are NRI questions.

But the starting point remains simple:

> *First test the policy. Then test withholding. Then test DTAA. Then test the country of residence.*

4.6 DTAA MADE SIMPLE

Most advisors use the word DTAA in one of two ways.

Some use it too casually:

> *"DTAA hai, tax nahi lagega."*

Others avoid it completely because it sounds too technical.

Both approaches are wrong.

A DTAA is neither a magic exemption nor an unknowable monster. It is a structured agreement between two countries. At its core, it solves a collision.

One country may tax because the income arises there. This is the *source country*. Another country may tax because the person lives there. This is the *residence country*. When both systems apply to the same income, double taxation may arise. The DTAA decides how that overlap should be handled.

The simplest way to read a DTAA is in three movements.

Step 1—Allocate

First, the treaty asks: which country has the right to tax this income? Sometimes only the residence country can tax. Sometimes only the source country can. Sometimes both can, but the source country is capped.

Step 2—Relieve

If both countries tax the same income, the treaty asks: how will double taxation be relieved? This is where exemption or credit enters.

Step 3—Document

The taxpayer must prove treaty eligibility. This is where the TRC, the treaty declaration (Form 41, the post-2026 replacement for Form

10F under the Income-tax Rules, 2026), PAN, the TDS certificate, and proof of tax paid come in. The document does not create the treaty benefit. It supports the claim.

4.7 THE THREE DTAA METHODS

Most practical DTAA results fall into three methods.

Exhibit 4.3 · Three Ways a Treaty Relieves Double Tax

Method	Simple meaning	How it feels to the client	Key documents
Exemption method	One country steps aside because the treaty gives taxing right to the other country	"India should not tax this because the treaty gives the taxing right to my country of residence."	TRC, Form 41, PAN (where applicable), income-character support
Credit method	Both countries may tax, but the residence country gives credit for tax paid in the source country	"India has deducted tax. My country of residence may tax me too, but may give credit for the Indian tax."	TDS certificate, proof of tax paid, foreign-tax-credit form where India grants credit, such as Form 44 for resident assessees claiming foreign tax credit.
Special rate method	Source country may tax, but only at a lower treaty rate	"India can deduct tax, but only at the treaty rate if documents are accepted."	TRC, Form 41, PAN (where applicable), beneficial-ownership declaration

This is enough for an advisor to understand the DTAA conversation. The advisor does not have to interpret every treaty article. The advisor has to know that DTAA is not one answer. It is a method.

It may exempt. It may reduce. It may give credit. It may require a refund claim. It may require documents. And in some cases, it may not help at all.

4.8 A SIMPLE DTAA FLOW FOR ADVISORS

Read the DTAA conversation in this order:

1. **Is the policy receipt taxable in India?** If no, India may not deduct tax—but the foreign country may still tax or require reporting. If yes, move to the next step.
2. **Is the recipient a tax resident of another country?** If yes, check whether India has a DTAA with that country.
3. **What does the DTAA do?** It may give exemption, a lower rate, or credit relief.
4. **Are the documents available?** Usually the TRC, Form 41, PAN where applicable, declaration, TDS certificate, and proof of tax paid.
5. **If the payer does not apply the treaty at source, what is the route?** The client may need a lower or nil-deduction certificate, or may claim refund through the Indian tax return.
6. **What happens abroad?** The country of residence must separately confirm taxability, reporting, and credit.

That is the practical DTAA conversation.

Not frightening. Not casual. Structured.

4.9 THE DOCUMENTS THAT USUALLY MATTER

In real life, DTAA relief often fails not because the treaty is unavailable, but because the document file is incomplete. For most advisor-level conversations, remember these documents.

- **Tax Residency Certificate (TRC).** Proves that the client is tax-resident of the treaty country.
- **Treaty declaration—Form 41 / Form 10F,** as applicable under the rules in force for the relevant tax year. It supports the treaty claim where prescribed details are not fully covered by the TRC.

- **PAN.** Often required for Indian tax and withholding processes.
- **TDS certificate.** Proves tax deducted in India.
- **Policy statement and payout computation.** Proves the nature of the receipt and the taxable component.
- **Foreign tax proof.** Needed where foreign tax credit is claimed.
- **Return / assessment records.** Useful for refund, credit, and any future scrutiny in either jurisdiction.

Do not overstate the role of any one document. The TRC is important, but the TRC is not the whole answer. It proves residence. It does not by itself prove that the treaty article gives exemption, or that credit is available, or that the foreign country will accept the Indian character of the receipt.

4.10 CREDIT IS NOT A REFUND SCHEME

Foreign tax credit is often misunderstood.

If India taxes income and another country also taxes the same income, the country of residence may give credit for tax paid in India, depending on its domestic law and the applicable DTAA. But credit is not a refund of every rupee paid abroad.

It is usually limited. It usually requires proof. It usually applies only when the same income is taxed in both countries. And it usually has timing rules.

This matters especially for NRIs who later return to India and become Resident and Ordinarily Resident. At that point, India may start taxing global income, and foreign tax credit may become relevant. Chapter 7 will examine that return-to-India problem in detail.

For Chapter 4, the lesson is simple:

> *DTAA relief is not automatic. It must be claimed, documented, and matched to the right income.*

A DTAA does not run a clock of its own. It speaks only after India and the country of residence have each applied their domestic law; the treaty then decides how the overlap is allocated, relieved or credited.

4.11 THE COUNTRY-OF-RESIDENCE OVERLAY

Now we return to Aditya in San Jose.

India may have one answer. The United States may have another. That is not because India is wrong. It is because two countries are asking different questions.

India asks:

Is this receipt excluded from total income under Section 11 read with Schedule II, Table: Sl. No. 2?

The foreign country may ask quite different questions. Is this a qualifying life insurance contract under our law? Is there inside build-up? Is there annual reporting? Is it an investment product? Is it a foreign financial asset? Is there a surrender value? Is there estate or inheritance exposure? Was income taxable before any cash was received?

These are not Indian questions. But they are real questions.

The advisor should not answer foreign law.

The advisor should know when foreign law must be asked.

4.12 COUNTRY-OF-RESIDENCE RISK MAP

This table is not a foreign tax manual. It is a risk-location map. Its purpose is to tell the Indian advisor where to pause, what to flag, and when to ask the client to obtain local-country advice.

Exhibit 4.4· Where the Foreign Question Bites

Country/ region	Lower-sensitivity policies	Higher-sensitivity Indian policies	Foreign-law reference point	Advisor takeaway
United States	Pure term insurance with no cash value	ULIPs, endowment, money-back, whole-life, single-premium policies, annuities, policies with surrender value or policy loans	US life-insurance qualification, cash-value treatment, foreign financial asset reporting, FBAR / Form 8938, possible PFIC / Form 8621 review for investment-linked structures	If the policy has fund value, cash value, surrender value, or investment linkage, Indian exemption is not the final answer for a US-resident client.

Country/ region	Lower-sensitivity policies	Higher-sensitivity Indian policies	Foreign-law reference point	Advisor takeaway
Canada	Pure term insurance with no cash value	Endowment, money-back, whole-life, ULIP, single-premium, annuity and participating policies	Exempt-policy testing, annual accrual rules, disposition rules, adjusted cost basis, foreign-property reporting such as T1135	Canada may look at value accumulation and policy disposition, not merely Indian maturity exemption.
United Kingdom	Pure term insurance	Endowment, money-back, ULIP, whole-life, single-premium policies, surrender, maturity and partial withdrawals	Chargeable-event gain regime, time-apportioned reduction, 5% cumulative withdrawal allowance, top-slicing relief, personal portfolio bond rules and post-6 April 2025 residence-based FIG / remittance-basis reforms where relevant.	UK-resident clients should not assume Indian exemption controls the UK result. Foreign policy gains may need UK chargeable-event review even if India exempts the payout.
New Zealand	Pure term insurance with no investment value	ULIPs, endowment, whole-life, single-premium policies, foreign policies with surrender value or fund value	Foreign Investment Fund rules, foreign life-insurance policy interest, de minimis threshold, transitional-resident rules	New Zealand can tax attributed income even before maturity or surrender. "No cash received" may not always mean "no tax."

Country/ region	Lower-sensitivity policies	Higher-sensitivity Indian policies	Foreign-law reference point	Advisor takeaway
Australia	Pure term insurance	Endowment, participating policies, investment-linked policies, surrender or maturity of policies with bonus / profit element	Life-assurance bonus and profit rules, especially short-term policy treatment under Australian tax law	Australia's issue is often the timing and character of policy profit, bonus, surrender or maturity proceeds.
France	Pure term insurance	Endowment, whole-life, ULIP, single-premium, policies with surrender value, partial surrender or maturity proceeds	Foreign life-insurance reporting, redemption / surrender taxation, social contributions and succession consequences	French-resident clients should not treat Indian savings policies as invisible merely because India may exempt them.
Germany	Pure term insurance	Capital-forming life insurance, endowment, whole-life, ULIP, surrender-value policies	Taxation of capital-forming life insurance, including gain between proceeds and premiums, subject to policy conditions	Germany may focus on the investment element of the policy. Indian tax character does not control the German result.

Country/ region	Lower-sensitivity policies	Higher-sensitivity Indian policies	Foreign-law reference point	Advisor takeaway
Netherlands	Pure term insurance	Endowment, whole-life, ULIP, capital-forming policies, policies with value accumulation	Box 3 wealth-based taxation of non-exempt policy value—currently a deemed-return regime, with transition towards actual-return taxation—and capital-insurance exemptions, depending on facts.	Dutch tax concern may arise from policy value, not only from maturity or surrender. The Box 3 transition should be checked close to the year of reporting.
Singapore / Hong Kong	Pure term and many ordinary policies	ULIPs, cash-value policies, annuities, surrender-value policies, policies likely to continue after relocation	Singapore foreign-income and capital-receipt rules; Hong Kong territorial-source rules; reporting requirements if any; and future relocation risk.	Current tax treatment may often be lighter, but policies with investment value should still be checked, especially if the client may later move to a high-tax country.

This table should create awareness, not panic. For many clients, the foreign consequence may be manageable. For some, it may be immaterial. For others, it may be significant. The advisor's duty is to avoid the dangerous sentence:

> *"It is tax-free."*

The safer sentence is:

> *"It may be exempt in India. Please also have your country-of-residence tax advisor confirm local tax and reporting."*

4.13 GULF NRIs—THE TOMORROW PROBLEM

The Gulf deserves separate treatment because it is the easiest place for advisors to become casual.

A client in Dubai, Doha, Muscat, Kuwait, Riyadh, or Manama may have little or no personal income-tax exposure in the country of residence during the period of stay. The Indian policy may appear simple. Premiums go from NRE. The policy continues. Maturity may be exempt in India. Nothing seems urgent.

But the complication is not always today.

It is tomorrow.

Many Gulf NRIs do not retire permanently in the Gulf. Some return to India. Some move to Canada, the UK, Australia, New Zealand, Singapore, or the United States to join children or extend professional life. A policy bought during a tax-simple Gulf phase may mature during a tax-complex Western phase.

That changes the analysis.

A maturity benign in Dubai may be reportable in Toronto. A ULIP ignored in Doha may need review in New Zealand. A policy treated casually in Riyadh may become a US classification question after relocation.

The advisor should therefore ask one extra question in Gulf cases:

> *"Where are you likely to be tax-resident when this policy matures, is surrendered, or is claimed?"*

The answer may not be certain. But the question itself improves the advice.

4.14 WHAT ADVISORS SHOULD STOP SAYING

Credibility is often built not by what the advisor says, but by what the advisor refuses to overstate.

Exhibit 4.5 The Sentences Worth Replacing

Avoid saying	Say instead
"This policy is tax-free."	*"This policy is generally excluded from total income in India if the Section 11 read with Schedule II conditions are satisfied."*
"NRI taxation is different."	*"The Indian taxability test is broadly similar. The NRI difference is usually withholding, documentation, DTAA and foreign-country treatment."*
"DTAA means no tax."	*"DTAA may give exemption, credit, or a lower rate, depending on the treaty and documents."*
"If India does not tax, nobody taxes."	*"Indian exemption does not decide foreign tax treatment."*
"Gulf client has no tax issue."	*"Current Gulf taxation may be simple, but future relocation must be considered."*
"The insurer will handle everything."	*"The insurer may deduct or report as required; the client still needs tax advice for India and the country of residence."*
"TRC is enough."	*"TRC proves residence. The treaty claim and supporting documents still need to match the income."*

This table may be one of the most useful pages in this chapter. Read it. Practise the second column out loud. The client does not remember rate tables. The client remembers tone. The advisor who speaks with quiet precision builds a relationship the client returns to at every life event.

4.15 THE ADVISOR'S SIMPLE INSURANCE-TAX FILE

The advisor does not need to prepare a legal opinion. But the advisor should encourage the client to keep a clean file. For most significant NRI insurance cases, the following are enough to begin with.

- Policy bond and proposal form.
- Premium schedule and payment source (NRE / NRO / foreign account, as relevant).
- Sum assured confirmation and any endorsements.
- Maturity / surrender / claim computation.
- Residential-status note for the year of receipt, surrender or claim—FEMA, the Indian Income-tax Act and country-of-residence tax residence, each kept separate.
- TRC and treaty declaration (Form 41) where treaty relief is claimed.
- TDS certificate where tax is deducted.
- Foreign tax advice note where the client is resident abroad.

This file does not make the advisor a tax practitioner. It makes the advisor credible.

4.16 THE CHAPTER IN ONE PAGE

When a client asks whether an Indian life insurance policy is taxable, the advisor should not begin with fear and should not begin with overconfidence. Begin with the four-step rule.

Step 1—Test the policy. Is the policy generally excluded from total income under Section 11 read with Schedule II, Table: Sl. No. 2, or is it a taxable payout?

Step 2—Test the withholding. If taxable, is the recipient resident or non-resident? Is the resident withholding route under Section 393(1), Table: Sl. No. 8(i) relevant, or does the non-resident withholding route under Section 393(2), especially Table: Sl. No. 17, enter?

Step 3—Test the treaty. Does a DTAA reduce, exempt, credit, or otherwise affect the tax? Are the documents available?

Step 4—Test the country of residence. Does the foreign country tax, report, accrue, deem, or classify the Indian policy differently?

That is the chapter in one page.

Closing—The Sentence That Protects the Advisor

The best advisors are not the ones who make every answer sound simple. They are the ones who know which part is simple and which part is not.

For Indian tax purposes, many NRI insurance cases are less complicated than advisors fear. The exemption test is often the same as it is for residents. A death claim remains a death claim. A maturity remains a maturity. A surrender remains a surrender. The policy must be tested under Indian law.

But once the recipient is non-resident, the handling changes. Withholding changes. Documentation changes. Treaty relevance changes. Foreign tax review changes. Future relocation changes the risk.

So the advisor needs one disciplined sentence:

"This is generally excluded from total income in India if the policy satisfies the Indian conditions. Because you are an NRI, we must separately check withholding, DTAA and your country-of-residence tax treatment."

That sentence does not weaken the sale. It strengthens the trust.

Because the client does not need an advisor who says "tax-free" quickly.

The client needs an advisor who knows exactly where India's answer ends—and where the rest of the world begins.

End of Chapter 4

PART III

THE INDIA DECISION

CHAPTER 5

NRI INVESTMENT REALITY CHECK

Why India Is Easy to Love,
But Not Always Easy to Invest In

It is a Sunday afternoon in Dubai, and Rahul is sitting at his desk with four browser tabs open.

The first is a property listing for a two-bedroom flat in Pune. The photographs are doing what property photographs are designed to do: sunlight on the balcony, a child in the garden, a gym he may never use, and a carpet area that requires more attention than the brochure would like him to give.

The second tab is an NRE fixed deposit calculator. The rate looks respectable. The maturity value looks neat. The bank name is familiar. The product feels like something his father would approve of.

The third tab is a mutual fund platform in India. His cousin has sent him the name of a fund that has done well over the last five years. The factsheet is attractive. The onboarding process is less attractive.

The fourth tab is his overseas brokerage account. There, he can buy an India-focused fund without calling his banker in Mumbai, without uploading his OCI card again, and without explaining why his foreign tax identification number must match the country where he files his return.

His annual bonus has just been credited. After conversion, it is roughly forty lakh rupees.

Four options. All plausible. None complete.

This is the modern NRI investment problem. The NRI does not lack choice. He is surrounded by choice. The difficulty is that every choice has a second life—a tax life, a FEMA life, a banking life, a repatriation life, a reporting life, and finally, a family life.

Rahul is not merely asking, *"Where will I earn more?"*

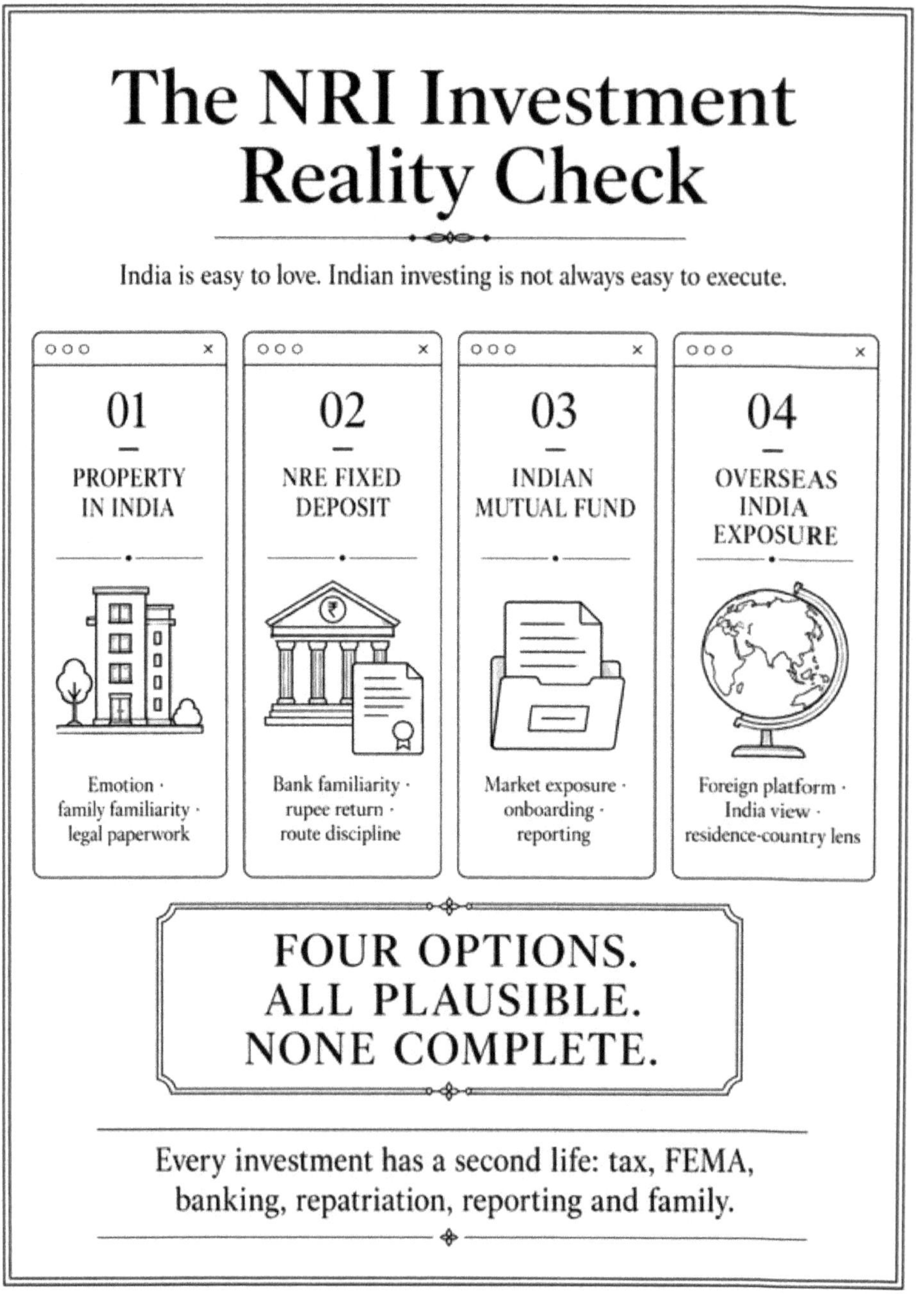

He is asking something larger, even if he has not yet said it aloud.

Where should the money I earned abroad finally belong?

That question is not mechanical. It comes with memory. It comes with parents. It comes with a future return that may or may not happen. It comes with the pressure of children growing up abroad and parents growing older in India. It comes with the pride of earning in a foreign currency and the instinct to bring part of that success home.

The NRI is the hero of this chapter.

Not because every decision he makes is correct. Often, it is not. But because he is trying to solve a problem most resident investors never face. He is trying to make one financial life work across two countries, two currencies, two tax systems, two emotional geographies, and sometimes two futures.

India is easy to love.

Indian investing, for an NRI, is not always easy to execute.

That is the distinction this chapter must make clear.

5.1 WHY INDIA COMES FIRST

For many NRIs, India is not one market among many. It is the default market.

The reason is not only economic growth. Growth can be found elsewhere. It is not only return. Returns are never guaranteed anywhere. It is not even only patriotism, though pride certainly plays its part.

India comes first because India is understood emotionally before it is understood financially.

The NRI knows the city. Or thinks he does. He knows which suburb is "coming up." He knows which builder his uncle trusts. He knows which bank branch his father uses. He knows where the new airport is expected, where the metro is coming, where the cousin bought a flat, where the family doctor lives, where the school is good, and where his parents would feel comfortable.

This familiarity is powerful.

It is also dangerous if mistaken for technical knowledge.

A person can know Pune emotionally and still misunderstand the TDS on a property sale. He can know Mumbai socially and still use the wrong account route. He can know Ahmedabad from childhood and still fail to report the asset correctly in his country of residence. He can understand India deeply and still not understand Indian compliance.

For an NRI in Dubai, Doha, Singapore, London, Toronto, California, Sydney or Nairobi, India may represent several things at once. It may be a retirement base. It may be the place where parents need support. It may be the place where weddings, medical needs, religious duties, ancestral property, and family expectations still sit. It may be where the client expects to return one day, even if that day keeps moving.

So the question is not, *"Why India?"*

For most NRIs, that question has already been answered in the heart.

The better question is:

Once India is chosen, how should the NRI enter India correctly?

Because in NRI investing, the first mistake is often made before the asset is selected. It is made when the client assumes that because the money is his, he can move it, convert it, invest it, redeem it and repatriate it as he pleases.

That is not how cross-border investing works.

5.2 THE FIRST REALITY: INDIA MEANS RUPEES

Let us state the point plainly.

If an NRI wants to invest in ordinary onshore India—a flat in Bengaluru, a mutual fund in India, listed shares on Indian stock exchanges, an Indian life insurance policy, an Indian fixed deposit, an Indian PMS, an AIF, a SIF, or most domestic Indian assets—the investment is ultimately an Indian rupee investment.

The client may earn in dollars. He may think in dirhams. His bonus may arrive in pounds. His children's future education may be priced in Canadian dollars. His retirement spreadsheet may have two columns, one in rupees and one in foreign currency.

But the ordinary Indian asset does not care.

A Pune flat is not purchased in dollars.

An Indian domestic mutual fund is not subscribed in dollars.

A domestic Indian insurance policy is not a dollar contract merely because the premium came from abroad.

Indian listed shares are not held as dollar assets merely because the investor lives in the United States.

The money may begin its life abroad. But once it enters the ordinary Indian financial system for domestic investment, it generally enters through the permitted banking channel and becomes rupee money.

That conversion is not a footnote.

It is the investment decision.

The NRI who converts dollars into rupees today has taken a currency call, whether he admits it or not. If the future liability is in India—parents' support, retirement in India, Indian property purchase, Indian family needs—rupee exposure may be sensible. If the future liability remains abroad—children's education in the US, retirement in Canada, relocation to Australia—then rupee conversion may become a future friction point.

This is why the advisor must never discuss Indian investments as if they are merely asset choices. They are currency choices first.

There is one important exception to this domestic rupee architecture, and that exception deserves its own chapter: GIFT City. The IFSC route can allow certain India-linked products and structures in freely convertible foreign currency. But that is a separate architecture, with its own rules, limits, opportunities and tax questions.

This chapter is about ordinary onshore India.

And ordinary onshore India begins with this sentence:

Your dollars do not buy Indian assets directly. They first need the correct Indian route.

5.3 THE SECOND REALITY: THE ROUTE DECIDES THE EXIT

Chapter 3 explained the banking rails. This chapter applies that rule to investments.

In NRI advisory work, NRE, NRO and FCNR(B) are not administrative labels. They are legal routes. The same client, the same amount, and the same investment can produce different exit outcomes depending on the account through which the money entered.

NRE is the repatriable rupee bridge. Foreign earnings enter India through normal banking channels, are converted into rupees, and retain repatriable character. The NRE account is useful when the client wants India exposure without losing, at least in principle, the ability to take money back abroad later.

NRO is the India-linked rupee account. It is used to receive and manage India-source income: rent, dividends, pension, sale proceeds, local credits, and other India-side money. It is useful, practical and often operationally simpler for domestic Indian transactions. But it is not as flexible as NRE. Repatriation from NRO is controlled, documentation-heavy, and subject to conditions, limits and tax compliance.

FCNR(B) is different again. It is not an ordinary operating account for daily investment transactions. It is a foreign-currency term deposit maintained with an Indian bank. It helps the client keep money in foreign currency while remaining within the Indian non-resident banking framework.

The advisor's first investment question should therefore not be:

"Which product do you like?"

It should be:

"What must this money be capable of doing later?"

If the money must come back to Dubai, London, New York, Toronto or Singapore, the route matters from day one. If the money is meant for parents in India or retirement in India, NRO may be adequate. If the client wants to preserve currency denomination, FCNR(B) may be relevant. If the client wants repatriable listed equity exposure, the NRE PIS route may enter the picture.

The route is not clerical. The route is strategy.

This is especially important in real estate. In theory, FEMA permits repatriation of sale proceeds of eligible immovable property in specified cases, subject to conditions. For residential property acquired from eligible foreign exchange, NRE or FCNR(B) sources, the repatriation of sale proceeds is restricted to not more than two such residential properties, and the amount eligible is linked to the permitted funding source. For property acquired out of rupee funds, inheritance, legacy or other India-side sources, the NRO remittance-of-assets framework generally applies, including the familiar USD 1 million per financial year route, subject to documentary evidence and tax compliance.

But the practical advisor must not make this sound easy.

In real life, when an NRI sells Indian immovable property, the sale proceeds usually do not glide into the NRE account as if nothing happened. They usually move into the NRO account. The bank asks questions. The source of acquisition matters. The sale deed matters. The tax deduction matters. The capital-gains computation matters. The remittance certification may matter. The authorised dealer's comfort matters. The repatriation limit may matter. The two-property condition may matter in eligible residential-property cases.

So the practical sentence is this:

Sale proceeds of Indian immovable property are not freely repatriable merely because the original investment came from abroad. They may be repatriable if conditions are satisfied, but the working route usually passes through NRO, tax compliance, documentation and bank scrutiny.

That sentence is less glamorous.

It is also more useful.

The rail always remembers.

It remembers how the money entered. It remembers whether the funds were repatriable or non-repatriable. It remembers whether the premium was paid from NRE, FCNR(B), eligible foreign remittance, NRO or another rupee source. It remembers whether listed shares were bought through NRE PIS or NRO. It remembers whether the property was purchased from foreign funds, rupee funds, inheritance, or mixed sources.

Years later, when the client sells, redeems, surrenders, receives maturity proceeds or tries to repatriate, the rail returns to the conversation.

The product may be new. The route is old. And the route often decides the exit.

5.4 RETURN, ROUTE AND RECORD

The frame for this chapter is simple.

Every NRI investment is three things at once: a return, a route, and a record.

Return is what the client sees first. CAGR, rental yield, interest rate, maturity value, capital appreciation, dividend income, projected corpus.

Route is what the client often sees last. Which account funded it? Was it NRE, NRO, FCNR(B) or direct foreign remittance? Is the asset held on a repatriable or non-repatriable basis? Can the sale proceeds go abroad? What documents will the bank ask for when the client tries to move the money?

Record is what the client underestimates. How is the asset reported in India? How is it reported in the client's country of tax residence? Does FATCA apply? Does CRS apply? Will the Indian financial institution report the account? Will the country-of-residence return require disclosure? Will a tax exemption in India be recognised abroad?

An investment that works on return but fails on route becomes a FEMA or banking problem.

An investment that works on route but fails on record becomes a tax or disclosure problem.

A serious NRI advisor must examine all three.

Return tells you whether the investment looks good.

Route tells you whether the money can lawfully move.

Record tells you whether the investment will survive scrutiny.

Only when all three work together does the investment make sense.

5.5 THE NRI INVESTMENT MENU

Broadly, an NRI looking at India has several investment paths. Real estate. Bank deposits. Mutual funds. Direct equity through the permitted route. SIFs. PMS. AIFs. Bonds and fixed-income instruments, where eligible. Government savings and retirement products such as PPF and NPS, where permitted. Overseas India exposure. Indian life insurance.

Each has a place. Each has a problem.

Real estate satisfies emotion but burdens exit.

Deposits give comfort but carry reinvestment risk, currency questions and limited growth potential.

Mutual funds offer diversification and SIP discipline, but may create foreign-tax, FATCA, CRS and onboarding complications for certain NRIs.

Direct equity gives control but requires the PIS, demat, broker and bank architecture.

SIFs may open a new middle lane between mutual funds and more sophisticated strategies, but eligibility, route and product documentation must be checked carefully.

PMS and AIF structures may suit sophisticated investors, but they bring higher ticket sizes, documents, taxation, reporting and jurisdictional filters.

Certain bonds, government savings products and sovereign-linked instruments may be available to residents but not to NRIs, or may be available only under specific conditions.

Overseas India funds may be simpler for some foreign residents but may not solve Indian family, rupee, protection or succession objectives.

Insurance can combine protection, discipline, tax planning, predictable outcomes, market-linked participation in some products, retirement income in others, and succession utility—but only when it matches the client's facts.

The advisor who makes this a beauty contest between products will miss the chapter's point.

The question is not, *"Which asset class is best?"*

The question is:

Which asset survives the client's full journey?

Funding. Holding. Reporting. Taxation. Exit. Repatriation. Return to India. Death. Succession.

That is the real comparison.

5.6 REAL ESTATE: THE ASSET THAT FEELS SAFEST BECAUSE IT FEELS LIKE HOME

When an NRI thinks of investing in India, the first instinct is rarely a bond, a fund, or a policy.

It is usually property.

A flat. A shop. A plot. A second home. Something visible. Something the family can visit. Something the parents can point to. Something that says, "We have not left India completely."

To understand NRI real estate, one must begin not with price per square foot, but with sacrifice.

Many NRIs left India with a picture in their mind. Not always a picture of wealth. Sometimes just a picture of dignity.

A father who spent thirty years in a rented apartment. A mother who never complained about the leaking ceiling. Parents who used their best years, their savings, their sleep, and sometimes their health, to educate the child who eventually left. A son who watched them adjust, compromise, postpone, and say, "Tu bas padhai kar." A daughter who knew that the family's dreams had been quietly transferred into her suitcase.

For such an NRI, buying a home in India for parents is not an investment.

It is repayment.

No spreadsheet can defeat that emotion. No CAGR calculation can explain the day the parents step into a home bought by the child they sent into the world. No financial planner should reduce that moment to rental yield.

That is one kind of property decision. This chapter respects it.

But this chapter is not evaluating that decision. This chapter is evaluating property as an investment.

The distinction matters. If a client is buying a home for parents, the analysis is not only return. It is duty, dignity, comfort and love. But if a client is buying the third flat in a growing suburb because "prices will double," then the asset must stand in the witness box like every other investment.

Return. Route. Record.

There is another layer too.

For many NRIs, Indian property is not only an emotional asset. It is a landing strip.

A foreign life can look permanent from the outside and fragile from the inside. Visa rules change. Projects close. Industries become obsolete. AI and automation rewrite job descriptions. Sponsorships end. Tax authorities abroad become more aggressive. Children adapt to the host country faster than parents do. A long-term residence permit still has conditions. A job loss can turn a confident foreign life into a countdown.

Some NRIs carry a private fear they rarely admit in public:

If I have to pack my bags, where will I land safely?

India answers that question differently from any other country.

For an Indian citizen, India is not a visa category. It is home. For an OCI cardholder, India is not citizenship, and the OCI is not a substitute for full constitutional rights; it has legal limits. But practically, the OCI often feels warmer than most foreign visa systems. In many situations, it gives the Indian-origin person a long-term right of connection that feels like what one may jokingly call "son-in-law treatment"—welcomed, accommodated, allowed to remain connected, though always subject to the boundaries of law.

So when an NRI buys property in India, he may not be buying square feet. He may be buying a safe landing.

That emotion must be honoured. But once the property is presented as an investment, the analysis must become rigorous.

5.7 PROPERTY PERMISSION AND PROPERTY ROUTE

Under FEMA, the clean purchase lane for Indian immovable property is not available to every person who has an emotional connection with India. An Indian passport holder resident outside India is an NRI—in other words, an Indian citizen living abroad. An OCI cardholder is a foreign citizen of Indian origin who has obtained the OCI status recognised by Indian law. These are the two broad categories that can generally acquire residential and commercial immovable property in India without prior RBI approval, subject to the restrictions on agricultural land, plantation property and farmhouses.

A foreign citizen of Indian origin who has not obtained OCI should not be casually placed in the same bucket. Indian lineage may explain the emotional connection, but the legal permission must still be checked. A PIO in the older cultural sense, without OCI status, does not automatically stand in the same clean purchase lane as an Indian citizen or OCI cardholder. If the person does not fall within the permitted category, prior RBI approval or another specific legal route may be required.

That is why advisors must not ask only, "Are you Indian-origin?" The correct question is sharper: "Are you an Indian citizen, an OCI cardholder, or a foreign citizen requiring a separate permission check?"

One final caution: the clean NRI/OCI purchase lane should not be extended mechanically to every foreign national with an Indian connection. Citizens of specified countries face separate RBI restrictions on acquiring or transferring immovable property in India, unless they are covered by OCI status or another permitted route. In property advice, citizenship and OCI status must be checked before comfort is given.

The acquisition must be funded through permitted banking channels, such as inward remittance through normal banking channels or debit to permitted NRE, FCNR(B) or NRO accounts, depending on the facts. The fact that the money originally came from abroad does not make the property a foreign-currency asset. The property is bought, held, rented and sold in rupees.

These distinctions expose three common misconceptions.

First, an NRI cannot simply arrive with foreign currency notes and buy property casually.

Second, the property is not a dollar asset merely because the NRI funded it from dollars.

Third, the funding rail affects what happens when the property is sold.

The NRI may buy the flat in rupees. The builder receives rupees. The stamp duty is paid in rupees. The registration value is in rupees. The rent is in rupees. The buyer at exit pays rupees. The tax deduction is in rupees. The sale proceeds arrive in an Indian bank account, usually NRO in practice.

If the client wants the money abroad later, the work begins much earlier than the sale date. It begins at purchase.

The source of funds must be clean. The bank trail must be preserved. The sale deed must be preserved. The tax records must be preserved. The evidence of inward remittance or NRE / FCNR(B) funding must be preserved. If rupee funds were used, that too must be documented.

The problem is not that repatriation is impossible. The problem is that repatriation is not casual.

5.8 THE DOUBLED-IN-SIX-YEARS ILLUSION

Property conversations in Indian families have their own mathematics.

"We bought it for fifty lakh. Now it is one crore."

The statement sounds powerful. It may even be true. But it is not yet an investment return.

Let us take the popular version: the property doubled in six years.

There is an easy way to convert this family-style statement into an approximate annualised rate for comparison. The Rule of 72 says that if money doubles over a period, the approximate annual return is 72 divided by the number of years.

So if the property doubled in six years:

72 ÷ 6 = approximately 12% per annum.

Now the conversation becomes more honest.

The property did not simply give "double." On the Rule of 72 approximation, it implies an annualised return of roughly 12% before costs, before tax, before currency movement, and before effort.

Now ask the real questions.

After stamp duty, did the return remain 12%? After registration cost, did it remain 12%? After brokerage, did it remain 12%? After society maintenance, did it remain 12%? After repairs, painting, leakage, vacancy and tenant change, did it remain 12%? After property tax, legal charges and management cost, did it remain 12%? After capital-gains tax and TDS cash-flow blockage, did it remain 12%? After rupee depreciation against the client's earning currency, did it remain 12%?

This is where the comparison changes.

Physical assets are usually discussed in doubling language. Financial assets are usually discussed in annualised-return language.

That makes the conversation unfair.

A property owner says, "My flat doubled." A mutual fund investor says, "My fund gave 11% CAGR." A fixed deposit investor says, "My rate was 7%." An insurance illustration says, "This is the maturity benefit or IRR under this structure."

These are not the same units of measurement.

Before comparing assets, bring them to the same measurement platform. Convert the property's doubling period into an approximate annualised return. Then compare that number with the reported CAGR, yield or IRR of other assets only after adjusting for costs, tax, currency movement, liquidity and timing. The point is not to pretend that Rule of 72 is an exact IRR calculation. The point is to stop comparing property in "doubling language" and financial assets in "annualised-return language."

The Rule of 72 helps when money doubles.

The Rule of 114 helps when money triples. If an asset has tripled, dividing 114 by the number of years gives a rough annualised return. If someone says, "This property became three times in ten years," the implied return is about 11.4% per annum before costs.

Again, the question is not whether the asset rose. The question is what it earned annually, net of everything, and whether that return justified the risk, illiquidity and compliance burden.

Property is not bad. Bad comparison is bad.

5.9 RENTAL INCOME: PASSIVE INCOME THAT IS NOT PASSIVE

The next comfort sentence is equally familiar:

"At least rent will come."

Yes. Rent may come.

But rent is not always passive income in the life of an NRI. It is often active headache disguised as passive income.

Who will find the tenant? Who will verify him? Who will sign the agreement? Who will collect the deposit? Who will coordinate police verification where applicable? Who will handle the society office? Who will answer when the tenant says water is not coming? Who will call the plumber when the bathroom leaks? Who will handle the air-conditioner breakdown in May? Who will repaint after the tenant leaves? Who will inspect whether the property has been damaged? Who will negotiate with the broker every eleven months? Who will chase the rent when the tenant delays payment?

The NRI sitting in Singapore or Dubai may own the flat. But someone in India must manage the flat.

Sometimes that someone is a parent. Sometimes a sibling. Sometimes a broker. Sometimes a property management company. Sometimes nobody, until the problem becomes expensive.

There are property management companies that handle these tasks professionally. They can be useful. But they are not free. Their cost must be included in rental-yield calculations.

The NRI should not calculate rental return by saying, "I get ₹50,000 per month."

The correct calculation is:

Gross rent, minus vacancy, minus maintenance, minus property tax, minus repairs, minus brokerage, minus society charges, minus legal cost, minus management cost, minus tax, minus currency impact, minus the mental cost of managing an asset from another country.

Only then does the rental yield become real.

Now comes the tax layer.

Rental income from Indian property is Indian-source income. When the landlord is an NRI, rent payment generally falls under the non-resident withholding framework. This is not the same as the simplified resident-landlord TDS conversation many tenants are familiar with.

Where the payment is taxable at slab rates in the hands of a non-resident individual, withholding is commonly applied at 30% plus applicable surcharge and cess. Where no surcharge applies, the effective rate becomes 31.2%. This means that if a tenant is paying rent to an NRI landlord, the tenant may have to deduct tax at this rate, obtain a TAN, deposit the TDS, file TDS returns, and issue the relevant TDS certificate.

This is not a small operational point.

Many tenants do not want this responsibility. Many do not understand it. Some may prefer a resident landlord simply because the compliance is easier. That affects marketability, tenant negotiations and cash flow.

Some NRIs try to solve this discomfort by asking the tenant to pay the rent directly to their parents in India, treating it as monthly support or a pension-like arrangement. The intention may be noble, but the legal character of the rent does not change merely because the money is routed to a parent. If the property belongs to the NRI, the rent remains the NRI's India-source income; the withholding, reporting, FEMA banking route and documentation questions must still be examined separately. Family support is one conversation. Recharacterising rental income is another.

If the final taxable income is lower after deductions, standard deduction, interest, or other allowable claims, the NRI may recover excess tax through the Indian return process. But that refund comes later. The cash-flow deduction happens now.

For the NRI landlord, rental income is therefore not merely "monthly rent."

It is tenant compliance, withholding, bank credit, tax return, refund possibility, and eventual repatriation review.

That is the real rental yield conversation.

5.10 SALE OF PROPERTY: THE CASH-FLOW SHOCK

The largest real-estate shock usually comes at sale.

A resident seller and an NRI seller are not treated operationally in the same way.

When an NRI sells Indian property, the buyer must examine withholding under the non-resident tax deduction framework. This is where many transactions become painful.

For many financial assets, withholding usually operates on the income component or according to the special-rate character of the income. If a mutual fund redemption gives rise to a capital gain, the withholding discussion is generally linked to the gain and its applicable rate. If interest is paid, the withholding is on the interest. If a dividend is paid, withholding is on the dividend.

Property is different in practice.

In the case of immovable property sold by an NRI, unless a lower or nil deduction certificate or proper determination is obtained, the buyer often deducts TDS on the entire sale consideration to protect himself from being treated as an assessee-in-default. The economic tax may ultimately be on capital gains. But the cash-flow deduction may hit the gross sale value.

That distinction must be understood clearly.

Tax is not necessarily on the entire sale value. But TDS may be deducted on the entire sale value if planning is not done.

Take a simple example.

An NRI sells a property for ₹1 crore. He assumes that after some tax, he will receive most of the money and then repatriate it abroad.

That may not happen.

Depending on the nature of gain, holding period, applicable rate, surcharge, cess, documents and buyer's advisor's comfort, roughly ₹14–15 lakh or another applicable amount may be deducted and deposited as TDS in his PAN. The seller does not receive that money in his bank account. It moves into the tax system.

Then the waiting begins.

The financial year must close. The TDS credit must reflect. The return must be filed. The capital gain must be computed. The exemption, if any, must be claimed. The refund, if due, must be processed. Only after that does the client realistically think of further repatriation, supported where applicable by the remittance declaration and certification framework—broadly, **Form 145**, the remitter's declaration, and **Form 146**, the accountant's certificate, under the Income-tax Rules, 2026, replacing the earlier Form 15CA and Form 15CB terminology for remittances governed by the new taxation regime—together with the authorised dealer bank's documentation and review.

So the issue is not only tax. It is cash-flow timing.

The NRI may be entitled to refund. But a refund after return processing does not help a client who needed sale proceeds now to buy a home abroad, repay a loan, fund children's education, or reinvest elsewhere.

The solution is advance planning.

If the NRI does not want excessive withholding on gross sale consideration, he must consider applying for a lower or nil deduction certificate before the sale transaction is completed. This is not automatic. It requires computation, documents, proposed sale deed, cost records, purchase deed, improvement cost evidence, capital-gains working, tax residency facts, past return-filing status, PAN, and a clear explanation before the jurisdictional officer.

The form may be online. The process is still document-heavy.

The officer must be satisfied. The certificate must cover the relevant transaction and amount. Only then can the buyer deduct tax at the lower rate specified in the certificate.

The buyer does not reduce TDS because the seller says, "My CA told me tax is lower." The buyer reduces TDS because the law-backed certificate permits him to do so.

Therefore, for an NRI selling Indian property, the advisory line should be direct:

Do not sign the sale agreement first and call the CA later. Call the CA before the transaction is structured.

In property sale, sequence is money.

Family arrangements often fail at the banking trail. If three brothers jointly own a property and one resident brother offers to "handle everything," the intention may be clean, but the route must still be clean. A power of attorney can authorise him to sign, coordinate and deal with the buyer; it does not allow the NRI brothers' sale proceeds, TDS credits, capital-gains records and repatriation trail to be collapsed into his personal bank account. Even if a later family transfer may look harmless, or even qualify as a gift under income-tax principles, FEMA does not run on family intention. It runs on source, ownership, account route and documentation. Good faith is not a substitute for a compliant trail.

5.11 INDIAN REINVESTMENT EXEMPTIONS DO NOT TRAVEL AUTOMATICALLY

A further trap appears when the NRI sells one property and reinvests in another.

Indian tax law may provide specific capital-gains exemptions where the taxpayer reinvests in another residential house or in specified assets such as capital-gains bonds, subject to the relevant provision, conditions, amount limits, timelines and documentation.

But the legal mechanics must be understood.

Even in India, the taxable event first occurs. The property is sold. The capital gain arises. Then the taxpayer claims an exemption because Indian law contains a specific provision saying that if prescribed reinvestment conditions are satisfied, the capital gain may be exempted to that extent.

The sale did not disappear. The exemption applied.

This distinction matters even more outside India.

Suppose an NRI tax-resident in another country sells Indian property and reinvests the proceeds in another Indian house or capital-gains bonds. India may allow exemption if the conditions are satisfied. But the residence country may see two separate events.

First event: sale of Indian property and realisation of capital gain.

Second event: investment of proceeds into another asset.

The second event may create a new reportable asset. It may not erase the first event. The residence country may tax the capital gain according to its own domestic law, cost basis, currency conversion rules, foreign tax credit rules, treaty rules and reporting framework.

India may say, "You have satisfied our reinvestment exemption."

The foreign country may say, "A taxable capital gain arose under our law."

Both can be true.

This is the same principle Chapter 4 established for insurance taxation. An Indian exemption is not a global exemption. A benefit under Indian domestic law does not automatically bind the country where the NRI is tax-resident.

Therefore, the correct advisory sentence is:

India may allow you to avoid paying capital-gains tax because Indian law contains a specific reinvestment exemption. Your country of tax residence is not bound to give the same relief unless its own law provides similar treatment.

That one sentence can prevent a very expensive misunderstanding.

5.12 FIXED DEPOSITS: THE COMFORT OF THE FAMILIAR

After property, the most familiar Indian investment is the fixed deposit.

For generations, Indian families have trusted fixed deposits. Before mutual funds became household language, before equity portfolios became app-based, before everyone had an opinion on asset allocation, the fixed deposit was the default symbol of safety.

A bank FD had a certain respectability. It was simple. It was visible. It had a rate. It had a maturity date. It did not argue. It did not flash red and green every morning. It gave the family a sentence everyone understood: "Paise FD mein rakhe hain."

For NRIs, that comfort becomes even stronger. The bank is known. The RBI-regulated system inspires confidence. Indian banking has institutional depth, compliance architecture and familiarity. Parents understand it. Spouses understand it. Advisors understand it. Compared with property registration, PIS accounts, FATCA declarations, PMS agreements or foreign tax classifications, an FD feels clean.

But even fixed deposits are not one thing for an NRI.

There are three broad deposit conversations: NRO, NRE and FCNR(B).

An NRO fixed deposit is used for India-source rupee funds. Rent, pension, dividends, local credits, sale proceeds, or other India-side money may sit in NRO and be placed into deposit. The interest on NRO deposits is taxable in India. Since it is income payable to a non-resident, tax withholding is generally heavy. In many ordinary cases, withholding on such interest is applied at 30% plus applicable surcharge and cess; where no surcharge applies, the effective rate is commonly 31.2%.

So the NRI should not compare the NRO FD rate with a resident FD rate casually.

The relevant number is post-tax, post-withholding, and post-repatriation-documentation where the funds are later to be moved abroad.

An NRE fixed deposit is different. Foreign earnings are remitted into India through the permitted route, converted into rupees, and placed in an NRE deposit. Interest on qualifying NRE deposits is generally exempt from Indian tax while the account holder remains eligible under the NRE framework. The principal and interest are freely repatriable.

That is attractive. But it is not free of analysis.

First, the money has been converted into rupees. If the client ultimately needs the money abroad, currency depreciation can reduce the effective foreign-currency return.

Second, NRE term deposits have a minimum stipulated period of one year to earn interest. If the deposit is withdrawn before completing that minimum period, interest may not be payable, and the bank's premature-withdrawal policy will apply. So the NRE FD is not merely "tax-exempt interest." It is tax-exempt interest subject to eligibility, tenure and account-status discipline.

Third, the FD rate is not permanent. Fixed deposits are cyclical and resettable. The rate is locked only for the tenure. On maturity, the next deposit will earn whatever rate is available at that time. If rates have fallen, the NRI faces reinvestment risk.

This is different from market risk. The FD may not fluctuate daily, but the future income stream is not guaranteed forever. Every maturity date is a new negotiation with the interest-rate cycle.

FCNR(B) deposits solve a different problem. They are foreign-currency deposits maintained with Indian banks in permitted currencies. The client does not take immediate INR conversion risk because the deposit remains denominated in foreign currency. Interest on qualifying FCNR(B) deposits is generally exempt from Indian tax for eligible non-residents. But FCNR(B) deposits too are term products. Here also, the minimum stipulated period is one year. If the deposit is withdrawn before completing that period, no interest may be payable, and the bank may apply its premature-withdrawal policy. So FCNR(B) protects the currency layer better than NRE, but it does not remove tenure discipline or reinvestment risk.

So the deposit comparison is not simply:

Which rate is highest?

The proper comparison is:

What is the source of funds? What currency does the client need? Is Indian tax exemption available? What is the post-tax return? Is the money repatriable? What happens if the deposit is broken early? What happens when the deposit matures and rates reset? What is the foreign-country tax treatment? What happens on death?

That last question is often ignored.

A fixed deposit can have a nominee. But nomination is not estate planning. Nomination helps operational transmission; it does not necessarily settle the ultimate beneficial ownership question in every family situation. If the NRI wants clean legacy protection, especially where family members are spread across countries, a registered will and proper succession documentation become important.

We will examine nominee versus legal heir in detail later. For now, the fixed deposit point is simple:

FDs are useful. FDs are familiar. FDs are often necessary. But FDs are not a complete cross-border wealth plan. They are banking tools with tax, currency, reinvestment, repatriation and succession consequences.

5.13 MUTUAL FUNDS: INDIA'S FAVOURITE MARKET VEHICLE, WITH A CROSS-BORDER TWIST

For the resident Indian investor, mutual funds have become the elegant middle path between doing nothing and doing everything oneself.

They are simple to understand at the first level. They are regulated. They are professionally managed. They offer different flavours: equity-oriented funds, debt-oriented funds, hybrid funds, index funds, sector funds, international funds, liquid funds, and more. They allow the ordinary investor to participate in markets without selecting every stock or bond personally.

The systematic investment plan, or SIP, is one of the great behavioural innovations of Indian personal finance.

It allows the investor to invest monthly. It allows entry into the market at different levels. It converts salary or surplus into disciplined accumulation. It removes the pressure of finding the perfect day to invest. A resident Indian earning every month can invest every month and build wealth silently over time.

From an Indian tax perspective, mutual funds are also efficient in a simple way: tax generally arises when there is a taxable event such as redemption, transfer or realisation of capital gains. Merely watching the NAV move upward does not usually create annual tax in India for the resident investor.

No wonder Indian investors love the structure.

It is SEBI-regulated. It is accessible. It is diversified. It is scalable. It has brought market participation into households that would never have opened a direct equity portfolio.

But when the investor is an NRI, the sentence changes.

What is simple for a resident Indian may not remain simple for a tax resident of another country.

The mutual fund is Indian. The investor is abroad. The tax return may be filed elsewhere. The reporting rules may belong to another country. The classification of the Indian mutual fund may not follow Indian language.

This is where many NRIs get surprised.

The real break in the mutual-fund story appears when the client is tax-resident in the United States, Canada, the United Kingdom, Australia, New Zealand or another worldwide-tax / foreign-reporting jurisdiction. Here, the issue is not merely longer KYC or heavier paperwork. The residence country may require reporting of foreign financial assets, tax worldwide income, classify the Indian mutual fund differently, or apply mark-to-market, deemed-income, anti-deferral, foreign-fund or punitive reporting rules.

The US PFIC regime is one example. PFIC stands for Passive Foreign Investment Company. Without going into technical detail, many foreign pooled investment vehicles can create adverse US tax and reporting consequences for US persons. An Indian mutual fund may look like a normal mutual fund in India but may create a difficult US tax reporting problem for a US taxpayer. The issue is not that India has done anything wrong. The issue is that the US tax law may classify and tax the foreign fund in its own way.

This is why the first mutual fund question for an NRI is not:

"Which fund is best?"

It is:

"Where do you file your tax return?"

Not where were you born. Not where is your PAN. Not where are your parents. Where are you tax-resident now?

The answer can change the investment route.

There is another advanced point. Some NRIs hear that under certain DTAAs, capital gains on Indian mutual fund units may not be taxable in India and may instead be taxable only in the country of residence. The UAE is the best-known example in many NRI conversations because the UAE does not currently levy personal income tax on individuals in the ordinary manner. But the discussion is not limited to the UAE alone. Depending on the exact treaty language, asset character, documentation and facts, similar treaty conversations may arise in relation to jurisdictions such as Singapore, Saudi Arabia, Mauritius, Luxembourg, Kuwait, Qatar, Oman, Cyprus, the Netherlands, Japan, Korea, Malaysia, Switzerland, Germany, Italy, Philippines, Nepal and other treaty countries.

But this is not a country-list shortcut. The treaty article, the nature of the mutual fund unit, the type of gain, the client's tax residency, TRC, Form 41, beneficial ownership, limitation-of-benefit or principal-purpose provisions, and the actual practice of the AMC or withholding agent all matter. The advisor should therefore never say, "You live in this country, so mutual fund gains are automatically tax-free." The correct sentence is: "This treaty may create a planning opportunity, but the treaty position must be checked and documented before redemption."

But this is not a WhatsApp-forward strategy.

It requires careful planning, proper treaty documentation, correct tax residency proof, timely submission to the AMC or withholding agent, and a defensible return-filing position. Even then, the residence country must be checked separately. A country with no personal capital-gains tax may make the result attractive. A country with worldwide taxation may not. The treaty can change the Indian tax result; it does not automatically settle the foreign-country result.

Then comes the onboarding problem.

Indian AMCs and platforms ask for FATCA/CRS declarations, tax residency details and foreign tax identification numbers because cross-border reporting obligations exist. Many Indian AMCs do not onboard US and Canada-linked NRIs, not necessarily because Indian law absolutely prohibits every such investment, but because the fund house may not want the operational burden, foreign reporting exposure, compliance complexity or risk of dealing with those investor categories.

That distinction is important.

The problem is not always permission. Sometimes the problem is provider willingness.

Even where a fund house or platform accepts a US-linked investor, the advisor must not celebrate too early. PFIC or residence-country tax analysis may still make the investment inefficient or painful.

So mutual funds remain excellent vehicles. But for NRIs, excellence depends on route, residence country, documentation, tax classification and reporting.

For resident India, mutual funds may be simple. For the NRI, they are simple only after the cross-border questions are answered.

5.14 FATCA, CRS AND THE END OF INVISIBLE INVESTING

This is the right point to pause and discuss the record.

FATCA and CRS have changed the visibility of cross-border financial assets.

FATCA is the US-driven reporting regime. CRS is the broader global information-exchange framework adopted by many jurisdictions. Indian banks, brokers, AMCs and insurers ask for tax-residency declarations, foreign tax identification numbers and self-certifications because financial assets no longer sit quietly inside one country's paperwork.

The NRI may think the investment is "in India."

The record may travel to the country where he is tax-resident.

This does not mean every Indian investment is taxable abroad in every case. Taxability depends on the residence country's domestic law, treaty, asset classification, timing, income character and facts. But reportability and visibility are now serious realities.

The client may ask:

"Why does my Indian insurer need my foreign TIN?" "Why is the bank asking where I am tax-resident?" "Why does the AMC care whether I live in Canada?" "Why should my Indian account be reported abroad?"

The answer is calm and simple.

This is no longer personal. It is infrastructure.

That infrastructure is also becoming faster. Recent reporting on India's revamped foreign tax information-exchange framework indicates that, from July 1, 2026, requests from foreign tax jurisdictions are to be treated as high priority, with information to be shared within 15 days where it is available with the Income Tax Department, and an interim report required within the same period where full information is not yet available. The practical lesson for the NRI is simple: we no longer live in an invisible world. Cross-border financial information may move between tax administrations in weeks, not years.

The cross-border financial system is designed to know where the taxpayer belongs. A false declaration, incomplete self-certification or casual address update can create problems later.

For advisors, the rule is clear:

Ask tax residency. Collect correct declarations. Do not guess the client's TIN. Do not treat FATCA/CRS as formality. Do not tell the client that Indian tax exemption means foreign reporting is irrelevant. Do not tell the client that the asset will not be visible abroad. Do not answer foreign tax questions beyond your competence.

A form filled casually today can become an explanation tomorrow.

5.15 DIRECT EQUITY AND THE PIS ROUTE: CONTROL WITH REPORTING

Some NRIs do not want funds. They want direct shares.

They want to own the familiar names they have watched for years—Reliance, TCS, Infosys, HDFC Bank, ICICI Bank, Larsen & Toubro, Hindustan Unilever, Bharti Airtel, Maruti Suzuki, Titan, Asian Paints and other well-known listed Indian companies. This is not a recommendation to buy any of them. It is simply the emotional truth of direct equity: the NRI does not feel he is buying an abstract asset class. He feels he is buying a piece of India's most visible corporate story.

Direct equity gives that feeling.

But for an NRI, direct equity is not the same as a resident Indian opening an app and casually trading.

If the NRI wants to invest in listed Indian shares on a repatriable basis, the traditional route is the Portfolio Investment Scheme, or PIS, through a designated bank. Payment for purchase of shares or convertible debentures on repatriation basis is required to come through inward remittance or from NRE / FCNR(B) funds; where purchases are on non-repatriation basis, NRO funds can also be used.

What does this mean practically?

The NRI opens a PIS account through a designated bank. This account is not merely a bank account with a different label. It is the reporting gate through which eligible listed equity transactions are routed. The bank links the PIS account with the demat account and broker. Trades are monitored and reported because NRI investment in listed Indian companies is subject to prescribed limits. The system exists so that aggregate NRI holdings in a company can be tracked against those limits.

This is why the NRE PIS route often costs more and feels heavier at the onboarding stage than ordinary resident investing. The bank is not merely holding money. It is monitoring, reporting and controlling the route. The friction usually appears in account opening, bank approval, demat linkage, broker mapping, documentation and operating charges.

The advantage of NRE PIS is repatriable character. The client is investing foreign-origin money converted into rupees through the NRE route, with a cleaner ability to take eligible sale proceeds abroad subject to tax and rules.

The NRO route is different. NRO-based equity investment may be operationally simpler in some cases, especially where the money is already India-source rupee money. But the investment character is different. For investment purposes, NRO-based equity investment should be treated as non-repatriable. The sale proceeds do not acquire NRE character merely because the investor is an NRI. They remain in the NRO / non-repatriable lane.

Current income is a separate conversation. Dividends or interest credited on such investments may be remittable as current income, subject to tax deduction, documentation and authorised dealer bank comfort. But that does not make the underlying NRO investment itself freely repatriable.

This distinction must be kept clean. NRE PIS is the repatriable route. NRO investment is the non-repatriable route. Mixing the two in language creates the exact misunderstanding that later becomes a banking and repatriation dispute.

The trading restrictions also matter. Delivery-based investment is generally permitted. Intraday and speculative trading are generally not the normal NRI PIS route. The client who wants active resident-style trading must be told that NRI direct equity investing comes with boundaries.

Direct equity therefore gives control.

But control comes with infrastructure.

PIS account. Designated bank. Demat. Broker. Reporting. Limits. Tax. NRE versus NRO classification. Higher operational cost. Residence-country reporting.

The NRI must know the price of control before choosing it.

5.16 SIF: THE NEW MIDDLE LANE

A SIF sits between ordinary mutual funds and higher-ticket structures such as PMS and AIFs. It is designed for investors who need more flexibility and strategy depth than a regular mutual fund, but who may not want the full-ticket size and complexity of PMS or AIFs. The threshold itself tells the story: the minimum aggregate investment across SIF strategies is generally ₹10 lakh at PAN level, materially higher than ordinary retail mutual funds but far below the PMS and AIF corridors. For that reason, the advisor should not treat SIF as merely "another mutual fund." It is a middle lane, but it is still a specialist lane.

The ticket-size ladder is therefore important: ordinary mutual funds may begin small, SIFs generally begin at ₹10 lakh, PMS begins at

₹50 lakh, and AIFs generally begin at ₹1 crore for most investors.

For the NRI, the first point is not excitement. It is eligibility.

Because SIFs sit within the SEBI-regulated investment product universe, an NRI should not assume that every SIF strategy will automatically accept every non-resident investor. The fund documents, AMC policy, FEMA route, tax status, country of residence, FATCA/CRS declarations and platform capability must be checked.

Where permitted, the funding route will again matter.

If the client invests through NRE funds, the intention may be repatriable exposure. If the client invests through NRO funds, the investment may sit in the non-repatriable or controlled-repatriation bucket. If the client is US or Canada-linked, the provider's onboarding policy and foreign-tax consequences must be checked separately.

The SIF may be new. The old questions remain.

Return. Route. Record.

What strategy is being used? What risk does it take? Is it open-ended, interval-based or close-ended? What is the exit structure? Is the investor eligible? Which bank account funds it? Is it repatriable? How is it taxed in India? How is it reported abroad? Will the residence country classify it like a fund, a foreign investment vehicle, or something else?

A new product does not remove old compliance. It only changes where the questions must be asked.

5.17 PMS: PERSONALISED PORTFOLIO, HIGHER TICKET, HIGHER DISCIPLINE

Portfolio Management Services, or PMS, occupy a different place.

In a PMS, a SEBI-registered portfolio manager manages a portfolio of securities for the client according to a strategy and agreement. The portfolio may be discretionary, non-discretionary or advisory in nature depending on the arrangement. Unlike a mutual fund, the client generally owns the underlying securities in his own demat account, and the portfolio is managed more directly.

PMS is not a small-ticket product. The minimum investment threshold for PMS is ₹50 lakh, making it a product for investors with larger portfolios who can understand and bear the risks involved.

For NRIs, PMS may appeal because it feels more customised than mutual funds. A client with a larger corpus may like the idea of a named manager, a defined strategy, regular reporting, and direct portfolio visibility.

For an NRI, the PMS route must also be tested through the same NRE/NRO lens. If the PMS portfolio is to be built on a repatriable basis and the underlying transactions involve listed Indian securities, the NRE PIS architecture may still enter the picture. That means designated bank coordination, PIS reporting, demat and broker linkage, and additional time before the investment becomes operational. A resident investor may see PMS as a manager-selection decision. An NRI must see it as a manager-plus-route decision.

PMS and direct equity may also appear more natural to some US- or Canada-linked NRIs because Indian mutual fund onboarding can be restrictive and, for US persons, foreign pooled funds can create PFIC-style tax and reporting pain. A portfolio of directly held Indian listed securities may avoid some mutual-fund-specific issues, but it does not remove cross-border reporting, capital-gains taxation, PIS mechanics, or residence-country tax analysis. So PMS may be an alternative to mutual funds in some cases. It is not an escape from compliance.

But customised does not mean simple.

The NRI must examine:

Can the PMS provider onboard the client's country of residence? Will the portfolio be built on repatriable or non-repatriable basis? If repatriable, is NRE PIS required? If non-repatriable, will the NRO route be used? What demat and broker structure is required? How will each transaction be taxed in India? What TDS applies? How will the residence country view directly held Indian securities?

Will every underlying security have to be reported abroad? What happens if the client returns to India? What happens on death?

For a resident investor, PMS may be a portfolio decision. For an NRI, PMS is also a cross-border reporting system.

5.18 AIF: SOPHISTICATED CAPITAL, SOPHISTICATED CONSEQUENCES

Alternative Investment Funds, or AIFs, are privately pooled investment vehicles established or incorporated in India that collect funds from sophisticated investors, Indian or foreign, for investment according to a defined policy.

AIFs are generally high-ticket products. In ordinary AIF conversations, the minimum commitment is usually far above the retail mutual fund or SIF level, commonly ₹1 crore for most investors, subject to the category, structure and applicable regulatory conditions. That alone tells the advisor something important: this is not a mass-market NRI product.

At a broad level, AIFs are divided into three categories.

Category I generally covers funds such as venture capital, SME, social venture and infrastructure-oriented funds—areas often seen as economically or socially beneficial.

Category II includes funds that do not fall under Category I or III and generally do not undertake leverage other than permitted operational requirements. Private equity funds, debt funds and real estate funds often sit here.

Category III covers funds that may employ diverse or complex trading strategies, including short-term trading strategies and, where permitted, leverage. The three categories are not marketing labels. They decide the broad investment universe, strategy, risk profile, leverage possibility, taxation discussion and suitability conversation.

AIFs are not ordinary retail products. They may have higher minimum investment amounts, longer lock-ins, capital calls, drawdowns, complex tax pass-through or fund-level tax issues, valuation questions, illiquidity, and heavier documentation.

There is also a separate accredited-investor framework in the Indian securities market. That route may matter for very serious and financially sophisticated investors, especially where product access, minimum investment conditions or suitability treatment is being evaluated. But this chapter is not written for the rare NRI who already has a family office and an investment committee. It is written for the broader NRI and advisor who must first understand the ordinary investment map. The accredited-investor route should therefore be treated as a specialist conversation, not as the default NRI investment pathway.

For NRIs, every one of those points becomes cross-border.

A US taxpayer investing in an Indian AIF may have foreign reporting and classification issues. A UAE-based NRI may have fewer personal tax issues locally, but still has Indian tax, FEMA, banking and documentation questions. A UK resident may face a separate set of reporting and tax rules. A Canadian resident may face yet another.

The product brochure will not solve these questions. Sophisticated products require sophisticated advice.

The advisor's sentence must be clear:

An AIF may be suitable for a sophisticated NRI, but it is not suitable merely because the NRI has money.

Wealth is not the same as suitability.

5.19 REITs AND InvITS: PROPERTY EXPOSURE WITHOUT PROPERTY OWNERSHIP

REITs and InvITs may also arise in sophisticated NRI conversations because they offer listed exposure to real estate or infrastructure without directly buying a flat, shop or land parcel. But they should not be oversold as a simple replacement for property. The investor does not get the emotional control of owning a family flat in Mumbai or a retirement home in Coimbatore. He gets units in a regulated investment vehicle, with market price movement, distribution rules, taxation, demat holding, broker/platform eligibility, FEMA route, KYC and residence-country reporting to be checked separately. For some NRIs, that may be cleaner than direct property. For others, it will not solve the emotional or family objective at all.

5.20 BONDS, GOLD BONDS AND PRODUCTS NOT MEANT FOR EVERY NRI

A resident Indian investor often assumes that if a product exists in India, an NRI can also invest in it.

That assumption is wrong.

The NRI investment menu is not identical to the resident Indian investment menu.

Some instruments may be available to NRIs, but only through a specific account route. Some may be available only on an NRO / non-repatriable or controlled-repatriation basis. Some may permit NRE or repatriable participation only under product-specific conditions. Some may be restricted by FEMA, some by the issuer's terms, and some by the platform's own onboarding policy. The advisor must therefore ask not only, "Is this product allowed for an NRI?" but also, "Through which account, with what repatriation character, and under what exit rules?"

Sovereign Gold Bonds are a useful example. Fresh subscription to SGBs is generally a resident-investor route. If a person subscribed while resident and later became non-resident, he may be allowed to continue holding the bonds until redemption or maturity, subject to the applicable terms. That is very different from saying that an NRI can freely subscribe to new SGB issues.

Similarly, some government savings schemes, bonds or fixed-income products may be resident-only or may have specific NRI eligibility conditions. Certain corporate bonds or debt instruments may allow NRI participation, while others may not, depending on the instrument, issuer terms, FEMA permissions and platform rules.

PPF is a classic example. An NRI should not treat PPF like an ordinary resident savings product. A fresh PPF account cannot be opened after becoming non-resident. If the account was opened while the person was resident in India, it may generally continue until original maturity, and contributions may continue during that period on a non-repatriation basis, subject to the prescribed annual limit, currently ₹1,50,000. But extension after maturity should not be assumed for an NRI. The larger lesson is clear: many government savings products are not simply "allowed" or "not allowed"; they are status-limited, route-limited and maturity-limited.

5.21 NPS: A RETIREMENT CORRIDOR, NOT JUST ANOTHER INVESTMENT

The National Pension System may also enter the NRI conversation, especially when the client's mind has begun to travel ahead of his body.

He may still be in Dubai, Singapore, London or Toronto. His salary may still be abroad. His children may still be studying there. His tax return may still be filed there. But somewhere quietly, another question has started.

When I slow down, where will my retirement money belong?

That is where NPS becomes relevant.

NPS is not like buying a flat because one day the family may return. It is not like opening an NRE fixed deposit because the rate looks neat. It is not like investing in a mutual fund because India feels like a growth story. NPS is a different kind of structure. It is a retirement corridor.

Once money enters that corridor, it does not behave like ordinary investment money. It carries discipline. It carries restriction. It carries an exit design. It carries retirement-linked withdrawal rules. It may carry an annuity decision. It may carry India tax questions. For an NRI, it may also carry the usual cross-border questions: contribution route, bank account, repatriation, foreign reporting and residence-country taxation.

That is why NPS should not be casually sold as "another option" in the investment basket.

It is not merely asking:

How much return will I get?

It is asking:

Am I building a retirement relationship with India?

That is a much deeper question.

Under the current PFRDA framework, NRIs and OCIs may participate in NPS subject to applicable eligibility, KYC, account and regulatory conditions. But the advisor must not stop at eligibility. Eligibility only opens the door. It does not explain the journey inside.

The advisor must understand the nature of the commitment. Can the client live with the retirement-linked lock-in? What happens when he exits? What portion is withdrawn? What portion moves into annuity or other permitted retirement payout structure? How will India treat that payout? How will the country of residence read it? What happens if the client returns to India before exit? What if he never returns, but the retirement asset remains in India?

These are not objections.

They are the real questions of a cross-border retirement product.

So the advisor's sentence should be careful.

Not:

"NPS is better."

Not:

"NPS is not useful for NRIs."

But:

"NPS can be useful where the client wants an India-linked retirement structure, but it must be understood as a retirement corridor, not a liquid investment. Eligibility, contribution route, exit, annuity or withdrawal, Indian tax, foreign-country treatment and repatriation must all be checked before comfort is given."

That is the correct place of NPS in the NRI investment discussion.

It is not a bad product.

It is not a universal product.

It is a disciplined product.

And disciplined products are powerful only when the client understands the discipline before entering.

The principle is simple:

Do not assume resident eligibility equals NRI eligibility.

And do not use a proxy.

If an NRI is not permitted to invest in a product directly, the solution is not to route the investment through a resident relative, friend, employee or driver. That may create FEMA issues, tax issues, beneficial ownership issues, benami concerns, succession disputes, banking problems and documentary contradictions.

A restriction cannot be casually bypassed by putting someone else's name on the form.

The advisor must be firm here.

If the product is not available to the client in his legal status, do not manufacture eligibility through someone else's name. A resident relative's bank account is not a compliance strategy. It is a future ownership, tax, FEMA, succession and evidence problem.

5.22 OVERSEAS INDIA EXPOSURE: INVESTING IN INDIA WITHOUT INVESTING FROM INDIA

There is another route that must be discussed fairly.

Some NRIs, especially in countries with mature investment platforms, may find it easier to get India exposure from outside India.

A US resident may buy a US-listed India ETF. A Canadian resident may use a Canada-available emerging market or India allocation. A UK resident may invest through a local platform fund. A global investor may already have India exposure inside a broader emerging-market portfolio.

This route may avoid Indian AMC onboarding friction. It may simplify residence-country reporting. It may be easier for the foreign tax preparer to classify. It may allow the client to keep money in the currency and reporting system of residence.

That does not make it automatically superior.

The India exposure may be diluted. Costs may be layered. The fund may not match the desired allocation. The client may not get India-specific product choices. The investment may not help with Indian family protection, rupee liabilities, succession planning or insurance needs.

Still, for some NRIs, the abroad route is rational.

A credible advisor should not dismiss it merely because it does not create an Indian transaction.

The right answer may be:

"For pure India market exposure, your home-country platform may be operationally easier. But for India-linked family protection, rupee liabilities, retirement in India, succession and insurance planning, Indian products may still have a role."

Balance builds trust.

5.23 TDS: THE NRI'S FRONT-END CASH-FLOW COST

Indian taxation for NRIs has one recurring practical feature: withholding often happens before final tax comfort.

This is why TDS becomes such a cash-flow issue.

For resident clients, tax is often experienced at filing time. For NRIs, tax is often experienced at transaction time.

Interest may suffer TDS. Rent may suffer TDS. Mutual fund redemptions may involve withholding. Insurance proceeds may involve deduction where exemption conditions are not satisfied. Property sale consideration may face substantial deduction pressure. NRO remittances may require tax documentation before funds move.

The advisor does not need to memorise every rate. Rates change. Surcharge and cess matter. Treaty positions matter. PAN matters. Product character matters. The applicable income-tax law for the year matters.

But the advisor must understand the operating pattern.

For income taxable at slab rates or general rates, withholding for NRIs often happens at the highest slab-style rate, generally 30% plus applicable surcharge and cess in many ordinary cases. Where surcharge does not apply, the effective rate is commonly 31.2%.

For income taxable at special rates, the withholding mechanism often attempts to align with that special-rate character. Capital gains, dividends, interest and other income categories may each need separate analysis.

Property, again, is the practical troublemaker. Because the payer is worried about non-resident withholding exposure, deduction may happen on gross consideration unless lower deduction planning is completed.

Once withholding happens, the money that reaches the NRI's bank account is already net of Indian tax deduction. The client may later claim refund or adjustment through the Indian return, depending on the final tax liability. But the cash flow has already been affected.

For NRIs, therefore, tax planning is not only about final tax. It is about timing of cash.

5.24 DTAA: RELIEF, NOT MAGIC

A DTAA does not erase compliance.

It does not automatically stop TDS.

It does not convert India-taxable income into globally tax-free income.

It does not make the foreign country follow India's exemptions.

A DTAA may allocate taxing rights. It may cap source-country rates for certain income categories. It may allow foreign tax credit. It may prevent double taxation. It may provide relief.

But relief has conditions.

The client may need a Tax Residency Certificate. Form 41 / Form 10F, as applicable under the rules in force for the relevant tax year, may be required where the prescribed particulars are not fully available in the Tax Residency Certificate. Declarations and documentation may be needed by the payer. The claim may need to be reflected in the Indian return or defended in the foreign return.

The dangerous sentence is:

"DTAA hai, tax nahi lagega."

The correct sentence is:

"DTAA may provide relief depending on the income type, treaty, documents, residential status and local-country tax treatment. Let us verify before assuming."

This applies equally to interest, dividends, capital gains, rent, insurance proceeds and other investment income.

5.25 THE FOREIGN EXEMPTION TRAP

The most important cross-border tax principle in this chapter is this:

Indian tax treatment stops at India's border.

If India exempts something, India has made an Indian tax decision.

It has not made a Canadian tax decision. It has not made a US tax decision. It has not made a UK tax decision. It has not made an Australian tax decision. It has not made a New Zealand tax decision. It has not made a Singapore tax decision.

This principle must be applied to every investment.

If NRE interest is exempt in India, the country of tax residence may still tax it.

If an insurance maturity is exempt in India, the residence country may still tax or require reporting.

If a capital gain is exempt in India because of reinvestment in another house or specified bonds, the residence country may still tax the gain.

If an Indian mutual fund gain is treated favourably in India, the residence country may classify the fund differently.

If an Indian asset is not foreign from India's point of view, it may still be foreign from the client's residence-country point of view.

The Indian advisor's professional boundary is clear.

Explain the Indian position. Flag the foreign-country dependency. Refer for local advice.

That is not weakness. That is credibility.

5.26 WHERE INSURANCE FITS

Now we come to the question that naturally follows.

If property is emotional but heavy, deposits are comfortable but limited, mutual funds are efficient but cross-border sensitive, direct equity needs PIS discipline, SIFs are new, PMS and AIFs require sophistication, bonds may have eligibility restrictions, and overseas India exposure may not solve India-family goals—where does life insurance fit?

It fits where the problem is not only investment return.

Insurance is not one product. It is a product family.

There are protection-led products where the central purpose is life cover. There are guaranteed-return products where the client values predictability, defined benefits and contractual certainty. There are immediate annuity products where the client wants retirement income to begin now. There are deferred annuity and pension-linked structures for retirement planning. There are ULIPs where the client gets market-linked participation inside an insurance contract, giving a mutual-fund-like investment flavour but with a different legal, tax, cost, liquidity and insurance structure. There are savings-oriented traditional plans where the client values discipline, long-term commitment and family-linked outcomes.

So the advisor must not say, "Insurance is better than mutual funds." That is too shallow.

The correct statement is:

Insurance solves a different problem.

It can combine protection, discipline, premium trail, maturity planning, beneficiary planning, claim architecture and, in some structures, market-linked or guaranteed outcomes. It can be useful where the NRI has India-linked responsibilities: parents, spouse, children, liabilities, retirement in India, succession concerns, or a desire to build a structured rupee corpus.

There is also an operational point advisors should not understate. Insurance does not require a PIS account. It does not require the client to build a demat-linked trading architecture merely to begin. Mutual funds may still need AMC onboarding, KYC, FATCA/CRS declarations and platform acceptance. PMS and AIF structures may involve higher-ticket documentation, manager onboarding and provider-specific eligibility filters. An insurance contract has its own underwriting, KYC, premium-source and tax questions, but in many NRI cases the purchase, servicing, premium payment, nomination update and policy communication can be handled through a more familiar and centralised process. That operational simplicity should never replace suitability; it should only ensure that insurance is considered seriously and fairly in the comparison.

If the client's long-term plan is to return to India, the protection conversation becomes even more important. Life cover protects the family's financial continuity; health insurance and relevant add-on covers may protect the return plan itself. A return-to-India plan that discusses property, deposits and investments but ignores protection is incomplete. The advisor should therefore discuss insurance not only as an investment-linked or tax-linked product, but as part of the client's India-readiness architecture.

But insurance must be positioned with clarity.

It is not a trading account. It is not a short-term parking product. It is not automatically globally tax-free. It is not always the lowest-cost route to market exposure. It is not suitable where the client needs full liquidity or cannot commit to premiums.

Insurance fits when the client's life problem matches the product's design.

This is where the discipline established in Chapter 3 returns. The premium is the seed. The account is the soil. The claim is the harvest. NRE soil generally gives a cleaner repatriable harvest, subject to the policy terms, the tax position, the documentation and the bank's review. NRO soil keeps the harvest within the controlled-repatriation framework. The advisor cannot treat the source of premium as a clerical detail today and then promise a different exit at maturity or claim.

The rail remembers in insurance the same way it remembers in property, deposits and equity. Years later, when the policy matures, surrenders or pays a claim, the route through which the premium entered will quietly resurface in the documentation, the bank credit, and the repatriation discussion.

And the NRI advisor must think beyond domestic limits mechanically.

For resident Indian conversations, advisors often get trapped in specific premium limits, exemption thresholds, or product-level tax rules. Those limits matter. Indian tax law must be respected. But the NRI conversation cannot stop there.

The NRI's world is larger than Indian exemption limits.

If the client is tax-resident abroad, the residence country may not care that India gives a particular exemption up to a particular threshold. The foreign country may classify the policy differently. It may tax accrual, surrender, maturity, fund growth, or death proceeds differently. It may require reporting of cash value. It may not recognise the Indian distinction in the same way.

So when discussing insurance with an NRI, the advisor must speak in the client's real terms:

What is the client's country of tax residence? What currency does the client earn in? What currency will the family need? What is the premium source—NRE or NRO? Is the maturity or claim intended to be repatriable? What is the product type—guaranteed, annuity, ULIP, term, savings? What is the liquidity expectation? How will India tax it? How might the residence country classify it? What happens if the client returns to India? What happens on death?

This is where the knowledge from the first four chapters comes alive.

Papers. Signal. Toll.

Who is the client? Which route is the money using? How will the income or benefit be taxed?

Insurance is not the answer because it is insurance.

Insurance is the answer only when it survives these questions better than the alternatives.

5.27 STRUCTURING, NOT PITCHING

Consider a client who wants to invest ₹12.5 lakh per year into India.

A domestic advisor may immediately think in terms of Indian exemption thresholds and product limits. That is necessary, but insufficient.

A cross-border advisor thinks structurally.

Should a portion go into a guaranteed plan for predictable India-linked outcomes? Should a portion go into a ULIP for market-linked participation, subject to Indian tax rules and foreign tax review? Should a smaller portion stay within a specific exemption threshold where appropriate? Should the rest go into mutual funds, deposits, overseas India exposure or another route? Should the client avoid a structure because the residence country taxes it harshly? Should the premium be from NRE to preserve repatriable character? Would NRO funding complicate the future claim or maturity route? Does the client need liquidity before committing to long-term premiums?

This is advisory thinking.

The objective is not to force the largest policy. The objective is to understand the client's life path and structure around it.

Here is where the cross-border advisor must learn to think bigger than the domestic advisor.

The domestic advisor's instinct is to optimise for Indian exemption brackets. Premium below the threshold, exemption preserved, conversation closed. That instinct is not wrong for a resident client. It is incomplete for an NRI client.

The reason is simple. For many NRIs, the Indian exemption is an illusion abroad.

An Indian exemption answers an Indian question. It does not answer the residence-country question. A maturity that India treats as exempt may be taxed, accrued, deemed or reported in the country where the NRI files his return. The client who chose a policy strictly to fit within an Indian threshold may still find the gain taxable in the United States, Canada, the United Kingdom or another residence jurisdiction. The Indian advisor who proudly preserved the Indian exemption may have preserved nothing for the client's actual tax bill.

That is one side of the picture.

The other side is equally important, and it cuts in the opposite direction.

Even where the Indian exemption is *not* available—perhaps the premium exceeded the Indian threshold, perhaps the structure does not satisfy the Indian conditions—the alternative is not automatically better. The relevant question is not, *did this product lose its Indian exemption?* The relevant question is, *what would the alternative have looked like after Indian tax, foreign tax, repatriation friction and reporting cost?*

Indian mutual funds may be taxed in India on capital gains. They may also create reporting and classification complexity in the residence country. A US-linked NRI may face a foreign fund classification problem. A Canadian-linked NRI may face residence-country accrual and reporting requirements. A UK-resident NRI may face yet another set of rules.

If the alternative is itself taxable in India, reportable abroad, and operationally heavier, then an insurance structure that has *also* lost its Indian exemption is not automatically worse than the alternative. It may still win on protection, on discipline, on premium-trail clarity, on succession utility, on currency-of-claim architecture, on rupee-liability matching, or on the operational simplicity of a defined-benefit contract.

So the question the advisor must ask is not, *is this good or bad?*

The question is, *what are the pros and cons of this asset for this client, and what are the pros and cons of the alternative for the same client?*

That single shift—from *good versus bad* to *pros and cons versus pros and cons*—is what separates the cross-border NRI advisor from the domestic advisor.

The domestic advisor recommends. The cross-border advisor compares.

One asset is taxable in India but free of foreign reporting friction. Another is exempt in India but reportable, accrued or taxable in the country of residence. One has predictable rupee outcomes but limited liquidity. Another has full liquidity but creates an annual foreign-tax reporting line. One protects family. Another optimises market participation. One survives a return to India. Another becomes inconvenient on return.

No client picks a portfolio in the abstract. Every NRI picks a portfolio for *his* life—*his* currency, *his* country of residence, *his* family, *his* exit, *his* succession.

The advisor's job is to lay out the trade-offs and let the structure emerge from the comparison. The largest policy is rarely the best policy. The smallest one is rarely either. The right answer is whichever asset, or combination of assets, survives the client's full journey.

This is also the moment to retire one habit common in domestic conversations: ranking products as superior or inferior. *Insurance is better than mutual funds. Mutual funds are better than FDs. Real estate is better than everything.* These are not advisory statements. They are slogans.

The cross-border advisor does not rank assets. He maps each asset against the client's facts and lets the facts decide.

An NRI may be abroad today, returning tomorrow, tax-resident elsewhere for ten years, ROR in India later, and leaving assets for family across jurisdictions after that. The product must be evaluated across that life path.

That is why cross-border insurance advisory is not product selling.

It is route design.

5.28 WHEN INSURANCE DOES NOT FIT

Insurance has to be brought into the conversation with honesty. It is not the answer to every NRI investment question.

If the client needs the money after two years, the advisor should not pretend that a long-term policy is the cleanest answer. If the client wants to trade actively, give him the direct equity conversation. If he wants only low-cost market exposure, say that plainly. If he cannot commit to premiums, do not convert his uncertainty into a policy. If his country of residence may treat the policy harshly, do not hide behind Indian tax comfort.

That does not reduce the place of insurance.

It defines it.

Insurance becomes powerful when the client needs what investment products alone may not provide: life cover, family protection, discipline, retirement income, defined outcomes, claim structure, succession support, and an India-linked financial promise that can continue even when the client is not there to manage it personally.

The advisor must therefore have the courage to say, "This is not the right fit," when it is not the right fit.

Because only then does his other sentence carry weight:

This may be right for you.

5.29 THE ADVISOR'S INVESTMENT FILTER

Before an advisor discusses any Indian investment with an NRI, he must first understand the room he is standing in.

He is not standing inside one law.

He is standing at a cross-border junction.

The client may be non-resident under FEMA, but differently classified under Indian income-tax. He may be tax-resident in Dubai, London, Toronto, Singapore or somewhere else. He may earn in dollars, dirhams or pounds, but need money later for parents in India, children abroad, retirement in India, or a house in a third country. The investment may be funded from NRE, NRO, FCNR(B), direct foreign remittance or another permitted route. It may be repatriable. It may be non-repatriable. It may be repatriable only after tax, documents, certification and bank comfort.

India may read the investment one way.

The country of residence may read it another way.

That is why the advisor must not begin with:

"Which product should I suggest?"

He must begin with better questions.

Who is this client under FEMA?

Who is he under Indian income-tax for this year?

Where does the foreign country treat him as tax-resident?

Which currency does he earn in?

Which currency will he need later?

Which account is funding the investment?

Can the money come back out?

What Indian tax or TDS can arise?

Will the same asset be visible, reportable or taxable abroad?

What happens if he returns to India, dies, changes citizenship or shifts to another country?

These are not academic questions.

They decide whether today's investment will remain clean tomorrow.

This discipline does not turn the advisor into a chartered accountant. It does not ask him to give legal opinions or foreign-tax advice. It simply makes him sharper. It tells him when to proceed, when to pause, when to document, when to refer, and when to avoid the most dangerous comfort sentence in NRI advisory:

"No issue."

In NRI work, "No issue" is rarely professional advice. It is usually a confession that the issue has not yet been checked.

5.30 THE FINAL COMPARISON

So where does that leave the NRI investment decision?

Real estate may be right where the client needs a home, a family base, a landing strip, a parent-support asset, a long-term rupee asset, or an emotional anchor. But when bought as an investment, it must be tested for CAGR, liquidity, title, rental management, TDS, capital gains, repatriation, documentation and foreign-tax consequences.

Deposits may be right where the client needs stability, banking comfort, emergency funds or predictable rupee parking. But they must be tested for post-tax return, currency risk, tenure, reinvestment risk, premature-withdrawal consequences and succession documentation.

Mutual funds may be right where the client wants diversified India exposure and the onboarding and foreign-tax position are manageable. But they must be tested for FATCA/CRS, US/Canada restrictions, PFIC-type issues, treaty documentation, TDS, redemption tax and residence-country reporting.

Direct equity may be right for a hands-on client who wants to own India's listed corporate story directly. But it must be tested for PIS route, NRE versus NRO classification, prescribed NRI investment limits, delivery-based trading restrictions, tax, costs, reporting and repatriation character. NRE PIS is the repatriable route. NRO investment should be treated as non-repatriable, with only current income examined separately for remittance.

SIFs may become a useful middle lane for investors who need more than ordinary mutual funds but less than PMS or AIF complexity, with a generally higher minimum threshold of ₹10 lakh. But each strategy must be checked for eligibility, route, liquidity, risk, repatriation and foreign classification.

PMS may be right for larger portfolios requiring customised management, especially where mutual fund onboarding or PFIC-style issues make pooled funds unattractive for certain NRIs. But PMS must be tested for minimum ticket size, manager risk, taxation, demat structure, country onboarding, reporting and, where repatriable listed equity exposure is intended, the NRE PIS requirement.

AIFs may be right for sophisticated capital, including serious investors who understand the accredited-investor or high-ticket framework. But they must be tested for category, strategy, minimum commitment, lock-in, leverage, tax, valuation, reporting, capital calls and residence-country consequences.

Bonds, PPF, SGBs and government-linked products may be useful where eligible. But resident eligibility must never be assumed to apply to NRIs. The route must be checked—NRE, NRO, repatriable, non-repatriable, fresh subscription, continuation till maturity or no extension—and proxy investing through relatives must be avoided.

NPS may be right where the client wants a disciplined India-linked retirement corridor. But it must be tested for eligibility, contribution route, lock-in, exit, annuity or withdrawal treatment, Indian tax, foreign-country treatment, repatriation and residence-country reporting.

Overseas India exposure may be right where the client wants market participation without Indian onboarding. But it must be tested for cost, exposure quality, tax, currency and whether it solves any India-linked family objective.

Insurance may be right where protection, long-term discipline, retirement income, guaranteed outcomes, market-linked participation through ULIPs, family security, health-cover readiness, premium-trail clarity, operational simplicity, tax planning and succession clarity matter. But it must be tested for product suitability, liquidity, premium source, underwriting, Indian tax, foreign tax, repatriation and claim route.

No asset wins in every case. The correct recommendation is the one that survives the full journey.

5.31 THE CLOSING THOUGHT

The NRI does not live in one financial world.

He earns in one place, remembers another, supports a third household, reports in one tax system, invests in another, and may retire in a country his children no longer fully understand.

That is why his investment decisions deserve more respect than a product brochure.

When he invests in India, he is not merely chasing return. He is negotiating belonging. He is building a bridge between the life he left and the life he built. He is asking whether foreign-earned money can still create Indian security.

The advisor's job is not to flatten that journey into a sales pitch. The advisor's job is to give it structure.

Return. Route. Record.

If the return is attractive but the route is wrong, the investment is incomplete. If the route is clean but the record is ignored, the investment is exposed. If the record is correct but the product does not match the client's life, the advice is hollow.

A good NRI advisor does not begin with, "This product is best."

He begins with, "Tell me where this money is coming from, where it must go, and what life it must protect on the way."

And once he listens, he does not answer in slogans. He answers in trade-offs. *These are the pros of this asset for you. These are the cons. These are the pros of the alternative. These are the cons.* The choice belongs to the client. The clarity belongs to the advisor.

That is when the conversation changes.

That is when trust begins.

That is when knowledge converts—not because the advisor pushed harder, but because he understood deeper.

Before the Next Doorway

This chapter has dealt with ordinary onshore India. Here, dollars generally become rupees before they become Indian assets. The client enters through NRE, NRO, FCNR(B) or another permitted banking route. The exit depends on the entry. The record follows the client across borders.

But a question remains for the NRI who earns, saves and reports in foreign currency.

What if he wants India-linked exposure without converting to rupees at the door? What if he wants a regulated India connection that can stay denominated in foreign currency? What if the problem is not India itself, but the route into India?

That is a different architecture—not a magic solution, not a tax-free escape, not a way to disappear from reporting. And in cross-border planning, architecture decides everything.

End of Chapter 5

CHAPTER 6

GIFT CITY: INDIA'S GIFT FOR NRIs

The International Finance Gateway Inside India

6.1 RAHUL'S NEXT QUESTION

Rahul was still at the same desk in Dubai.

The tabs from Chapter 5 had not disappeared. The Pune flat was still open. The NRE fixed deposit calculator was still open. The Indian mutual fund platform was still asking for documents. His overseas brokerage account still looked easier than everything else.

He had understood the problem now.

India was attractive.

India was familiar.

India was emotionally closer than any other market in the world.

But ordinary Indian investing was not always simple for a person whose financial life was outside India.

The moment Rahul entered ordinary onshore India, the questions changed.

Which account?

NRE or NRO?

Rupee or foreign currency?

Repatriable or non-repatriable?

PIS or non-PIS?

Will TDS apply?

Will Form 145 or Form 146 be needed later?

Will the money go back abroad cleanly?

Will his country of residence ask a different tax question?

None of these questions was wrong. They belonged to the ordinary Indian route.

But Rahul was asking a different question now.

What if I do not want every India-linked decision to begin with rupee conversion?

What if I earn in dollars, save in dollars, and want to invest from a dollar account?

What if I want the product, statement, redemption, maturity or claim also to remain in foreign currency, wherever the product permits?

What if I want access to India, but through an Indian-regulated international platform rather than through the ordinary domestic maze every time?

Then Rahul thought of Mark.

Mark sat two desks away from him in Dubai. He was British. He had no Indian passport, no OCI card, no parents in Pune, no ancestral house in Kerala, no emotional reason to send money to India.

But Mark had a financial view.

He believed India was one of the most important growth stories of the next decade. He wanted exposure.

Until now, Mark's practical choices were usually outside India. He could buy a US-listed India ETF. He could buy an emerging-market fund with some India exposure. He could invest in an offshore India fund managed from Singapore, Mauritius, Dubai, London or New York. If he wanted direct institutional access into Indian securities, the discussion could quickly become technical.

The opportunity was Indian.

The financial container was often foreign.

That is the gap GIFT City is trying to close.

GIFT City is India saying: if global capital wants India, and if Indian-origin capital wants India, why should the international financial gateway always sit outside India?

Why should the India story always need a Singapore wrapper, a Dubai platform, a Mauritius fund, or a London structure?

Why can India not build its own international finance gateway?

It has.

That gateway is GIFT City.

More accurately, for this chapter, that gateway is GIFT IFSC—the International Financial Services Centre inside GIFT City.

GIFT City is not outside India. It is not a loophole. It is not a tax-free island. It is not a reporting holiday. It is not an escape from the law of the country where the client lives.

It is India's international financial services platform: an Indian-regulated IFSC architecture designed for cross-border financial activity in freely convertible foreign currency.

For the advisor, the first sentence should be simple:

GIFT IFSC is India's international counter.

Ordinary India is the domestic rupee counter.

GIFT IFSC is the international foreign-currency counter.

Both are Indian.

But they are not the same route.

6.2 GIFT CITY, GIFT IFSC AND IFSCA

Clients will say 'GIFT City.'

Advisors must think more precisely.

There are three terms to separate.

Term	Meaning	Why It Matters
GIFT City	The physical city in Gandhinagar, Gujarat	The broader ecosystem: infrastructure, offices, domestic area, SEZ and IFSC
GIFT IFSC	The International Financial Services Centre inside GIFT City	The relevant financial route for banking, funds, exchanges, insurance and international products
IFSCA	International Financial Services Centres Authority	The unified regulator for financial products, financial services and financial institutions in the IFSC

This distinction matters because 'investing through GIFT City' is not one action.

It may mean opening a foreign-currency account with an IFSC Banking Unit. It may mean investing in an IFSC retail fund. It may mean subscribing to a restricted scheme. It may mean using IFSC PMS. It may mean buying insurance from an IFSC Insurance Office. It may mean trading through an IFSC broker. It may mean using the IFSC route for global products. It may mean a resident Indian remitting under LRS.

Same city. Different routes.

The correct question is not: 'Is GIFT City available?'

The correct question is: which IFSC product, for which client, through which route, in which currency, with what tax and exit consequence?

That is how an advisor becomes technically credible.

6.3 INDIA'S ONSHORE OFFSHORE CENTRE

The easiest way to understand GIFT IFSC is this: it is India's onshore offshore centre.

The phrase sounds contradictory, but the idea is powerful.

The centre is physically in India.

The legal and regulatory framework is Indian.

The regulator is Indian.

The jurisdiction is Indian.

But many financial activities inside the IFSC are designed for international finance: foreign currency accounts, international banking, offshore fund management, global securities, IFSC exchanges, reinsurance, foreign-currency insurance, leasing, bullion, fintech and cross-border financial services.

This is what global financial centres have historically done. Singapore, Dubai, Mauritius, London and New York did not become important only because investors lived there. They became important because money, products, regulation, tax treatment, professionals and market infrastructure came together in one financial container.

India's question was obvious. If Indian assets, Indian companies, Indian markets and Indian growth attract global attention, why should the financial container always be outside India?

GIFT IFSC is India's answer.

For NRIs and OCIs, it may become a bridge between Indian financial infrastructure and their global financial life. For foreign investors, it may become an India-based route to participate in India-linked opportunities. For resident Indians, it may become a regulated access point for permitted global products through the Liberalised Remittance Scheme. For institutions, it is India's attempt to compete with offshore financial centres in banking, funds, insurance, exchanges, leasing and structured finance.

That is why this chapter must not reduce GIFT City to 'dollar products for NRIs.'

That is too small.

GIFT IFSC is India's attempt to bring international finance home.

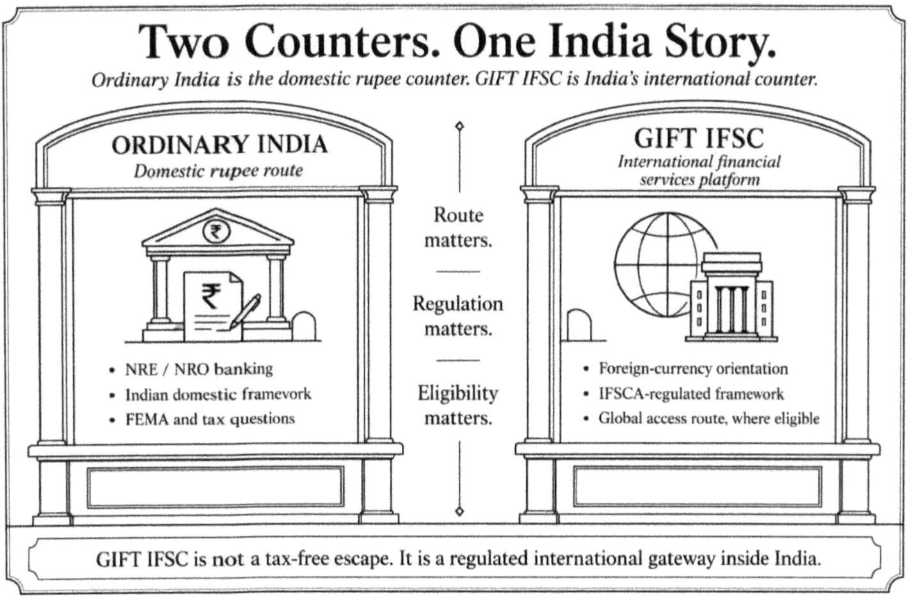

6.4 THE TWO MOVEMENTS: INBOUND AND OUTBOUND

Every GIFT City conversation begins with one question: which way is the money moving?

There are only two broad movements.

Inbound.

Outbound.

Once this is clear, most confusion disappears.

Inbound: Foreign Money Coming Towards India

Inbound means foreign money comes into the GIFT IFSC route.

Rahul in Dubai investing USD 50,000 into an India-focused IFSC fund is inbound. An OCI in Singapore investing through an IFSC PMS that gives Indian market exposure is inbound. A British investor like Mark investing into an IFSC India opportunity fund is inbound. A global family office investing into an IFSC fund that accesses Indian private markets is inbound.

The money starts outside India. It enters the IFSC framework as foreign money. Depending on the product, it may then access Indian securities, Indian debt, Indian private equity, Indian infrastructure, Indian real estate-related assets or other permitted opportunities.

This is the route most NRIs instinctively think about. They are saying: 'I have money outside India. I want India exposure. Can I use GIFT City?' The answer may be yes, subject to eligibility, product structure, documentation, tax treatment and the law of the country where the client lives.

Outbound: Using GIFT IFSC to Access the World

Outbound means the investor uses GIFT IFSC as an international financial services centre to access global opportunities. Here, the client may not be investing into India at all. He may be using an IFSC bank, broker, fund, PMS platform, insurance office or other regulated entity to access global securities, global funds, international insurance, treasury products or other permitted financial services.

For an NRI, this may feel similar to using Singapore, Dubai or another global platform. For a resident Indian, however, the route is different. A resident Indian cannot behave like an NRI. His money begins in India. If he wants to use GIFT IFSC to access global products, the Liberalised Remittance Scheme must be examined.

RBI's July 2024 circular permits authorised persons to facilitate LRS remittances to IFSCs for availing financial services or financial products under the IFSCA Act, and for current or capital account transactions in other foreign jurisdictions through a foreign currency account held in IFSC.

So the clean map is this:

Investor	Direction	Simple Explanation
NRI / OCI bringing foreign earnings into an IFSC India-linked product	**Inbound**	Foreign money enters the IFSC route
Foreign investor with no India connection investing into India-linked IFSC products	**Inbound**	Global capital accesses India through India's IFSC platform

Investor	Direction	Simple Explanation
NRI / OCI using IFSC for global products	**Outbound / international platform use**	IFSC works like an India-based global financial centre
Resident Indian individual using GIFT IFSC for permitted global products	**Outbound under LRS**	Indian resident money goes out under LRS
Resident Indian sending money out only to re-enter Indian assets through IFSC	**Problem area**	Round-tripping concern

This table is the advisor's first map. Without it, GIFT City becomes a slogan. With it, GIFT City becomes understandable.

A resident Indian using GIFT IFSC must be viewed differently from an NRI using GIFT IFSC. An NRI may be bringing foreign earnings into an IFSC product. A resident individual is generally sending Indian money outward under the LRS framework. Where a GIFT IFSC product gives global exposure, India exposure, or a combination of both, the advisor should not decide merely from the label of the product. The correct questions are: what is the remittance route, what does the product invest in, what do the product documents permit, what does FEMA allow, and how will the client report the investment? A developing market interpretation should not become a confident sales sentence.

6.5 ROUND TRIPPING: THE LINE THAT MUST NOT BE CROSSED

A resident Indian cannot use GIFT City as a backdoor to make Indian money look foreign.

That is round tripping.

Round tripping means Indian money leaves India and then comes back into India wearing a foreign label.

Imagine a resident Indian in Hyderabad saying: 'I will remit money under LRS to a GIFT City product, and that product will invest back into Indian securities. This way I can invest in India like a foreign investor.' That is not clean planning.

LRS is a window for permitted overseas investment and international financial products. It is not a tunnel to send Indian money out and bring it back into India in disguise.

This does not mean every IFSC structure with Indian exposure is prohibited. Regulated pooled funds, IFSC schemes and fund structures may have their own permissions, investor-category conditions, diversification rules, documentation requirements and investment restrictions. The concern is different. The concern is a resident Indian using LRS merely to convert Indian money into a foreign-looking route for investing back into India.

That is where the advisor must be firm.

Resident Indian money going out under LRS and NRI foreign money coming into IFSC are different routes. Do not mix them casually.

6.6 WHO CAN USE GIFT IFSC?

GIFT IFSC is not only for NRIs. NRIs are important users, but they are not the only users.

User	Possible IFSC Use	Advisor's Caution
NRI / OCI	Foreign-currency banking, deposits, funds, PMS, capital-market products, insurance	Check FEMA status, product eligibility, India tax and country-of-residence treatment
Foreign investor with no India connection	India exposure or global products through IFSC platform	Check onboarding, investor classification and local-country tax
Resident Indian individual	LRS route for permitted IFSC / global financial products	USD 250,000 LRS limit, TCS, Schedule FA, FEMA conditions and round-tripping risk
Resident company / firm / HUF / trust	Separate FEMA route—not LRS	Do not treat all resident Indians as one category

This last point is important. LRS is available to resident individuals, including minors. It is not available to corporates, partnership firms, HUFs or trusts. RBI's LRS framework states that resident individuals may remit up to USD 250,000 per financial year for permitted current or capital account transactions, and that the scheme is not available to corporates, partnership firms, HUFs or trusts.

Resident entities may have separate FEMA routes, including ODI, OPI or other permitted routes, depending on the entity, instrument, purpose and transaction. Those routes should not be collapsed into LRS. For this chapter, the advisor only needs to remember one rule: a resident individual, company, partnership firm, HUF, trust and family office are not the same FEMA person.

So the advisor must not ask only: 'Is the client resident or non-resident?' He must ask: 'Is the client an individual, company, trust, HUF, family office or another structure?'

In FEMA, the person matters before the product.

6.7 THE PRODUCT MAP

GIFT IFSC is not one product. It is a platform. Inside that platform, different product lanes exist. For this book, the advisor does not need to master every lane with institutional depth. But he must know the map.

Lane	Product Family	Reader-Level Explanation
1. Banking	Foreign currency accounts, deposits, remittances, treasury services	The foreign-currency banking counter inside IFSC
2. Capital Markets	IFSC exchanges, brokers, ETFs, debt instruments, permitted securities and derivatives	Market access through IFSC infrastructure
3. Fund Management	Retail schemes, restricted schemes, venture capital schemes, PMS, investment advisory, family investment funds and exchange-traded products where available	Managed investment structures under IFSC fund regulations
4. Insurance	Life, health, non-life, annuity and reinsurance through IFSC Insurance Offices and intermediaries	Foreign-currency protection and insurance solutions under IFSC framework

Lane	Product Family	Reader-Level Explanation
5. Institutional Finance	Aircraft leasing, ship leasing, bullion, finance companies, factoring, forfaiting, fintech	More relevant to institutional and corporate clients
6. Global Access / Global Market Access	IFSC as an India-based access point for permitted global securities, financial products and international market exposure through regulated IFSC intermediaries	The Singapore / Dubai / Mauritius-style role India is trying to build

For an NRI life insurance advisor, the most important lanes are banking, funds, PMS, capital markets and insurance. Insurance is not just one lane among many. For this book, it is the lane that must be examined most carefully.

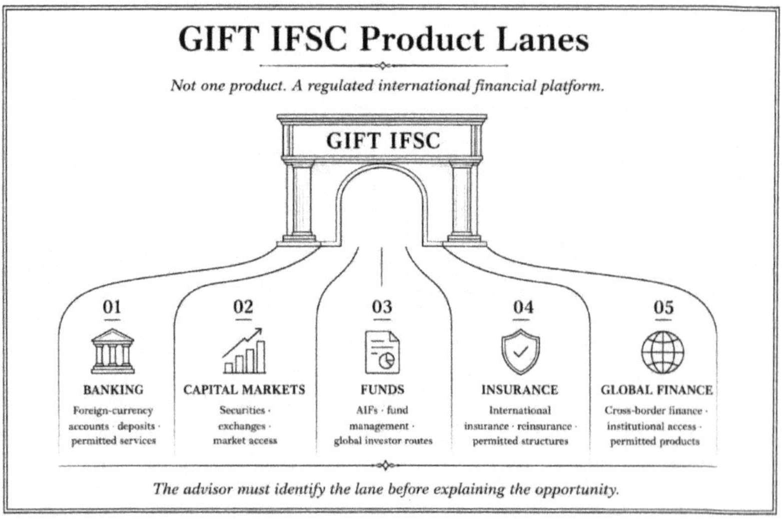

Exhibit 6.1 GIFT IFSC Product Entry Points: Not Everything Starts at USD 150,000[1]

One of the most common mistakes in GIFT City conversations is to say: 'Minimum investment is USD 150,000.' That is not

1 Entry points in this exhibit are drawn from regulation, from provider-level commercial terms, and from market practice observed in the field; the three are not the same. Before quoting any number to a client, the advisor must check the current scheme document, IFSCA regulation, banking terms or insurer terms for the exact product.

correct. USD 150,000 is relevant for certain restricted schemes for non-accredited investors. It is not the entry point for every IFSC product. Some GIFT IFSC entry points may be retail-friendly, some may begin at modest ticket sizes, and some are clearly meant for sophisticated or institutional capital. The entry point depends on the product, the investor category and the provider's commercial terms.

Product Category	Typical Investor	Entry Point/Minimum
IFSC bank account / foreign currency deposit	NRI, OCI, foreign investor, eligible resident individual under LRS	Bank- and product-specific. No single GIFT-wide minimum should be assumed. Some bank account or deposit products may begin as low as USD 1,000, but that is a product-level commercial minimum, not a regulatory rule. The advisor must check the bank's current terms, account type, currency, tenor, onboarding conditions and eligibility rules.
Exchange-traded securities / permitted listed products	NRI, foreign investor, eligible resident under LRS	Broker, exchange, product, lot-size or margin based. No single GIFT-wide minimum should be assumed.
Retail scheme under IFSC fund framework	Retail and eligible investors	Product-specific. Do not assume that retail IFSC schemes start at USD 150,000. At the time of industry review, some live retail schemes had entry points as low as USD 500, with additional investment as low as USD 100; other live schemes typically started around USD 5,000, with additional investment around USD 500. The USD 10,000 threshold is relevant for specified close-ended retail scheme situations; it is not the minimum for every retail scheme. The advisor must check the current scheme document before quoting any number to a client.

Product Category	Typical Investor	Entry Point/Minimum
Restricted scheme / AIF-style product	Sophisticated / accredited investors	USD 150,000 for non-accredited investors. Accredited investors may be exempt from this regulatory minimum. In market practice, accredited-investor tickets may be lower; industry experience suggests USD 50,000 is commonly seen, and some schemes may go down to around USD 25,000, though lower tickets are unusual. Certain employees, directors or designated partners of the FME may have the lower USD 40,000 threshold. The scheme document must be checked before quoting the entry amount.
Venture capital scheme	Startup / VC investors	USD 250,000 for non-accredited investors. Accredited investors may be exempt from this regulatory minimum. Certain employees, directors or designated partners of the FME may have the lower USD 60,000 threshold. The scheme document must be checked before quoting the entry amount.
Portfolio management services	HNI / sophisticated investors	Generally USD 75,000, unless an applicable exemption or product-specific condition applies. Check the PMS agreement and client eligibility.
Investment advisory	Similar eligible clients	Do not assume a PMS-style USD 75,000 minimum automatically applies to every advisory arrangement. Investment advisory may operate differently depending on the applicable IFSCA registration category, engagement terms, platform terms and product route. The advisor should verify the actual advisory arrangement before quoting any minimum.
Family Investment Fund	Single family / family office	Minimum investment of USD 10 million within the prescribed period.

Product Category	Typical Investor	Entry Point/Minimum
Insurance through IFSC Insurance Office	NRI, OCI, foreign national, eligible resident individual depending on product	Product-specific. Check insurer terms, underwriting, premium currency, policy currency, claim currency, beneficiary location, payout route and local-country tax or reporting rules.

This exhibit matters because it prevents two errors. The first error is to make GIFT IFSC sound only for ultra-HNIs. The second error is to make every IFSC product sound retail. Both are wrong.

Some doors may open at modest ticket sizes—even USD 500 or USD 1,000 in some product categories or market offerings. Some doors are clearly meant for sophisticated investors, accredited investors, HNIs, family offices or institutions. Some numbers come from regulation. Some numbers come from the provider's commercial decision.

The advisor's job is not to memorise every ticket size. His job is to understand the category, check the document, and avoid making one product's minimum sound like the rule for all of GIFT IFSC.

6.8 THE FIRST PRACTICAL BENEFIT: THE STARTING COUNTER CHANGES

In ordinary onshore India, the NRI usually begins with a banking question.

NRE or NRO?

Repatriable or non-repatriable?

Should FCNR(B) be used?

Will PIS apply?

Will proceeds go back abroad later?

Will Form 145 and Form 146 be needed?[2]

2 Form 145 and Form 146 should be read as applicable under the Income-tax Rules, 2026 for relevant remittance reporting and certification under the new framework. For earlier periods, the familiar Form 15CA and Form 15CB framework applied. The correct form should be verified against the rules in force for the date of remittance.

Will the authorised dealer bank agree?

These questions are necessary in the domestic route. But GIFT IFSC changes the starting counter.

In many eligible IFSC products, the client may be able to fund the product from an overseas bank account or through an IFSC Banking Unit in foreign currency, depending on the product, bank, onboarding requirements and regulatory conditions.

The conversation changes. In ordinary domestic India, the first question is often: 'Which Indian account will you use?' In GIFT IFSC, the first question may become: 'Which foreign currency route will fund the product?'

That is a major simplification.

It does not mean no KYC. It does not mean no source-of-funds check. It does not mean no FATCA or CRS. It does not mean tax residency is irrelevant. It does not mean the client can ignore the country where he lives. It means the starting architecture is different.

For a globally mobile NRI, that difference matters. A person earning in dollars, saving in dollars, educating children in dollars, and still unsure whether retirement will be in India, Dubai, Singapore, Canada or somewhere else may not want every India-linked decision to begin with rupee conversion.

GIFT IFSC gives him another route. Not always. Not for every product. Not without conditions. But where the product permits, the psychology changes.

The NRI does not feel that he is leaving the international system to enter a domestic maze. He feels he is entering India through an international gate.

6.9 THE SECOND PRACTICAL BENEFIT: INDIA ACCESS WITHOUT BECOMING THE MACHINERY

Many foreign individual investors want Indian exposure. They do not want to become experts in Indian market plumbing.

Mark does not want to study Indian domestic mutual fund onboarding. He does not want to open Indian domestic accounts. He does not want to understand PIS, NRO, repatriation files or institutional FPI mechanics. He wants a regulated way to participate in India.

That is where IFSC funds, brokers, platforms, PMS structures and other eligible products become important. The investor may not be saying: 'Make me a foreign portfolio investor.' He may simply be saying: 'Give me a regulated route through which I can access India.'

That is the strategic value.

Earlier, Indian opportunity often needed a foreign container. GIFT IFSC allows India to create its own international container.

For NRIs, this is emotionally meaningful.

For foreign investors, it is commercially meaningful.

For India, it is strategically meaningful.

For advisors, it means the conversation should not stop at NRE, NRO and domestic mutual funds. There is now another counter.

6.10 DOLLAR DENOMINATION IS NOT DOLLAR IMMUNITY

This is the most important caution in the chapter.

Chitra sees an IFSC India fund.

Subscription currency: USD.

NAV: USD.

Redemption: USD.

She relaxes. In her mind, the currency problem has disappeared. It may not have.

The advisor must ask one question: what does the product own after Chitra's dollars enter?

If the product owns US Treasury securities, dollar bonds or global dollar assets, the economics may remain substantially dollar-linked. But if the product owns Indian equities, Indian debt, Indian infrastructure or Indian private-market assets, the underlying economic exposure is still rupee-linked.

The wrapper is dollar.

The engine may be rupee.

Suppose Chitra invests USD 100,000 into an IFSC India equity fund. The fund shows its NAV in dollars. Behind the curtain, the fund gets exposure to Indian securities. Those securities trade in rupees. Their value moves in rupees. At NAV calculation, the rupee value is translated back into dollars.

Assume the Indian portfolio rises 10% in rupee terms. But during the same period, the rupee depreciates 6% against the dollar. Chitra's dollar return is not simply 10%. The currency has spoken.

The client may not see a separate line item called 'rupee depreciation loss.' The impact may be absorbed into the dollar NAV. But it exists.

Dollar entry and dollar exit do not always mean dollar economics.

GIFT IFSC may reduce route friction. It does not repeal currency economics.

Before recommending an IFSC product, the advisor must ask: What is the subscription currency? What is the reporting currency? What is the redemption currency? What is the currency of the underlying assets? Is the currency exposure hedged? If hedged, who pays the hedging cost? If unhedged, is the client comfortable with INR movement? Where are the client's future liabilities—India or abroad?

A salesman says: 'It is a dollar product.' An advisor asks: **'What is the underlying currency exposure?'**

That is the difference.

6.11 THE COST QUESTION: WHY GIFT IFSC IS NOT AUTOMATICALLY BETTER

After hearing the benefits, the client may ask: 'If GIFT City is so useful, why should every NRI not use it?' The answer is cost.

A smoother route is not always a cheaper route. A foreign-currency structure is not automatically better than a rupee product. An IFSC product may carry costs that are not obvious at first glance.

The advisor must examine the total cost of the route.

Cost Layer	What to Check
Product cost	Fund management fee, policy charges, mortality charges, allocation charges, surrender charges
Route cost	Custody, platform fee, brokerage, banking charges, administration cost
Currency cost	Conversion spread, hedging cost, bid-ask spread, FX movement
Compliance cost	Indian tax filing, foreign tax reporting, advisor fees, local-country specialist review
Exit cost	Liquidity, lock-in, surrender penalty, redemption conditions, claim documentation

Domestic Indian products may be cheaper for plain-vanilla needs. A domestic Indian mutual fund may have lower expenses than a specialised IFSC fund. A domestic rupee insurance policy may be more cost-effective where the family's needs are in India. A simple NRE deposit may be adequate where the client only wants rupee exposure.

So the advisor should not say: 'GIFT City is better.'

He should say: GIFT IFSC may be better when the client needs the international route.

That is the correct sentence.

Question	Domestic India May Work Better When...	GIFT IFSC May Work Better When...
Currency	Future liability is in rupees	Future liability is foreign currency or uncertain
Cost	Client needs low-cost plain exposure	Client values foreign-currency route and international access
Complexity	Client is comfortable with NRE / NRO / PIS / domestic process	Client wants IFSC route and foreign-currency continuity

Question	Domestic India May Work Better When...	GIFT IFSC May Work Better When...
Insurance	Family claim need is in India	Family claim need is outside India or currency-linked
Market access	The client only needs a simple domestic mutual fund, listed share, deposit or rupee insurance route.	The client needs foreign-currency access, IFSC fund / PMS route, global exposure, or an India-linked international structure.
Tax	Ordinary domestic tax treatment is acceptable and simpler.	The IFSC route gives a specific India-side tax advantage, exemption, concessional treatment, withholding benefit or capital-market efficiency for that product and investor.
Foreign reporting	Local-country treatment is manageable	Local-country treatment must still be reviewed either way

The comparison is not domestic India versus GIFT City.

The comparison is route versus need. That is how an advisor must think.

6.12 INSURANCE THROUGH GIFT CITY: THE PROTECTION COUNTER

At most gateways, people first notice the departure boards. Flights. Destinations. Gates. Movement.

But for a family, the most important counter is sometimes not the investment gate. It is the protection counter.

That is how advisors should think about GIFT City insurance.

An IFSC Insurance Office is the insurance gateway inside GIFT IFSC. It is the regulated IFSC platform through which eligible insurance products may be offered under the IFSCA framework.

This matters because GIFT City insurance is not an unregulated offshore product being sold from somewhere unknown. It is international in currency. But it sits inside India's IFSC regulatory framework. That combination gives it relevance.

IFSCA identifies insurance as a major IFSC activity and notes that insurers based in GIFT IFSC can offer products for global Indians, including foreign-currency term life, health and annuity plans.

Why IFSC Insurance Matters for NRIs

Domestic Indian insurance is usually INR-denominated. Even if the premium comes from abroad, the product is usually expressed in rupees. The premium is converted into rupees. The sum assured is in rupees. The maturity is in rupees. The claim is paid into the applicable Indian banking route.

As Chapter 3 explained, the account rail remembers. That works where the client's life is India-rupee linked.

But many NRIs do not live purely in rupees.

Their income may be in dollars.

Their liabilities may be in dollars.

Their children's education may be abroad.

Their spouse may live outside India.

Their retirement country may be undecided.

Their estate may one day be spread across jurisdictions.

For such a family, the question is not only: 'How much life cover do I need?' It is also: 'In which currency should my family receive protection?'

GIFT City insurance can answer this question differently.

Premium in foreign currency, where the policy permits.

Policy value in foreign currency, where the product is designed that way.

Death claim in foreign currency, subject to policy terms.

Maturity in foreign currency, subject to product design.

Annuity in foreign currency, where product terms permit.

For a globally mobile NRI, the biggest advantage may not be return. It may be currency continuity.

The ordinary domestic rail says: foreign currency enters, rupee policy begins, future benefit follows the rupee route.

The GIFT IFSC rail may say: foreign currency enters, foreign-currency policy begins, future benefit may remain in foreign currency.

That is not a return guarantee.

It is route integrity.

Term, Savings, Investment-Linked, Health and Annuity Products

Term insurance is the cleanest protection product. A Dubai-based NRI with spouse and children outside India may not want only rupee cover. A US-based NRI with a dollar mortgage, dollar school fees and dollar household expenses may not want the family's protection to depend entirely on future rupee conversion. A Singapore-based professional may want cover that does not force an early India decision.

The correct question is: where will the family need the money if the income earner is gone? If the answer is outside India, the currency of cover matters.

Savings and guaranteed products require a different discipline. The word 'guaranteed' sounds comforting, but an advisor must ask: Guaranteed in which currency? Guaranteed by which insurer? For what tenure? At what cost? With what surrender value? With what liquidity? With what India tax treatment? With what residence-country treatment? A guarantee is useful only if the client can hold the product properly.

Investment-linked contracts require even more care. The policy may be denominated in dollars. The fund options may be India-linked, global or mixed. The client may value the combination of protection and investment. But the advisor must examine charges, fund options, underlying currency exposure, liquidity, surrender rules, tax treatment, foreign reporting and claim route.

For US-connected clients, pooled funds and insurance-linked

structures may require US tax classification review. The advisor should not certify that analysis unless qualified to do so. The correct professional sentence is: 'This requires US tax review before you invest.'

Health insurance in the GIFT City context should be explained as geography planning. Where does the client live? Where can treatment happen? Where will claims be reimbursed? Which hospitals are covered? What is excluded? What is the currency of premium and claim? Will the policy remain useful if the client returns to India?

Annuity and retirement products raise similar questions. Where will retirement be spent? Where will the spouse live? Can annuity be paid abroad? What happens on death? What happens if the client becomes resident in India? For NRIs, health and retirement are not only financial questions. They are geography questions.

The Claim File Is Designed at Purchase

Naina in Singapore was not asking about yield.

She was asking about her family.

If she bought a foreign-currency policy through an IFSC Insurance Office, paid premiums from Singapore, and named her husband and daughter as beneficiaries, where would the claim go if something happened to her?

Singapore?

India?

An IFSC account?

NRE?

FCNR?

A foreign bank account?

Would the daughter's residence matter?

Would the nominee's bank account matter?

Would the insurer, bank and tax advisor all ask the same question?

Would Indian law, Singapore law or both become relevant?

This is where GIFT City insurance must be explained carefully. The product may be issued in foreign currency. The policy may be regulated through India's IFSC framework. But the claim route still depends on policy terms, claimant status, currency, beneficiary location, documents, banking route, tax law and foreign-country consequences.

The advisor who asks these questions before the policy is bought may sound slower at first.

Later, he sounds wise.

The ordinary advisor celebrates policy issuance.

The NRI advisor thinks about the claim file from day one.

That is the difference.

6.13 TAXATION: INDIA-SIDE EFFICIENCY, NOT GLOBAL TAX-FREE

GIFT IFSC has tax advantages. But it should never be described as universally tax-free.

That sentence must be removed from the advisor's vocabulary.

The correct approach is to separate three levels.

First, the IFSC unit may have entity-level tax incentives under Indian law. But those incentives sit at the level of the eligible unit and its qualifying income. They do not automatically become the personal tax exemption of the NRI investor using that platform.

Second, certain IFSC products or transactions may have specific exemptions or concessional treatment. This may include specified funds, certain capital-market transactions, fund structures, leasing structures, insurance provisions or other IFSC-specific regimes, depending on the exact provision and facts.

Third, the investor's own tax position must be checked. An NRI in Dubai, a US taxpayer in California, a UK resident in London, a Canadian resident in Toronto and a Singapore resident do not live under the same tax system. India may provide favourable treatment to a qualifying IFSC product. That does not settle the tax answer in the country where the client lives.

For insurance, this distinction matters most of all. In India, life-insurance proceeds may be exempt but only where the policy meets the statutory conditions, including premium-threshold and issue-date rules, with the usual exceptions. A policy issued by an IFSC Insurance Office to a non-resident may fall outside the ordinary premium-threshold ceiling, subject to conditions. The exemption is a statutory outcome, not a slogan.

That does not mean the advisor should say: 'This policy is tax-free everywhere.'

He should say: the Indian tax treatment may be favourable if the policy qualifies, but your country-of-residence treatment must be checked separately.

That is the safe sentence. It is also the honest sentence.

6.14 RESIDENT INDIANS: LRS, TCS AND SCHEDULE FA

Resident Indians require a separate explanation. They may be able to access permitted IFSC financial services or products through LRS, but GIFT City is not a bypass around LRS.

The resident individual must consider:

USD 250,000 annual LRS limit.

Authorised dealer bank process.

PAN and Form A2 declarations.

TCS under the Income-tax Act, 2025.

Indian return reporting of foreign assets and foreign income, including Schedule FA where the relevant asset, account or interest is reportable under the applicable return instructions.

Taxability in India on global income.

Round-tripping restrictions.

Product eligibility.

A GIFT IFSC product should not receive a blanket Schedule FA answer merely because it is denominated in foreign currency or sits inside GIFT IFSC. The reporting position depends on the taxpayer's residential status, legal character of the product, account location, asset location, fund domicile, return-form instructions and the view taken by the taxpayer's advisor. The advisor should not say either 'Schedule FA definitely applies' or 'Schedule FA never applies' without a product-level review.

The RBI LRS framework confirms the USD 250,000 annual limit for resident individuals and clarifies that unused or unspent foreign exchange, unless reinvested, must generally be repatriated and surrendered within 180 days.

GIFT IFSC gives you an India-based route to access permitted international financial products, but your money still goes out under LRS. The LRS limit, TCS, FEMA conditions and Indian tax reporting remain relevant.

That is the resident Indian position. Do not mix it with the NRI position.

6.15 PIS IS NOT PFIC

Two acronyms must never be confused.

PIS and PFIC.

They sound similar enough to confuse less technical advisors. They belong to completely different worlds.

PIS is an Indian capital-market route issue. It deals with how NRIs invest in domestic listed Indian securities through the permitted banking and reporting architecture.

PFIC is a US tax classification issue. It deals with how the United States may classify and tax certain foreign pooled investment vehicles held by US persons.

Anand in California saw a GIFT City fund denominated in dollars and asked: 'If this is in dollars and regulated from GIFT City, does that solve the PFIC issue?' The answer is not automatic.

GIFT IFSC may solve or reduce the ordinary domestic PIS route problem. It does not automatically solve PFIC. A GIFT City pooled fund may still require US tax review for a US person. A dollar label and IFSC address do not decide US tax classification.

For an IFSC-issued life insurance contract, the analysis may be different. But the advisor should not certify that position unless qualified under US law.

The professional sentence is: this requires US tax review before you invest.

The advisor's job is not to answer every foreign tax question. His job is to know that the question exists.

6.16 WHAT GIFT CITY SOLVES—AND WHAT IT DOES NOT

GIFT IFSC solves many India-side route issues.

It may reduce the need to begin with the ordinary NRE / NRO route for certain products.

It may allow foreign-currency funding.

It may provide India exposure through IFSC funds, PMS, platforms or exchanges.

It may offer access to global products from an India-based international financial centre.

It may offer foreign-currency insurance solutions.

It may reduce some domestic friction around account selection, currency, repatriation and operational routing.

But it does not solve everything.

It does not remove underlying INR risk where the asset is rupee-based.

It does not make every product cheap.

It does not eliminate suitability analysis.

It does not remove foreign-country tax and reporting.

It does not allow resident Indians to round-trip money into India.

It does not make every product appropriate for every NRI.

GIFT City solves many India-side access and route issues. It does not remove currency economics, product cost, suitability review or residence-country tax consequences.

This is not a weakness of GIFT City. This is the reality of cross-border finance.

6.17 THE ADVISOR'S GIFT CITY CHECKLIST

Before discussing any GIFT City product, the advisor should be able to answer twelve questions.

Question	Why It Matters
Who is the client?	NRI, OCI, foreign national, resident individual, entity, trust or family office
Which route is being used?	Inbound, outbound, LRS, insurance, fund, PMS, bank or broker route
What is the funding currency?	Dollar, dirham, euro, pound, Singapore dollar or another currency
What is the product currency?	Policy, fund, account or security denomination
What is the underlying asset currency?	Dollar wrapper may still hold INR assets
Is currency risk hedged?	If yes, who pays hedging cost? If no, who bears INR movement?
What is the minimum entry?	Retail fund, restricted scheme, PMS, VC, bank deposit and insurance differ
What are the total costs?	Product, route, currency, compliance and exit costs
What is the India tax position?	Exemption, withholding, filing, section and product conditions
What is the residence-country position?	Tax, reporting, disclosure, estate and insurance classification
What happens on exit?	Redemption, surrender, maturity, annuity, claim or death
What if the client returns to India?	FEMA, Income-tax residential status and foreign-asset reporting may change

This test does not make the advisor responsible for every GIFT City product nuance. It makes him a credible first filter. That alone changes the quality of the conversation.

6.18 THE RETURN-TO-INDIA CAUTION

One final caution belongs here because it prepares the next chapter.

A GIFT City product bought during non-resident years should not be forgotten when the client later returns to India. The consequences on return depend on FEMA status, Income-tax residential status, product structure, asset location, income character, reporting requirements and foreign-country residue.

Foreign-currency denomination does not, by itself, answer the Indian tax or disclosure question after return. The same caution applies to foreign-origin assets such as employer stock, overseas brokerage accounts or foreign policies. Those items belong to a separate return-to-India review.

A person who becomes Resident and Ordinarily Resident in India may have to examine global income, foreign assets, foreign accounts, foreign policies and Schedule FA reporting.

The product must be reviewed again when the client moves from non-resident life to resident life.

The advisor who understands this does not treat return as an afterthought. He treats it as part of the original route map.

6.19 THE CLOSING THOUGHT

Chapter 5 showed the NRI the maze.

GIFT City shows him that India is building a gateway.

That matters.

For years, the NRI who wanted India exposure often had to choose between two imperfect worlds. On one side was the domestic Indian route—familiar, regulated, close to family, but rupee-based and full of NRE, NRO, PIS, TDS and repatriation questions. On the other side were offshore centres—international, foreign-currency, efficient, but not Indian in regulatory identity.

GIFT IFSC brings these worlds closer.

It tells the NRI: you do not always have to leave India's regulatory comfort to find international architecture. You do not always have to convert every dollar into rupees before every India-linked conversation. You do not have to assume that India's financial system ends at the ordinary domestic route.

It tells the foreign investor: India now has an international financial gateway of its own.

It tells the resident Indian: you may access permitted global opportunities through the proper LRS route, subject to conditions.

But it also tells the advisor:

Do not confuse inbound and outbound.

Do not sell round tripping as planning.

Do not call dollar NAV dollar immunity.

Do not compare tax without comparing cost.

Do not recommend insurance without thinking about claim currency.

Do not say tax-free when you mean India-side efficient.

Do not turn one product minimum into a GIFT-wide rule.

Do not ignore live market ticket sizes.

GIFT City is not magic. It is a route. Used well, it can preserve currency continuity, reduce ordinary domestic route friction, offer IFSCA-supervised products, create new insurance possibilities, and make India more accessible to global Indians. Used carelessly, it becomes another slogan.

NRIs do not need another slogan.

They need a route map.

A good advisor does not stand at the GIFT City gateway and say: 'This is the answer.' He says: 'This is a different route. Let us first see whether it fits your status, your money, your currency, your tax country, your family and your exit.'

That is when the conversation becomes mature.

That is when GIFT City becomes not a buzzword, but advice.

BEFORE THE LABEL IS TESTED

But a route only tells us how money moves. It does not tell us where the person finally belongs in law.

The client may still be in Dubai, Singapore, Toronto or London, still calling India home, still saying, 'One day we will return.' On the day life moves again, the legal reading begins to change. His FEMA position and his Indian income-tax residential status may not change on the same date. Bank accounts are read differently. Foreign assets are read differently. Policies and investments built during non-resident years may need a fresh Indian review.

So the good advisor does not stop at the gateway. He looks at the person walking through it and asks the quieter question that protects both the client and the institution:

If this life moves again, will this advice still stand?

That question waits at the threshold of return—and it is where the next part of this book begins.

End of Chapter 6

PART IV

RETURN, LEGACY AND EVIDENCE

CHAPTER 7
RETIRING IN INDIA

Myth, Masterplan and the Trap of Return

The return to India is not a flight. It is a financial migration.

The first time the thought arrives, it does not arrive as a tax question. It arrives quietly—after a phone call from home, after a hospital visit abroad, after one more visa renewal, or during a Diwali evening in New Jersey when the house is decorated perfectly, the lights are warm, the sweets are ready, the children are busy with their own lives, and the silence in the room feels louder than the celebration.

An NRI in his late fifties looks around the life he built with so much discipline and begins to ask a different question. Not, "How much have I accumulated?" Not, "What is the market doing?" Not even, "What will my pension look like?" Something older. Something softer. Something he may not say loudly at first: How many more years?

How many more years of living by visa dates, contract renewals, school calendars, tax deadlines, medical insurance renewals, and short visits to India that begin with jet lag and end before the heart has settled? How many more festivals on video call? How many more emergency flights for parents? How many more years of saying, "Next year we will think seriously," when everyone in the family knows that next year has been arriving for ten years?

This is when retirement becomes real. Not when the spreadsheet opens, but when emotional timing overtakes professional momentum. And that is exactly where many advisors make their first mistake. They treat returning to India as a financial event. It is not. It is a life event that creates financial consequences. It is an emotional decision that must pass through legal gates. It is a family choice that must survive banking, taxation, FEMA, pensions, insurance, healthcare, documentation and disclosure.

> *The client sees a flight ticket. The advisor must see a migration of status.*

Over the years, in countless conversations with NRIs planning to return to India, one pattern has repeated itself with almost painful consistency. The thought of return lives in the mind for years. It is discussed in fragments—after dinner, during a visit to India, after a parent falls ill, when a child says, "I don't think I will move to India," or when the client realises that the house abroad is comfortable, but the heart is still unsettled. But when the actual decision is finally made, it is often made in haste.

Out of every ten return-to-India conversations, hardly one or two happen two or three years before the planned return, when the best planning is still possible. Most calls come much later—after the client has already landed, after the NRE account question has become urgent, after the foreign pension withdrawal has begun, after the first Indian return as a resident is approaching, after the flight ticket is booked or after the client has realised that the emotional decision was correct but the financial migration was not designed.

> *That is the tragedy of many returns. The desire was not sudden. Only the planning was.*

That is the real question of this chapter. Why does retiring in India remain a beautiful dream for so many NRIs, and become a workable masterplan for only a few? Because return is not one decision. It is many decisions pretending to be one. Where will you live? How will you draw income? What happens to your foreign retirement accounts? What happens to your NRE, NRO, FCNR(B) and foreign bank accounts? When will India begin to tax your global income? When will India ask you to disclose your foreign assets? And have you cleaned up the legal and financial trail of the life you built outside India?

Get that sequence right, and the return feels calm. Get it wrong, and even good assets start behaving badly.

7.1 THE PULL OF HOME

Say the word return to ten NRIs and you will not hear the same reason twice. For one man in Dubai, return is the apartment in Kochi that has been painted three times but lived in for only twenty-two days. For a woman in Toronto, return is the kitchen in Chennai where her mother still insists on cooking despite the doctor's instructions. For a couple in London, return is not only India; it is the possibility of growing old in a place where family does not feel like an appointment and companionship does not have to be planned weeks in advance. For a family in Singapore, return is practical—schools, parents, cost of living, ageing, property, help, access and language. For a businessman in Muscat, return is already built. The house is ready. The temple is nearby. The brothers live ten minutes away. The only missing item is the courage to call it the next chapter.

Home is not always rational. It is not meant to be. Home is where the doctor knows your father's history without asking for a file. Home is where someone can come home in ten minutes if your spouse feels dizzy. Home is where a cousin can arrange an attendant, a neighbour can recommend a nurse, and the pharmacist knows which medicine your mother actually takes and which one she only claims to take.

Abroad, systems may work better. India, at its best, holds you better. That is why the return question refuses to die. Even the NRI who says, "No, no, I am settled here," often keeps one property in India, one bank account in India, one locker in India, one doctor in India, one family WhatsApp group that never sleeps, and one unfinished sentence in the heart.

Maybe later. Maybe after the children settle. Maybe after one more promotion. Maybe after retirement. Maybe when parents need us. Maybe when we need India more than India needs us. Maybe when India learns to respect professional boundaries a little better, so that returning professionals are not expected to answer every manager's call after office hours or surrender every weekend to work. For many in the IT and corporate world, this is not a small hesitation. It is one of the quiet fears sitting behind the return decision.

> *The pull is real. But the pull is not a plan. That distinction decides everything.*

7.2 THE PUSH NOBODY DISCUSSES LOUDLY

Most advisors understand the pull. Fewer understand the push. The pull is emotional—parents, family, food, language, culture, belonging, familiarity, festivals, prayer, neighbours and the strange comfort of being understood without explanation. The push is more uncomfortable. It is the part of the NRI story that brochures do not photograph.

Not every NRI has American citizenship. Not every NRI has a European pension. Not every NRI has a permanent retirement home in the country where he spent his working life. For many Gulf-based Indians, residence has historically been connected to employment, sponsorship, eligibility or continuing compliance with local visa conditions. Some countries may offer long-term or retirement-linked residence options for eligible persons. But that is the key word—eligible. It is not the same as saying every expatriate worker has an automatic, permanent right to retire there.

So the Gulf NRI often lives with a truth that resident Indians do not fully understand. The country may reward his working life without necessarily promising to hold his ageing life. This changes the emotional mathematics. A man may work in Dubai for thirty years, but his retirement address may still be Thrissur. A nurse may spend half her adult life in Kuwait, but the home she imagines at sixty-five may still be in Mangalore. A technician may send remittances from Qatar for decades, but the house he builds is not in Doha. It is in Kollam, Surat, Patna, Jalandhar, Lucknow or the town where his father still knows every shopkeeper by name.

For such clients, return is not merely a dream. It is a date waiting to be forced. Sometimes the date is not even chosen by retirement.

It may be forced by a visa cancellation, a job loss, a geopolitical shock, a health emergency, or a family event back home that does not wait for the perfect tax year. In such moments, the client's first instinct is often to move money quickly and simplify everything. But sudden return should not become panic liquidation. The first protection is to know what is exposed; the second is to keep access, documentation and currency flexibility alive.

For NRIs in Western countries, the push may be softer, but it is still present. Children settle into their own lives. Healthcare becomes expensive or emotionally distant. Winters become longer. Friendships thin out. The house becomes too quiet. A client may have citizenship, pension rights and a comfortable portfolio, yet still ask whether this is where he wants to spend the next twenty-five years.

Success abroad does not automatically answer the question of ageing abroad. That is why return-to-India planning must begin with respect. The returning NRI is not confused because he is careless. He is carrying two countries in one life. He is trying to decide which country should hold the final decades.

7.3 THE MISTAKE OF CALLING IT RETIREMENT

The word retirement is too small for what is happening here. For a resident Indian, retirement may mean stopping work. For an NRI, retirement may mean stopping work, changing country, changing tax status, changing FEMA status, changing bank accounts, changing health systems, changing family dependency, changing currency exposure, changing estate documents, and explaining to two tax systems what happened in the same year.

That is not retirement. That is financial migration.

The NRI may say, "I am coming back." The law hears many other sentences. A person who was outside India may now become resident under FEMA. A taxpayer who was non-resident may enter RNOR and later ROR under the Income-tax Act. An NRE account may need redesignation. An FCNR deposit may need maturity-stage planning. A foreign pension may need classification. A foreign brokerage account may become reportable. A foreign retirement account may raise timing questions. A foreign tax paid later may need to be matched with Indian reporting. A foreign insurance policy may require a different analysis from an Indian policy. A nomination abroad may not solve succession in India. A child abroad may remain financially relevant even after the parents return.

The client says, "I want peace." The advisor must gently say, *"Then let us create sequence."* Because peace after return is rarely accidental. It is engineered.

And sequence is even more important when the return is sudden. A planned return allows time to choose. A forced return tests whether the family has access to money where the liabilities actually sit. Indian EMIs need Indian liquidity. Foreign loans, rent commitments, credit cards, insurance servicing or final settlement issues may need foreign-country liquidity. A balance visible on an app is not enough if the family cannot operate the account, receive notices, coordinate documents, or service the obligation when the client has already moved.

7.4 THE ADVISOR'S REAL ROLE

This is where the chapter must slow down. Not to become a tax manual, and certainly not to become a compliance checklist, but to place the insurance advisor in the right role.

A life insurance advisor serving NRIs does not have to become a cross-border tax professional. He does not have to compute RNOR, interpret every pension article in every treaty, complete Schedule FA, advise on liquidation of foreign securities, or decide whether a foreign retirement account qualifies for relief under the Income-tax Act, 2025. That is not the job. But he must know that these questions exist. He must know when an ordinary-looking retirement conversation is no longer ordinary. He must know when to pause the product conversation and ask for the return plan.

A good return-to-India conversation does not begin with a product. It does not begin with a tax rate. It does not begin with whether to liquidate dollars. It begins with one quiet question: What life are you bringing back?

That question changes the room. Because the client is not bringing back only money. He is bringing back bank accounts, brokerage accounts, retirement plans, employer stock, insurance policies, old tax returns, foreign addresses, pension rights, immigration history, travel dates, children's education commitments, ageing-parent responsibilities, memories that do not fit neatly into any form, a working style that may now feel alien to India's office culture, foreign mortgages or home-equity loans, house-property documents in another country, unpaid emotional debts, and sometimes, a spouse who is less ready to return than he is.

The advisor who understands this does not behave like a product presenter. He behaves like a trusted first listener. He may not solve every issue, but he can identify the shape of the issue. He understands that ownership and access are not the same. The client may own the asset, but who can access the policy details, bank communication, loan closure letter, nominee record, claim process or foreign account document when something goes wrong? In cross-border families, this distinction can decide whether money is merely visible or actually usable. He can ask whether the client has foreign retirement accounts before recommending retirement income. He can ask whether existing policies should be reviewed before suggesting fresh insurance. He can ask whether the client's status has changed before discussing account routes. He can ask whether the client is still an NRI under FEMA before assuming that NRE/NRO treatment continues. He can ask whether the client's foreign assets will become relevant once the client becomes ROR.

> *These questions do not turn the advisor into a tax consultant. They turn him into a serious NRI advisor.*

This is the distinction the reader must carry. The insurance advisor's role is not to give the final tax answer. It is to avoid giving a wrong answer too early.

7.5 TWO REFEREES: FEMA AND INCOME TAX

When an NRI returns to India, two referees step onto the field. One is FEMA. The other is the Income-tax Act. They are both

Indian laws, and both affect the client, but they are not reading from the same rulebook. This is where the **Compliance Highway Rule™** returns: Papers, Signal, Toll.

THE COMPLIANCE HIGHWAY RULE™—RETURN EDITION

Checkpoint	Governs	Return-to-India Question
Papers	Citizenship / Immigration Law	Is the client an Indian citizen, OCI, or foreign citizen? What is the passport status?
Signal	FEMA / Exchange Control	Has the client become resident under FEMA? Which accounts must be redesignated? What may be held, remitted or repatriated?
Toll	Income-tax Act, 2025	What is the residential status—Non-Resident, RNOR or ROR? What income is taxable? What must be disclosed?

Papers ask who the client is—Indian citizen, OCI, foreign citizen, resident, non-resident, person of Indian origin in a practical sense. Signal asks what FEMA permits on the date the client acts. Toll asks what income India may tax and what the tax return must disclose for the relevant year. The returning NRI often mixes these checkpoints. He says, "I am still RNOR for tax, so can I keep my NRE account as it is?" That is borrowing comfort from the wrong counter.

RNOR is an Income-tax concept. It is not a FEMA status. FEMA asks whether the person is resident in India for exchange-control purposes and, if so, what he may hold, operate, remit, invest, redesignate or continue. The Income-tax Act asks a different question: how many days was the person in India, what is his past residential history, and whether he is Non-Resident, Resident but Not Ordinarily Resident, or Resident and Ordinarily Resident for that year.

For the insurance advisor, the practical lesson is simple but important. Do not casually merge FEMA and income tax. Do not assume that because the client has a tax benefit, the banking route remains unchanged. Do not assume that because the client has an NRE account, he is still legally positioned as an NRI for every purpose. And do not make the client comfortable with the sentence, "Sir, nothing changes." In return-to-India cases, something almost always changes. The right question is what changes, when, and under which law.

This is not academic. Premium payments, maturity proceeds, claim credits, nomination, repatriation, annuity choices, and policy servicing may all sit on top of the client's status and account route. A wrong assumption at the status level can contaminate the entire conversation.

7.6 THE NRI KAALCHAKRA™: THREE CLOCKS, ONE TRAVELLER

There is a dangerous sentence hidden inside many return-to-India conversations.

It sounds harmless.

"I have come back."

To the family, it is an emotional sentence.

To the client, it is a sentence of relief. After years of airports, contracts, renewals, distance, elderly parents, school calendars and short India visits, he has finally done what he kept postponing. He has returned.

But the law does not hear only emotion in that sentence.

The law asks: returned for what purpose, from which date, under which status, through which account, with which assets, and under whose tax clock?

That is where the returning NRI often gets trapped. He thinks life has moved in one step. The law may move him in stages.

A simple road example explains this better than any definition.

Suppose Ramakrishnan has lived in the United States for twenty-two years. He is not careless. He is not uninformed. He has driven there for years, followed the rules there, paid his taxes there, filed his papers there, maintained his credit history there, and built a disciplined life there.

Then he returns to India.

One morning, he takes the car out.

For twenty-two years, his instinct has been trained differently. The side of the road, the turn, the mirror, the speed, the signalling, the way traffic behaves—his body remembers another system.

But now he is in India.

If Ramakrishnan starts driving on the right side of the road and says, "But I have come from America," the traffic constable will not argue with his biography.

He will look at the road.

That is the point.

Where Ramakrishnan came from explains his instinct.

It does not change the Indian road.

Cross-border financial life works in exactly the same way.

The returning NRI says, "I have come back to India."

FEMA asks, "For exchange-control purposes, how should India read you now?"

The bank asks, "Which account can hold this money, and what is its route?"

Indian income-tax asks, "For this financial year, are you Non-Resident, RNOR or ROR?"

The country he has left may still ask, "Are you still resident, reportable, taxable, domiciled or required to disclose anything here?"

The client experiences one return.

The law may read three different timings.

That mismatch is what I call **legal jet lag**.

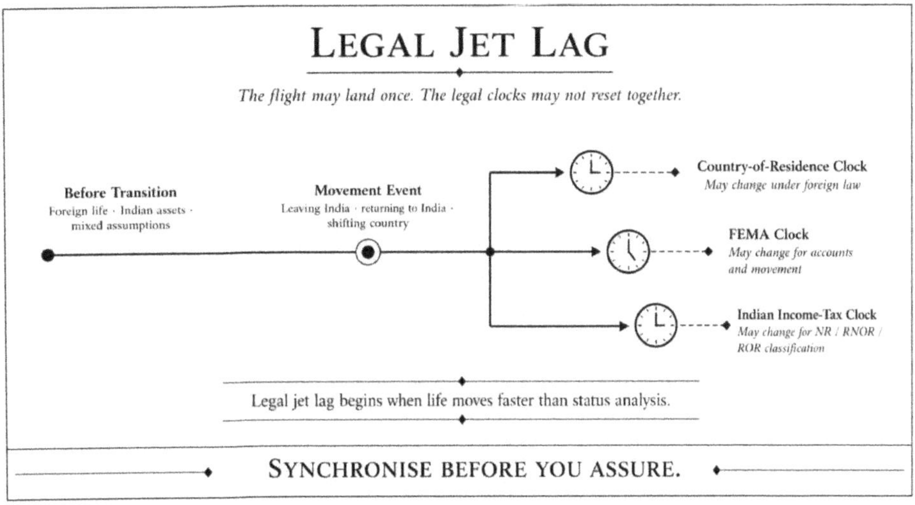

Ordinary jet lag happens when the body crosses time zones faster than it adjusts. Legal jet lag happens when a person crosses borders faster than his legal status, banking route, tax residence and reporting obligations adjust.

And legal jet lag is more dangerous because it does not announce itself at the airport.

It appears later.

At account redesignation. At repatriation. At pension withdrawal. At the first resident return. At foreign-asset disclosure. At maturity. At claim.

At the exact moment when the client thought the difficult part was already over.

This is why the return-to-India conversation needs more than the Compliance Highway Rule™. The Highway gives the advisor the map: Papers, Signal, Toll. But in a transition year, the advisor also needs a timing lens.

That timing lens is **The NRI Kaalchakra™**—the wheel of time, used here in its plain, professional sense. It is a way to understand how an NRI's legal status turns when life moves across borders.

The Kaalchakra watches three clocks.

The first is the **country-of-residence clock**. This clock asks when the foreign country starts or stops reading the person as resident, tax-resident, reportable, taxable, domiciled or ordinarily resident. This is the clock many returning NRIs forget, because emotionally they have left. But a country's tax or reporting system may not switch off merely because the flight has landed in India.

The second is the **FEMA clock**. This clock asks when India reads the person for exchange-control purposes—banking route, account status, investment permissions, remittance and repatriation. This clock is practical. It is concerned with where the person is now, what he intends, which account he is using, and how the money is moving.

The third is the **Indian income-tax clock**. This clock asks how India classifies the person for income-tax purposes—Non-Resident, RNOR or ROR—and what follows for taxability, TDS, return filing, global income and foreign-asset disclosure. This clock has its own method. It counts days. It reads past presence. It does not move merely because the client feels Indian again.

Although this chapter meets the Kaalchakra at the moment of return, the same three clocks turn in the other direction too. The year a person leaves India sets these clocks running just as decisively, and a major shift from one foreign country to another can reset them again. Return is where the mismatch is felt most sharply. It is not the only place where it exists.

One traveller. One return. Three clocks.

They do not always strike the hour together.

That is why the advisor's discipline in a transition year must be simple:

Synchronise before you assure.

Before saying, "No issue, sir," ask:

Which clock is reading this client as what, and from when?

Ramakrishnan's foreign history matters. It matters for his pension, reporting, foreign assets, tax residence, treaty position, account route and succession. But his foreign history does not replace the rulebook of the road he is on today.

The mistake is not that Ramakrishnan came from America.

The mistake is that he assumed arrival and adjustment were the same thing.

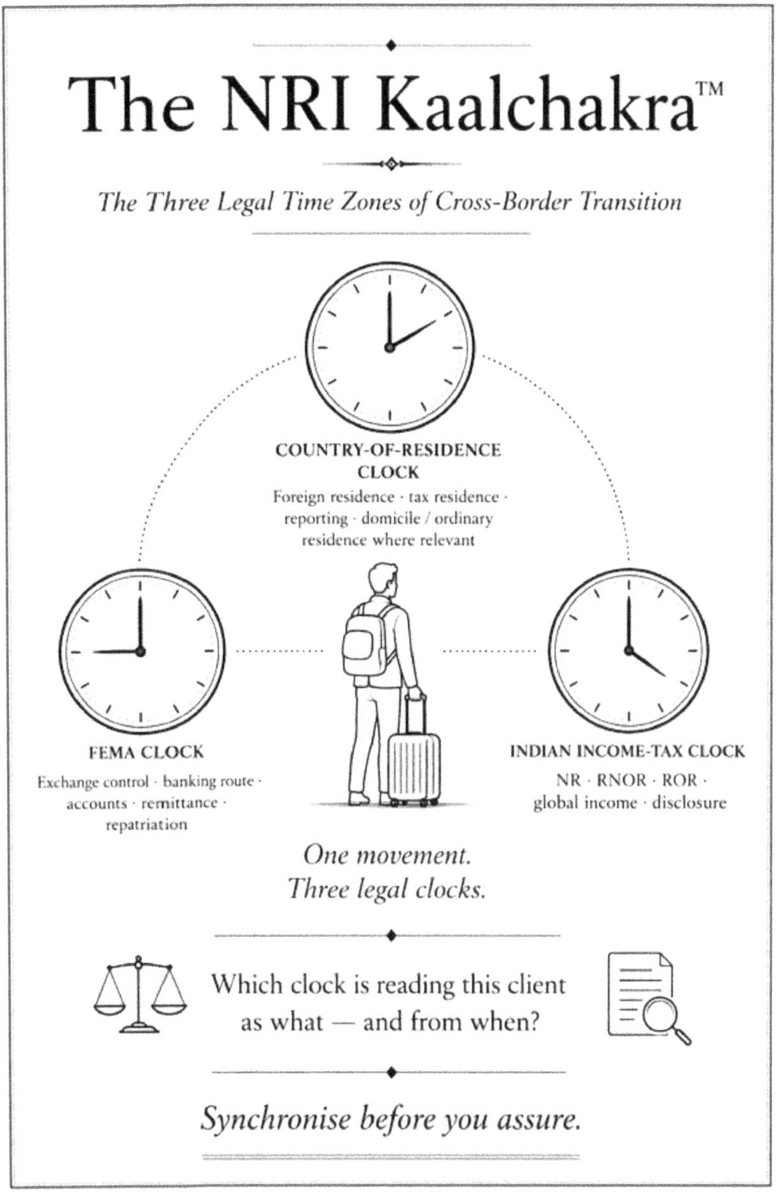

7.7 THE CONVENIENCE TRAP

Every experienced advisor has heard some version of this sentence: "I will just keep my NRE account for now." It sounds harmless. It sounds practical. It sounds like a small administrative delay. But in cross-border work, convenience is often where non-compliance enters wearing ordinary clothes.

The returning NRI has reasons. He may go back again. His children are abroad. His old mandates are linked. One last foreign salary credit may come. He does not want to disturb the bank. He has operated the account for twenty years. Emotionally, all of this is understandable. Legally, it may still require review.

Account type is not a lifestyle choice. It must match status. That principle is simple, but it is not small. When the client's FEMA position changes, the banking architecture has to be reviewed. The advisor does not need to redesign the entire structure himself, but he must recognise that NRE, NRO, FCNR(B), RFC, resident accounts, demat records, mutual fund folios, broker records, KYC declarations, FATCA and CRS statements may all become part of the status-clean-up conversation.

> *The correct professional attitude is not panic. It is hygiene. Do the legal hygiene first. Then optimise. That one sentence protects the client from a great deal of avoidable trouble.*

7.8 WHERE INSURANCE ENTERS THE RETURN PLAN

For an insurance advisor, this is the section that matters most. Return to India is not an invitation to force a new policy into every conversation. It is an invitation to read the client's life more carefully.

The returning NRI is often entering a stage where uncertainty reduces in one area and increases in another. His country of residence may now become India. His family base may now become India. His healthcare needs may now arise in India. His spouse may live in

India. His ageing parents may already be in India. His children may still be abroad. This is precisely why insurance must not be treated as a product pitch. It must be treated as part of the return architecture.

The first insurance conversation should usually be a reading exercise. What policies already exist? Were they issued in India or abroad? Who is the policyholder, life assured and nominee? From which account were premiums paid? When will the policy mature? Will the proceeds support retirement liquidity, spouse security, healthcare, legacy, or children abroad? Is the client assuming that "tax-free in India" means tax-free everywhere? Does a foreign-issued policy need a separate review once the client becomes ROR?

An advisor who has not understood the return-to-India journey may see only the immediate opportunity: a returning NRI, a fresh conversation, and a possible new policy. The difference this book should create is a change in the advisor's eye. He should now see the complete picture—the old policies, the changing residential status, the shifting banking framework, the healthcare exposure, the family dependencies, and the client's move from an NRI framework into an Indian retirement framework. After that reading, a genuine gap may emerge—spouse protection, income certainty, annuity discipline, liquidity, healthcare contingency, estate structure or claim-credit clarity. But the gap must be discovered, not manufactured.

One practical reality must be stated clearly. Healthcare in India is not what it was when many NRIs left. India may offer familiarity, family support and access to excellent doctors, but quality healthcare in India is no longer inexpensive by default. Large hospitals, specialised treatment, long-term medication, assisted care, attendants, nursing support and recurring diagnostics can create serious cash-flow pressure in retirement. The returning NRI may come back because care feels possible here, but care still needs funding.

This is where Indian insurance planning becomes meaningful again. Once the client is settling back in India and is likely to become an Indian tax resident in due course, the advisor can bring the full strength of Indian insurance planning into the conversation—protection, annuity, retirement income, liquidity, nomination, claim-credit clarity and domestic tax efficiency, subject always to the conditions of law. Policies that are designed within the Indian tax framework can now be discussed more naturally because the client's long-term financial life is moving back into India.

That does not mean every product becomes suitable. It means the advisor's familiar territory becomes relevant again. The question is no longer only, "Can an NRI buy this policy?" The better question is, "Now that the client is returning to India, what role should insurance play in the family's Indian retirement structure?"

That is a higher-quality conversation. It gives the advisor a legitimate place in the return plan without pretending that insurance solves every return-to-India problem.

7.9 WHEN FOREIGN RETIREMENT MONEY COMES HOME

Foreign retirement money is one of those areas where a returning NRI's confidence can be misleading. The account may look familiar to the client, but the moment India becomes part of the retirement story, its tax character may need a fresh reading.

A returning NRI may say, "I have a retirement account abroad." That sentence is not enough. It may refer to a US 401(k), IRA, Roth IRA, UK pension, Canadian RRSP, Irish pension arrangement, annuity, employer retirement plan, social security-style benefit, or even an ordinary brokerage account that the client mentally treats as retirement money. Each can have a different tax character.

The starting point is uncomfortable but important. A foreign pension or retirement account, even if recognised by the government or tax law of that country, is generally not treated as a recognised pension fund under Indian tax law merely because it is recognised abroad. Once the client becomes taxable in India on global income, the Indian question is not only whether money has been withdrawn. India may also ask whether income has accrued or arisen inside that account during the year. Interest credited to the account, dividends received by the account, realised gains on sale or switching of investments within the account, or other credited income may therefore require Indian tax analysis even if the client has not personally withdrawn the money and even if the amount has been reinvested inside the retirement wrapper. The foreign country may defer tax until withdrawal because it recognises the account as a retirement vehicle. India may not automatically grant the same deferral unless a specific Indian provision, treaty position or relief mechanism applies.

For the advisor, the practical lesson is this. Under the Indian income-tax framework, eligible income accrued in a specified foreign retirement benefit account maintained in a notified country may, where the prescribed option is exercised, be taxed in India in the year in which that income is taxed in the foreign country on withdrawal or redemption.

In simple terms, it may prevent India from taxing the returning resident today on retirement-account income that the foreign country itself will tax only later. But the benefit is conditional. The account must qualify, the country must be notified, the statutory framework must fit, and the prescribed option must be exercised in the prescribed form and within time. The notified countries are set by the Central Government and at present include the United States, the United Kingdom and Canada; the list can change, so it must be checked for the relevant year. The DTAA must also be read alongside, because pension and annuity articles may affect taxing rights and relief. The advisor need not give the final answer. He should recognise the red flag and say: "This is not a normal bank deposit. Before we build your Indian retirement-income plan around it, the Income Tax provisions and treaty position should be reviewed."

This is also where an informed advisor can add value without overstepping. Take a UK pension. In eligible cases, the United Kingdom's framework permits certain pension rights to be transferred to a qualifying recognised overseas pension scheme, and some such schemes operate in India. But this must never be presented casually as an available or suitable route. The receiving scheme must satisfy HMRC requirements, the recognised-scheme list is revised regularly, and overseas transfer charge can apply unless specific residence and scheme conditions are met—and can apply later if those conditions are broken within the relevant period.

The advisor need not promise that such a transfer is possible. But if he knows the question exists, he can place it before the right pension professional. For a client settling back in India, that itself is valuable: it shows the advisor is examining whether part of the retirement architecture can come home, not merely looking for a sale. A UK pension should therefore never be treated as an ordinary foreign investment or a normal annuity before the Indian retirement-income plan is finalised.

The mature sentence is simple: "Before we discuss how insurance should support your retirement in India, your foreign retirement accounts should be classified properly." That sentence protects the client and elevates the advisor.

7.10 RNOR, ROR AND THE TRAP OF RETURN

Picture this conversation.

A client has returned to India after twenty-five years abroad. The bags are unpacked. The flat is being repaired. The parents are relieved. The children are still overseas. The client smiles and says, "Now I am back in India. So everything should become simple, right?"

This is the moment where the advisor must not nod too quickly. He must gently bring the client back to the Toll.

The Signal may have changed when the client returned to India. FEMA may now read him differently because his intention, stay and financial conduct have changed. But the Toll—the Income-tax Act—does not decide tax residence merely from the emotion of return. It looks at days, history and statutory classification. At that Toll, the returning NRI may pass through one of three lanes.

The first is the Non-Resident lane. In this lane, India is mainly looking at the India wallet. Income received in India, income accruing or arising in India, and income deemed to accrue or arise in India may come into the Indian tax net. The client may still hold foreign bank accounts, foreign pension rights, foreign investments and foreign insurance, but India is not yet asking for the entire global balance sheet merely because those assets exist outside India.

The second is the RNOR lane—Resident but Not Ordinarily Resident. This is the transition lane, and it is one of the most valuable concepts in return-to-India planning. But it is also one of the most misunderstood. RNOR is not given because the client feels newly settled. It is decided from the client's past. The law looks back at earlier years: how long the client was non-resident, how many days he spent in India, and what his residential pattern shows. In practical terms, a long lookback can matter, which is why the return conversation should ideally begin before the flight is booked, not after the landing stamp.

For many returning NRIs, RNOR can provide a limited but precious runway. During this period, India generally continues to tax Indian income, while foreign income is taxed only in specific situations, such as income from a business controlled in India or a profession set up in India. Foreign assets also generally do not enter the foreign-asset disclosure framework (the Schedule FA-type reporting) in the same way they do for an ROR, subject always to the applicable return form and instructions for the relevant year. For a client with foreign retirement accounts, brokerage holdings, employer stock, foreign insurance, property abroad or old bank accounts, this is not a small distinction. It is breathing room.

But breathing room is not sleeping room.

RNOR is the last wallet before India asks for the full *hisaab kitaab*. It is the time to examine what sits abroad, what should remain abroad, what may need to come to India, what requires treaty review, which old insurance policies must be read, which nominations must be cleaned, and which accounts should not be carried blindly into the next stage. In suitable cases, this window may allow the client to realign or rebalance parts of the foreign financial life before India begins taxing and tracking the full global picture, subject of course to foreign-country tax, treaty position and specialist advice.

The third lane is ROR—Resident and Ordinarily Resident. This is where the Toll changes character. India is no longer looking only at the India wallet. India can now ask to see the global wallet. Global income may become taxable in India, subject to treaty relief where available. Foreign assets may need disclosure. The client's foreign bank accounts, vested RSUs, employer stock, brokerage assets, retirement accounts, foreign insurance, foreign property and signing authority can all become part of the Indian return conversation.

This is the compliance cliff of return. A client who uses the RNOR runway well can enter ROR with control: documents ready, assets mapped, policies reviewed, accounts understood and family liquidity planned. A client who wastes the runway may experience the same year as a *crash landing*—not because he returned to India, but because he arrived at the full-disclosure stage without a map.

For the insurance advisor, the lesson is not to calculate residential status. That is specialist work. The lesson is to recognise the lane. A client in the NRI lane, a client in the RNOR lane and a client approaching ROR are not the same advisory conversation. Insurance, annuity, claim-credit routes, nomination, liquidity and family protection must all be discussed with that changing lane in mind. The advisor who understands the Toll does not rush to the product. He first asks a better question: which lane is the client in, and how close is he to the cliff?

The advisor who understands this chapter does not need to become the client's tax consultant, FEMA lawyer, pension professional and estate planner all at once. That is not the role. His role is to see the return map before he recommends the product. Before discussing insurance, he should know whether old policies exist, whether the client is still in the NRI lane or moving towards RNOR/ROR, whether foreign retirement money needs review, whether healthcare and spouse protection are properly funded, whether nominations and claim-credit routes are clean, and whether the family can actually access the money when it is needed. This is the difference between an ordinary insurance conversation and a serious NRI advisory conversation. The ordinary advisor sees a returning client. The serious advisor sees a changing framework.

We began this book with the NRI as a person between two worlds, carrying distance, duty, ambition, memory and belonging in one life. This chapter brings that journey to its most delicate turn. The NRI who returns to India is not going back to the life he left; that life has changed, and so has he. Coming home does not erase the years built abroad. It brings those years into an Indian frame.

So when the client says, "I want to come back," the advisor must not rush to sell, reassure or simplify. He must sit with the sentence, respect it, and then say: "Let us make the return worthy of the life you built."

> *That is where myth becomes masterplan. That is where the trap becomes a runway. That is where homecoming becomes advice.*

End of Chapter 7

CHAPTER 8

LEGACY, LAW & LIABILITY

The Inheritance Trap for NRIs

The return to India is not the only moment when an NRI life is tested.

Sometimes the client comes home.

Sometimes only his file does.

The flight back, the change of status, the redesign of accounts, pensions, insurance, healthcare and disclosure are one kind of transition. They ask what happens when an NRI returns and the law begins to read him differently.

This chapter asks the question families postpone even more.

What happens when the NRI does not return at all?

Not because he changed his mind.

Because he is gone.

That is when the neatness of a financial life is tested.

The bank account.

The policy.

The property file.

The demat statement.

The nomination form.

The will that was discussed but never signed.

The second marriage everyone knew about but no one analysed.

The child born abroad.

The parent waiting in India.

The sibling who knows the banker.

The beneficiary named on paper but unsupported by law.

All of it comes together in one room.

And the client is no longer there to explain what he meant.

After a person is gone, intention has only one voice left.

Documentation.

That is the inheritance trap.

8.1 AMAR'S SILENT GAP

Amar had done what careful men usually do.

He had nomination forms filled. He had kept separate bank accounts for separate geographies. India was India. Kuala Lumpur was Kuala Lumpur. His Surat flat was in his own name. His Indian mutual funds and fixed deposits were neatly maintained. His Malaysian assets were held the way he wanted them held.

His financial life looked orderly enough to reassure a banker.

What he had not done was answer the only question that mattered after his death.

When you are gone, which law opens which drawer?

Amar is fifty-eight. He holds a Malaysian passport and an OCI card. For thirty years, Kuala Lumpur has been home. That is where he built his career, his second household, and the life that now feels most honestly his.

But Amar's story did not begin in Kuala Lumpur.

It began in Surat, in a house where decisions were not always spoken in the language of choice. His first marriage to Sunita had begun the way many marriages of an earlier generation began, arranged by families, accepted under pressure, and carried forward because duty was louder than desire. There was no dramatic rebellion. No villain in the room. No one thought they were destroying anyone's life. They were doing what families often did then: choosing stability, reputation and continuity, and asking the young couple to grow into the decision later.

Sometimes people do grow into such decisions.

Sometimes they only learn to live around them.

Sunita still lives in the Surat flat. Their two adult children live nearby. Amar did not abandon the Indian side of his life in a fit of irresponsibility. He remained connected. Money moved. Visits happened. Duties were performed. From the outside, enough remained intact for the family story to continue.

Then Malaysia stopped being a posting.

It became home.

Years passed. The children grew up. The visits to India became shorter. The life in Kuala Lumpur became fuller. Amar stopped merely living abroad and began belonging there.

Alia entered that life not as a footnote, not as a secret line item in a file, but as the person who shared his ordinary days. The morning tea. The clinic visits. The airport drops. The quiet evenings. The version of him that Surat did not fully know.

For this illustration, assume the relationship is legally recognised in Malaysia.

That does not end the analysis.

It begins it.

Whether, and how, that recognition reaches an Indian policy, an Indian flat, an Indian account, an Indian nomination or an Indian succession claim is a separate legal question.

On paper, to someone looking only from India, Amar's life may appear uncomfortable, even contradictory. One wife in Surat. One wife in Kuala Lumpur. Children in India. Assets in both countries. A Malaysian passport. An OCI card. A financial life split neatly; an emotional life split less neatly.

But life is not always built in the clean order in which forms expect it to be written.

Not every divided life begins with deception.

Sometimes it begins with a decision made for you, followed by decades of decisions you make for yourself.

This does not make Amar right.

It does not make him wrong.

It makes him human.

And that is precisely why the case is dangerous.

Because the law is not designed to complete the unfinished emotional sentences of a human life. The law will not sit with Amar's history, weigh his loneliness, understand his family pressure, recognise his silences, and then gently distribute his estate according to what feels fair.

The law will ask colder questions.

Which marriage is recognised for this purpose?

Which claimant has which right?

Which asset is located where?

Which document governs which property?

Which nominee is merely a nominee?

Which beneficiary is legally protected?

Which court, bank, insurer or authority must act?

That is where sympathy ends and documentation begins.

Alia's recognition and consequences under Indian law for succession, nomination, estate claims and insurance benefits cannot be assumed. Sunita's position cannot be ignored. The children's rights cannot be guessed. The Malaysian assets cannot be casually merged with the Indian estate. The Indian assets cannot be casually governed by Amar's Malaysian life.

Each drawer needs its own legal key.

His Indian estate is not small: a Surat flat worth about ₹2 crore, along with Indian mutual funds and fixed deposits worth another ₹1.5 crore. His Malaysian assets form the other half of his life.

His wish is neither unusual nor dramatic. He wants the Indian side to go to Sunita and the children. He wants the Malaysian side to remain with Alia. Above all, he wants nobody forced into the kind of meeting that begins with grief and ends with document files.

He has no will.

That one sentence is the whole problem.

A man can spend thirty years dividing his life across two countries and still leave no legally usable sentence explaining how the division must continue after him.

In conversation, everyone may know what Amar wanted.

At a claims desk, knowing is not enough.

At a bank, affection is not authority.

In court, intention without documentation is only a story someone has to prove.

He is not alone.

Most NRI estate failures do not begin with fraud. They begin with false substitution.

A nomination is mistaken for a will.

A bank mandate is mistaken for an estate plan.

A policy benefit is mistaken for a succession solution.

A family understanding is mistaken for legal clarity.

> *Family understanding is beautiful at dinner. It is weak at a claims desk.*

Before we go further, three instruments must be separated.

A nomination tells the insurer whom to recognise at the point of claim.

A will directs succession to estate assets such as property, bank balances, investments and other belongings, subject to applicable succession law.

An MWPA structure, where validly effected, can create a statutory trust over a specific life insurance policy for the wife, children, or any of them.

These are not three versions of the same thing.

They do different work.

They fail in different ways.

And when an NRI confuses one for another, the family pays for the confusion later.

8.2 THE MOST MISUNDERSTOOD WORD IN INDIAN PERSONAL FINANCE

The word is nominee.

Ask a hundred NRI clients what a nominee means, and most will answer the same way: the person who gets the money.

That answer is understandable.

It is also incomplete.

In life insurance, nomination is governed by section 39 of the Insurance Act, 1938. It gives the insurer a recognised person to deal with when the policy becomes payable on death. It reduces claim uncertainty. It does not, by itself, create a complete estate plan.

Think of a nomination as a claims bridge.

It helps the insurer cross from uncertainty to payment.

It is not always the final map of ownership for every family situation.

The 2015 amendment to section 39 changed the position for a defined family class. Where the holder of a life insurance policy on his own life nominates his parents, spouse, children, spouse and children, or any of them, Section 39 provides that the nominee or nominees shall be beneficially entitled to the amount payable by the insurer, subject to the other provisions of Section 39, and unless it is proved that, having regard to the nature of the policyholder's title to the policy, he could not have conferred such beneficial title.

This change matters.

But it must not be sold as a blanket answer to inheritance.

A family nomination under Section 39 can be stronger than an ordinary receipt nomination. But it still does not replace a properly thought-through succession plan. Assignment, creditor claims, MWPA policies, family disputes, wills, personal law and the facts of the policyholder's title may still matter. It does not mean every nominee is now an owner. It does not mean succession disputes have disappeared. It does not mean a nomination form can replace a will. It does not mean a foreign spouse, second spouse, stepchild, adopted child, partner, sibling, friend or business associate automatically receives the legal treatment the client emotionally assumes.

That is why Amar's case is dangerous.

If Alia is named on an Indian policy, the real question is not only what Amar intended. The real question is whether Indian law would recognise her, for that policy and that fact pattern, in the manner Amar assumes.

That answer does not sit on the nomination form.

It sits in legal analysis.

A nomination answers the insurer's first question.

It does not always answer the family's last one.

For NRIs, this problem is magnified by distance. They change countries, marriages, tax residencies, beneficiaries, trustees, bank accounts and family equations over decades. Yet the nomination on an old Indian policy often remains frozen in the year it was first signed.

A nominee may have died.

A marriage may have changed.

A child may have become a foreign citizen.

A sibling may no longer be close.

A parent may no longer be alive.

A spouse may no longer be the only spouse in the story.

The policy remains active. The premiums remain paid. On the surface, nothing looks broken.

Legally, something may already be broken.

One updated nomination during life is a form.

The same error after death is a file.

The advisor who says, *"Sir, nominee ka naam daal dete hain,"* is completing paperwork.

The advisor who asks, *"Sir, does this person's legal and family position still match your intention?"* is doing NRI advisory.

> *The first completes a form. The second protects a family.*

8.3 LEGAL HEIRS, PERSONAL LAW AND THE CROSS-BORDER ESTATE

Once nomination stops answering the question, the estate begins asking its own.

Who is the legal heir?

Which law decides?

Does the answer change for property, bank balances, insurance proceeds, movable investments and assets abroad?

This is where comfortable language becomes expensive.

For Indian assets, the applicable succession framework must first be identified properly. For many Hindu clients, intestate succession may be governed by the Hindu Succession Act, 1956. For Christians, Parsis and Jews, the Indian Succession Act, 1925 may become relevant. Muslim succession follows its own personal-law framework. Other fact patterns can require separate analysis.

But the advisor must not reduce succession analysis to a religious label and assume the work is done.

Intestacy, testamentary succession, domicile, marital status, recognition of foreign relationships, adoption, legitimacy, asset type, location and court process are separate layers. They must be kept separate.

The law is a poor reader of emotion.

It does not automatically know who was loved, who was dependent, who was promised, who sacrificed, who stayed back, who sent money, who kept the keys, or who sat beside the hospital bed.

It reads documents.

Two practical rules matter most.

For immovable property in India, location carries decisive weight. The flat in Surat is Indian property. The apartment in Gurgaon is Indian property. Foreign residence or foreign citizenship does not, by itself, convert Indian immovable property into a foreign succession asset. Indian legal documentation will matter.

For movable assets, the position can become more layered. Insurance proceeds, bank balances, demat holdings, mutual funds and other financial assets may raise institution-level documentation requirements and, in some cases, private-international-law issues. In practice, Indian insurers, banks, registrars and depositories usually require documents they can recognise and act upon under their Indian operating process.

Whatever Amar intends for Indian assets must be expressed through a legally workable Indian instrument.

Indian law will not infer delicacy merely because his life was delicate.

8.4 THE WILL: THE DOCUMENT NRIs RESPECT TOO LATE

A will is one of the most misunderstood documents in an NRI family.

People speak of it softly, if they speak of it at all. The moment the word is mentioned, someone in the room becomes uncomfortable. A parent says, "Why are you talking like this?" A spouse says, "Nothing will happen." A client smiles and says, "We will do it later."

Later is a very dangerous word in estate planning.

Because later assumes the person who must sign will still be available to sign.

A will does not make the client old. It does not invite death. It does not announce mistrust. It does not mean the family is broken.

In fact, it often means the opposite.

It means the client loves his family enough not to leave them with a puzzle at the worst moment of their lives.

> *A will is not about dying. It is about not making the living fight over what the dead person meant.*

That is the emotional truth advisors must understand before they explain the legal one.

A will answers, in advance, the questions grief is too tired to answer later.

Who receives what?

Who has authority?

Which asset is covered?

Which law applies?

Which person speaks for the estate?

Which family member is protected from confusion?

Which argument never needs to begin?

For a resident Indian family with one house, one bank account and everyone living in the same city, the absence of a will can still create damage.

For an NRI family, the damage travels.

The flat may be in Surat.

The bank account may be in Mumbai.

The mutual fund folio may be in India.

The spouse may be in Kuala Lumpur.

The child may be in Toronto.

The executor may be in Dubai.

The passport may be foreign.

The grief may be everywhere.

That is why an NRI will cannot be treated as a one-page formality signed in a hurry before a flight.

It must be thought through asset by asset and jurisdiction by jurisdiction.

Indian immovable property needs Indian legal attention. Indian bank accounts, demat accounts, mutual funds, partnership interests, business holdings and other India-held assets need India-side documentation. Foreign assets may require a separate foreign will or local estate document, depending on the country and the client's facts.

The advisor should be especially careful with the phrase, "Make one will and everything is solved."

That sentence is comforting.

It may also be careless.

A single global will can sometimes work. But it can also slow everything down if one jurisdiction holds the original, another requires probate, and a third asks for translation, notarisation, apostille, consular attestation or local court recognition.

Wills can also injure each other quietly. A later foreign will with broad revocation language may unintentionally revoke an earlier Indian will. An Indian will that ignores foreign assets may leave ambiguity. A foreign will that assumes Indian institutions will act automatically may disappoint the family at the exact moment speed is needed. A will naming an executor who lives abroad may still be valid, but the Indian process may become slower. A will that is never stored, indexed or retrievable may be legally elegant and practically ineffective.

> *A will locked in a drawer that no one can find is not planning. It is paper pretending to be protection.*

The safer sentence is:

"Make a coordinated estate plan, and ensure Indian assets are covered clearly."

That is less glamorous.

It is more defensible.

The advisor is not expected to draft wills.

That belongs to lawyers.

But the advisor must know when the absence of a will makes the insurance conversation incomplete. A policy may create money. A will gives that money and the rest of the estate a direction. Without direction, money does not always become security. Sometimes it becomes evidence in a dispute.

In Amar's case, the will is not a luxury.

It is the document that should have spoken when he no longer could.

It is the missing bridge between intention and law.

8.5 MWPA: THE POLICY THAT PROTECTS BEFORE THE FIGHT BEGINS

The Married Women's Property Act, 1874 is one of the strongest protection tools available in Indian life insurance.

For an NRI family, its value is not theoretical.

It is practical.

The wife may be in Dubai.

The children may be in Canada.

The policy may be issued in India.

The documents may be with someone else.

The beneficiary who needs the money most may be the farthest from the claim desk.

In such a family, the question is not merely, "Who has been named?"

The sharper question is, "Will the policy money stand protected for the people it was meant to protect?"

That is where MWPA becomes powerful.

A nomination gives the insurer a recognised person to deal with at claim stage. It is important, but it is primarily a claim-recognition mechanism.

MWPA goes further.

Under section 6 of the Married Women's Property Act, where a married man effects a policy on his own life and expresses it for the benefit of his wife, or of his wife and children, or any of them, the policy is treated as a trust for the benefit so expressed. So long as any object of that trust remains, the policy is not subject to the control of the husband, his creditors, or his estate.

> *That is the power. Nomination tells the insurer whom to recognise. MWPA gives the policy a protected statutory character for the wife and/or children. Naming a person is one thing. Creating protection is another.*

In an NRI claim, that difference can matter deeply. Relatives may ask questions. Documents may be in India while beneficiaries are abroad. Liabilities may be discussed before the family even understands the estate. A valid MWPA structure can help keep one important policy from being pulled into that noise.

It is not a decorative option on a proposal form.

It is a protection decision.

But protection has boundaries.

MWPA protects the specific policy validly brought within that structure. It does not protect the Surat flat, the mutual fund folio, the NRO account, or the rest of the estate. It does not protect parents, siblings, business partners, friends, or anyone outside the statutory beneficiary class. It does not replace a will.

That is not a weakness.

That is its design.

The policy is protected because it has been committed to that purpose. If the policy is validly expressed for the statutory beneficiaries, the structure must be respected during its life, at maturity, and at claim stage, subject to the policy terms and applicable law.

Strong law still needs clean execution. Beneficiary shares, insurer process, banking route, foreign-resident beneficiaries, tax reporting, remittance consequences, existing obligations and creditor issues must be reviewed.

For NRIs, these are not technical afterthoughts.

They are the difference between a protected policy and a disputed expectation.

So the advisor must not say, "MWPA solves inheritance."

That overstates it.

He must also not treat MWPA as routine paperwork.

That insults its value.

> *The right understanding is simpler. MWPA does not solve the whole estate. It can protect one of the most important parts of it.*

Three Instruments. Three Different Jobs.

Nomination, Will and MWPA must not be treated as the same thing.

01	02	03
NOMINATION	WILL	MWPA

Operational claim route	*Succession intention*	*Protective benefit structure, where validly used*
Helps the institution know whom to pay	Speaks after death through legal process	Can ring-fence policy benefits for intended beneficiaries
Does not automatically settle inheritance	Must align with assets and family facts	Not a general substitute for succession planning

The family does not need more papers. It needs papers that speak to each other.

Nomination helps payment. Succession decides ownership. Protection requires structure.

8.6 THE FOREIGN-CITIZEN CHILD: THE WILL AS A LETTER OF CARE

Some NRI inheritance conversations are not really about money. They are about a child.

A child born in Toronto, London, Singapore, Dubai, Sydney or New Jersey. A child with a passport that is not Indian. A child who knows India through summer holidays, grandparents, mangoes, temple visits, cousin weddings and video calls that always end with, "Come soon."

And somewhere in India, there are grandparents who have already decided, without ever needing to say it formally, that if life ever becomes cruel, the child will come home to them.

> *That is how Indian families think. Love first. Paper later. Sometimes never.*

Many NRI parents carry the same quiet assumption. If something happens to both of us, my parents will take the children. Or my sister will. Or my brother will. Everyone knows this. Everyone agrees.

That may be true around the dining table.

It may not be enough at the school office, the hospital counter, the immigration desk, the bank, or the foreign court.

This is the painful distinction.

A child is not an asset in the estate.

Parents do not leave children the way they leave flats, deposits, policies or jewellery.

They leave wishes.

They leave instructions.

They leave evidence of trust.

And if they are careful, they leave those wishes in a form the law can at least hear.

Through properly drafted documents, parents can record their guardianship wishes and, where the applicable law permits, appoint or nominate a testamentary guardian for the minor child's person, property, or both. Under Indian law, the Hindu Minority and Guardianship Act, 1956 recognises testamentary guardianship for Hindu minors in specified circumstances, subject to the structure and limits of that Act. The Guardians and Wards Act, 1890 provides the court framework for guardianship matters and requires the welfare of the minor to guide the court's decision. In the case of Hindu minors, the Hindu Minority and Guardianship Act also expressly makes the welfare of the minor the paramount consideration.

That phrase, welfare of the minor, must not be read like a dry legal expression.

It is the whole room.

It asks where the child will be safe. Who knows the child. Who can raise the child. Who can manage the money. Who can keep the child's life from collapsing twice, first by loss, then by confusion.

Now add the NRI complication.

If the child is a foreign citizen by birth, and especially if the child ordinarily lives abroad, the country of residence may have its own rules on guardianship, custody, child welfare, immigration, schooling, medical consent and court approval. An Indian will cannot simply order a foreign court, school, hospital, immigration officer or child-protection authority to hand over the child to a relative in India.

That would be comforting.

It would also be legally unsafe.

But this does not make the will unimportant.

It makes the will more important.

Because when the parents are no longer there, the will becomes their calmest remaining sentence.

It tells the court what they wanted.

It tells the family whom they trusted.

It tells the grandparents in India that they are not entering a foreign legal system empty-handed.

It tells the insurer, banker, trustee, executor and lawyer that the parents had thought beyond money.

> *A will does not pack the child's suitcase. It tells the world which home the parents wanted the child to reach.*

Consider Nikhilesh and Swati in New Jersey. Their daughter Tara was born in the United States. She is a US citizen by birth. Nikhilesh and Swati are Indian citizens. Their parents live in Jaipur. In every serious family conversation, it is understood that if something happens to both parents, Tara should be raised by Swati's parents in Jaipur.

Everyone knows it.

No one has written it.

Then imagine the unthinkable.

There is an accident. Tara survives. The insurance policies exist. The Indian property exists. The grandparents are ready. The family is united in emotion.

But the first question may not be, "Who loves Tara most?"

The first question may be, "Who has legal authority?"

Who can speak to the school?

Who can consent to medical treatment?

Who can access records?

Who can apply for travel documents?

Who can move the child across borders?

Who can receive or manage policy proceeds for the child?

Who will satisfy the foreign court that this arrangement is in Tara's welfare?

Love will answer all of this in one second.

Law will not move that fast.

For NRI parents with children born abroad, a will should therefore not be seen only as a distribution document. It is also a care document. It should record guardianship preference, backup guardian, asset-control structure, education funding, trustee or guardian identity, location preference, cultural and family wishes where relevant, and coordination with foreign-country documents.

This must be handled with professional advice in the country where the child lives, and in India where the family, assets or proposed guardian may be located.

The advisor must keep the sentence precise.

Not:

"Make a will and custody will automatically transfer to your parents in India."

That is comfort without defence.

The better position is:

"A will can record your guardianship wishes and, where the applicable law permits, appoint or nominate a testamentary guardian. But if your child is a foreign citizen or resident abroad, local law and the child-welfare jurisdiction of that country must also be checked."

This is not legal pessimism.

It is parental realism.

The insurance policy may fund the child's future.

The guardianship plan decides who stands beside the child while that future is being protected.

8.7 THE MINOR CHILD PROBLEM: OWNERSHIP IS NOT CONTROL

The most painful inheritance disputes are not always about who gets the money.

Sometimes the real problem is who controls it until the real beneficiary is old enough to understand what was done in his name.

Sanjay has been in Muscat for fifteen years. His son Rohan is eleven and studies in a boarding school in Dehradun. Sanjay calls him every Sunday evening. Some calls last twenty minutes. Some last four. But every call ends the same way.

"Study well. I am doing all this for you."

That sentence is not dramatic.

It is the private religion of many NRI parents.

Sanjay and his wife had been separated for years, but the marriage had never been legally dissolved. She lived in Mumbai and had formed a new household with another partner. Everyone in the family knew the reality. The documents, however, had not caught up with it.

That fact, by itself, is not the legal problem. Adults are entitled to rebuild their lives. The problem is narrower, more personal and more painful: Sanjay does not want Rohan's education fund, insurance money and Indian assets to be controlled by an adult household whose values, priorities and financial decisions he does not trust for his son.

He is not trying to punish his former wife.

He is trying to protect his child.

That distinction matters.

Because in family law and estate planning, emotion easily becomes accusation. A responsible advisor must not encourage that. The issue is not whether one adult's life choice is right or wrong. The issue is whether the parent funding the child's future has created a legally workable structure for how that future should be managed if he is no longer around.

Sanjay has an Indian life policy. He has named Rohan as nominee. He feels reassured because the name is correct.

But Rohan is still a minor.

A minor cannot walk into an insurer's office, sign discharge papers, manage claim proceeds, choose a bank account, pay school fees, invest funds, resist pressure, or explain to a court what his father would have wanted.

So the real question is not, "Is Rohan named?"

The real question is, "Which adult will control Rohan's money until Rohan can control it himself?"

That is where many NRI plans quietly fail.

> *The money may belong beneficially to the child. The practical control of that money belongs to the adult structure around the child. A child's name on a form can create comfort. It does not automatically create control.*

If Sanjay simply names Rohan on the policy, the insurer may still need an appointee, guardian, trustee, legal representative or court-supported process, depending on the structure and facts. The policy may eventually benefit Rohan, but the path between claim approval and Rohan's actual welfare may be controlled by someone else.

That is not a technicality.

That is the whole issue.

A properly structured MWPA policy with a suitable trustee may change the conversation where the statutory conditions are satisfied. A well-drafted will with guardianship and asset-control thinking may change it further. A trust or other structure may be needed in larger or more sensitive cases. But a bare nomination does not answer enough.

For cross-border families, minor-beneficiary planning must consider guardian identity, trustee competence, educational use, emergency access, foreign residence, currency movement, tax reporting and the possibility that the surviving parent or nearest adult may not be the person the client wants controlling the money.

The advisor does not need to judge the family.

He needs to identify the risk.

A minor nominee is not a complete plan. It is a question mark wearing a child's name. The advisor who avoids this question is not simplifying the conversation. He is leaving the hardest question for the family to answer when the father is no longer there to answer it himself.

8.8 THE PROPERTY FEAR

The question usually does not come when the NRI is healthy, busy and confident.

It comes after the first warning.

A chest pain in Dubai. A stent in Singapore. A collapse in a hotel lobby in Doha. A doctor in Toronto saying, "You were lucky this time."

For the first few days, the family speaks only of recovery. Diet. Medicines. Walking. Rest. No stress. Everyone becomes gentle for a while.

Then, one evening, when the house is quiet and the phone has stopped ringing, the NRI opens a file.

Not the investment file.

The India file.

The flat agreement. The society papers. The old electricity bill. The property tax receipt. The photocopy of the sale deed. The key that has travelled through three cupboards and two countries.

And suddenly the question is no longer theoretical.

"If something happens to me, what happens to this flat?"

When an NRI asks that, he is not asking only about real estate.

He is asking whether the India he built will remain safe after him.

For many NRIs, property is the closest asset to the heart. A bank balance is useful. A policy is protective. A mutual fund is efficient. But a flat in India is different.

It is not just an asset.

> *It is the proof that he did not leave India completely. It is the house where parents may still sit in the evening. The balcony where a father reads the newspaper. The cupboard where school certificates, wedding albums and donation receipts quietly age together. The address that relatives still use when they say, "Unka ghar yahin hai."*

His children may grow up abroad. His tax residence may change. His passport may change. His accent may soften in another country. His daily life may belong elsewhere.

But when he says, "Our flat in India," the word our carries something no valuation report can capture.

It carries belonging.

That is why the fear cuts deep.

He is not merely worried that someone may claim an asset.

He is worried that the one place he built to keep the family tied to India may become the reason the family stops speaking.

And this fear is not imaginary.

Indian immovable property does not move according to private emotion. Without a will, it may pass under the applicable intestate succession framework. It may not go neatly to "my wife," "my son," or "the child who stayed back in India." It may move to multiple heirs at once. What felt like one family home can become a shared legal file requiring consent, release, mutation, partition, settlement or court process before it can function cleanly again.

Then comes the second layer: possession.

In Indian property matters, the person with the keys can sometimes create more friction than the person with the law.

Legal title and practical control are not the same thing. The relative who has access to the flat, speaks to the society office, collects rent, manages tenants, knows the local broker, keeps original papers or lives fifteen minutes away can slow down a family for years, even where the legal position is ultimately clear.

The court may finally decide ownership.

But meanwhile, life waits.

Rent waits. Sale waits. Mutation waits. Repairs wait. The widow waits. The children abroad wait. The family WhatsApp group becomes a courtroom without a judge.

A will does not make every family noble.

It does something more useful.

> *It reduces the space in which confusion can become opportunity. Uncertainty gives disputes room to breathe. A clear will quietly closes that room.*

So when an NRI says, "I worry that relatives will claim the flat," the correct response is not, "Sir, don't worry."

That is sympathy without structure.

The better response is:

"Your Indian property needs estate documentation before your family needs it."

Usually, that means a properly drafted Indian will for Indian assets, supported by clean title papers, updated nominations and transmission records where relevant, family communication where appropriate, and a practical plan for who will handle the asset after death.

The advisor should not casually opine on title, tenancy, partition, probate, stamp duty, registration or litigation risk.

Those belong to a lawyer.

But the advisor must recognise the signal.

After the first heart attack, the NRI is not only afraid of dying.

He is afraid of leaving behind a fight in the one place that made him feel he still belonged.

That is why Indian property cannot be treated as just another line in the balance sheet.

For the NRI, it is often the last physical address of belonging.

And that address should not become the dispute he leaves behind.

8.9 TAX, TDS AND THE LAST MILE OF THE CLAIM

After death, families often ask one sentence in many forms: **"How quickly will the money come?"**

The honest answer is: entitlement is only half the journey.

The last mile still has tax, banking and documentation.

Four distinctions are enough for the advisor to remember.

First, succession is not income. Money or property received under a will or inheritance is generally not taxed in India merely because the asset has moved to the heir. But income earned after that, rent, interest, dividends, annuity income or gains on later sale, is a separate tax event.

Second, Indian exemption is not foreign exemption. A death claim or inheritance may have one treatment in India and a very different reporting, estate, inheritance or tax consequence in the beneficiary's country of residence. India's answer does not bind the world.

Third, withholding does not arise merely because the beneficiary lives abroad. Under Indian income-tax law, the question is not where the recipient lives, but whether the sum is chargeable to tax in India. Residence is relevant. Chargeability is decisive.

Fourth, death does not close the tax file automatically. If the deceased had Indian taxable income, pending filing obligations, refunds, TDS credits, capital gains, rent, interest or other reportable matters, the Indian return may need to be filed by the legal heir or representative assessee in accordance with the applicable income-tax law. This is not just compliance. It creates a clean record, supports credits and refunds where applicable, and gives the estate a cleaner exit.

The advisor need not become a tax lawyer at claim stage.

But he must not say, "No issue."

Insurers may still ask for KYC, claim documents, relationship proof, FATCA or CRS declarations and bank details. Banks may still ask for succession papers, a source trail, remittance reporting, certification or authorised dealer review, depending on the route.

When inherited money has to move from India to an NRI beneficiary abroad, it must travel through the permitted banking route, supported by the remittance documentation required for that payment and that date. Under the post-2026 framework, this may involve Form 145 and, where applicable, Form 146, along with authorised dealer bank review and source documents.

Chapter 3 made one point clear: bank accounts are not containers. They are rails.

After death, the rail still matters.

A claim to a resident heir, non-resident heir, minor, trustee, nominee or executor may not travel through the same route. NRE, NRO, resident accounts, remittance of inherited assets and foreign-resident beneficiaries all require the correct documentary path.

> *The claim is not truly complete when the insurer approves it. It is complete when the money reaches the right hands, on the right rail, with the right papers, and, where required, with the deceased person's Indian tax record properly closed.*

8.10 THE FINAL DISCIPLINE

By this point, the advisor does not need a longer checklist.

He needs discipline.

Before an NRI policy is treated as complete, four things should be checked for consistency: that the nomination matches the client's present family reality, that the will covers Indian assets clearly, that MWPA has been considered where a specific policy is meant to protect the wife, the children, or both, and that guardianship wishes are recorded where minor or foreign-born children are involved.

If these four speak against each other, the family inherits confusion.

If they speak together, the family inherits order.

The advisor is not expected to draft legal documents.

But he must not ignore their absence.

That is the professional line.

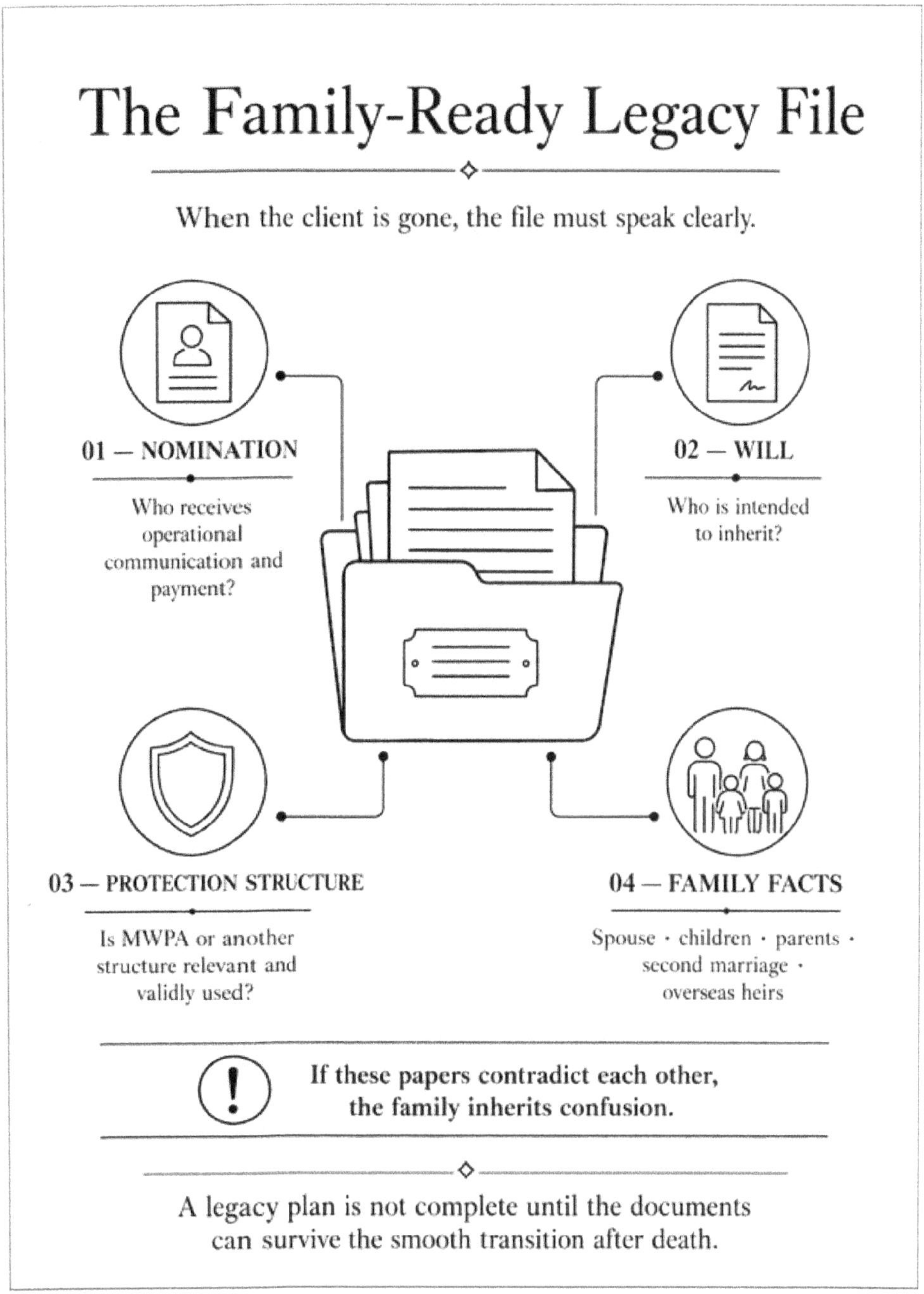
The Family-Ready Legacy File
When the client is gone, the file must speak clearly.
01 — NOMINATION
Who receives operational communication and payment?
02 — WILL
Who is intended to inherit?
03 — PROTECTION STRUCTURE
Is MWPA or another structure relevant and validly used?
04 — FAMILY FACTS
Spouse · children · parents · second marriage · overseas heirs
If these papers contradict each other, the family inherits confusion.
A legacy plan is not complete until the documents can survive the smooth transition after death.

8.11 WHAT MUST NEVER BE OVERSOLD

The advisor should never say:

"Nominee is enough."

"MWPA protects everything."

"Indian will solves foreign assets."

"Foreign-born child will automatically go to grandparents in India."

"Death claim is tax-free everywhere."

"If beneficiary is abroad, TDS always applies."

"Sir, no issue."

The better sentence is shorter and stronger:

> *"This depends on the facts, documents, residential status, beneficiary location, account route, guardianship position and applicable law. It should be reviewed before the claim becomes a crisis."*

That sentence may not sound like selling.

It sounds like credibility.

And in the NRI market, credibility is the sale before the sale.

8.12 BEFORE THE LABEL IS TESTED

Inheritance planning is not an emotional add-on to the NRI insurance conversation. It is often the reason the conversation matters.

A policy can be sold in one meeting. A claim can stay stuck for years. A child can be loved by everyone and still be caught between courts, passports and papers. A family can know exactly what the client meant and still fight over the document he never signed.

The final lesson is simple. Nomination is useful. A will gives direction. MWPA can protect powerfully within its limits. Guardianship wishes must be recorded. Tax must be kept apart from succession. The banking rail must be planned. Foreign residence does not make Indian legal work disappear.

The NRI who has built a life across borders has already accepted complexity in earning. What he postpones is complexity in ending. That postponement is the inheritance trap.

The advisor who helps him step out of it is not merely selling protection. He is restoring order to the one part of a financial life its owner will not be present to repair.

And once the family, the policy, the nominee, the will, the child, the account and the tax record have all been seen together, "NRI" can no longer be treated as a label. It has to be tested against the life behind it.

TECHNICAL SOURCE NOTE

This chapter should be read with reference to section 39 of the Insurance Act, 1938; section 6 of the Married Women's Property Act, 1874; the Hindu Minority and Guardianship Act, 1956 where applicable; the Guardians and Wards Act, 1890; applicable Indian succession and personal-law principles; FEMA and RBI banking, remittance and repatriation rules relevant to nominees, heirs, executors, trustees and non-resident beneficiaries; and Indian income-tax provisions relevant to insurance receipts, inheritance, later income, capital gains and payments to non-residents.

For tax years and remittances on or after 1 April 2026, the Income-tax Act, 2025 and the Income-tax Rules, 2026 apply, including the life-insurance exclusion under section 11 read with Schedule II, Sr. No. 2, and the remittance-reporting and certification framework using Form 145 and Form 146 where required. Exact provision and form mapping should be verified against the law in force on the relevant date before publication or client use.

Foreign-country consequences, especially guardianship, custody, immigration, estate, inheritance, reporting and tax consequences, must be confirmed separately in the relevant jurisdiction.

End of Chapter 8

CHAPTER 9

BEST PRACTICES THAT BUILD CREDIBILITY

The File That Protects the Client, the Family and the Advisor

Every old Hindi film courtroom had a familiar moment.

The lawyer would rise slowly. The file would open. Someone would say, "My Lord." The judge would adjust his glasses. The background score would become serious. One missing paper, one forgotten signature, one contradiction, and suddenly the entire case would turn.

Cinema made it dramatic.

Real life is usually quieter.

Today, the question may not come from a wooden courtroom at all. It may come through a virtual hearing, an income-tax portal, a bank compliance desk, an insurer's claim team, an AMC or RTA, a broker, a portfolio manager, an IFSC intermediary, a remittance query, a foreign tax advisor's email, or a family member asking a question after the client is no longer alive.

There may be no judge on a raised bench.

No dramatic pause.

No background music.

But the principle is exactly the same.

When the question comes, the file must answer.

Not memory.

Not confidence.

Not goodwill.

The file.

That is the discipline this chapter is about.

The earlier chapters have already given the advisor the technical landscape. He has travelled through identity, citizenship, FEMA, income tax, banking rails, treaty relief, foreign-country exposure, investment routes, GIFT IFSC, return to India, nomination, MWPA and succession.

By now, he has not merely collected information. He has walked through the full architecture of the NRI client's financial life.

This chapter is not meant to repeat that architecture.

It is meant to convert it into conduct.

Because a book can give knowledge.

But an advisor must develop judgment.

And judgment is visible not in how much the advisor can say, but in what he asks, what he records, what he qualifies, what he refuses to oversimplify, and when he brings the right professional into the room.

That is the point at which product knowledge, route awareness and documentation discipline become trusted advice.

In this chapter, insurance remains the most familiar example because many readers will first meet the NRI through a policy conversation. But the discipline is larger than insurance. The same file discipline applies when the NRI buys a mutual fund, opens a deposit, enters PMS or AIF, sells property, uses GIFT IFSC, receives rent, repatriates proceeds, names a nominee, prepares a will or returns to India.

The product changes.

The discipline does not.

In NRI advisory, credibility is not created by knowing one product deeply. It is created by knowing which questions must be asked before any product is placed into a cross-border life.

The NRI File Architecture

The file that protects the client, the family and the advisor.

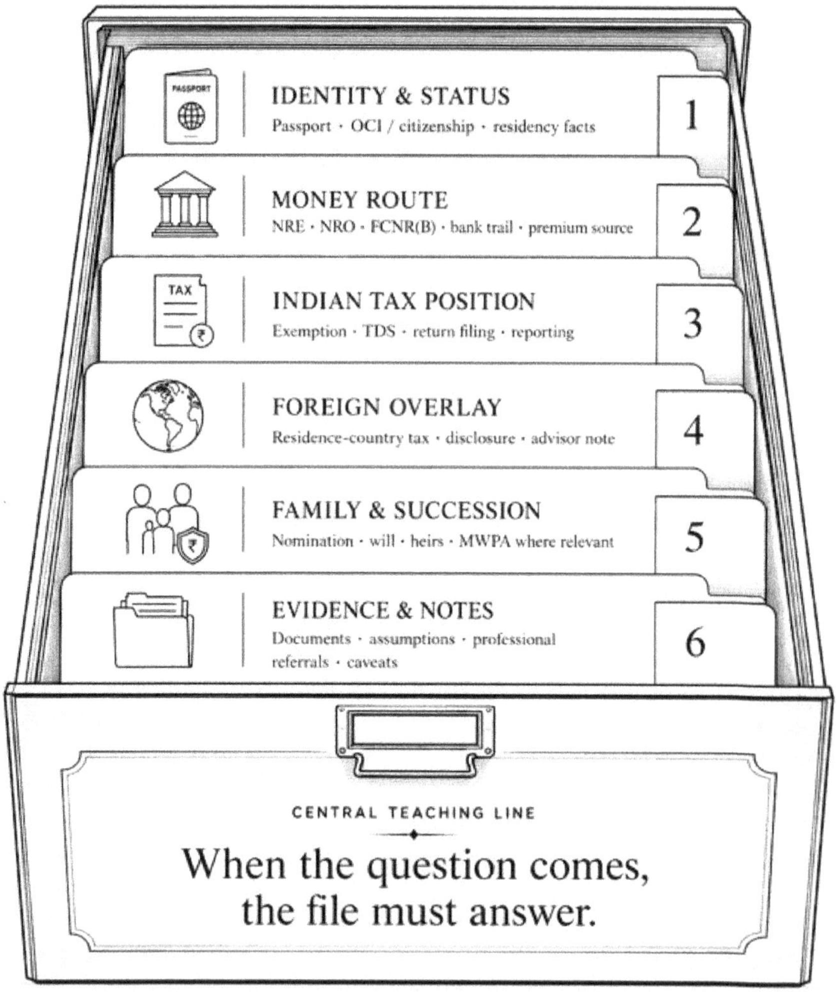

Not memory. Not confidence. Not goodwill. *The file.*

9.1 THE ADVISOR AFTER THE JOURNEY

A beginner wants more information.

A trained advisor wants a framework.

A trusted advisor develops instinct.

He does not look at an NRI client and see only a proposal form, application, subscription document or onboarding checklist.

He sees a person whose money, family, tax position, banking route and future plans may be spread across more than one country.

He understands that one sentence spoken casually in India may create a very different consequence abroad.

He understands that a financial product or asset that looks simple today may become complicated when the client returns to India, changes citizenship, changes country of residence, passes away, redeems, sells, repatriates or expects money to move across borders.

He understands that the NRI client is not a domestic client with an overseas address.

He is a cross-border financial person.

That is the shift this book has been building towards.

The advisor is no longer expected to behave like a product distributor with extra facts.

He is expected to behave like the first filter of cross-border risk.

That does not make him a Chartered Accountant, a FEMA specialist, a lawyer, a banker or a foreign tax advisor.

It makes him a trusted advisor.

There is a significant difference.

A trusted advisor does not pretend to know everything.

He knows what must not be ignored.

He knows when comfort is premature.

He knows when a matter must be documented.

He knows when a specialist must confirm the position.

That is professional maturity.

9.2 THE CENTRAL RULE: THE FILE MUST NOT DEPEND ON MEMORY

NRI advisory fails most often not because the advisor had bad intention.

It fails because important facts remain floating in conversation.

The client says he lives in Dubai.

The advisor hears "NRI."

But the file does not record the country of residence, tax residency, source of funds, account route, family structure, return-to-India plan, or whether foreign-country tax advice is required.

The client says the money will be paid from India.

In an insurance case, the advisor hears "premium paid." In an investment case, he may hear "subscription done," "purchase completed," "funding made" or "transfer processed."

But the file does not show whether the money came from NRE, NRO, FCNR(B), resident funds, foreign inward remittance, sale proceeds, rent, inheritance, redemption proceeds, maturity proceeds or another person's account.

The client says his wife will be nominee, joint holder, beneficiary, mandate holder or intended recipient.

The advisor hears "family arrangement done."

But the file does not show whether she is resident in India or abroad, whether her KYC is current, whether minor children are involved, whether a will exists, whether transmission will be smooth, or whether succession risk has been considered.

The client says the policy is tax-free, the interest is exempt, the capital gain is covered, the redemption is clean, or the remittance is allowed.

The advisor hears one legal answer.

But the file does not show whether the Indian position has been tested against the law in force, whether FEMA permits the route, whether withholding applies, or whether the client's country of residence may tax, report, accrue, classify or question the same receipt differently.

This is how gaps are created.

Not because anyone planned to mislead.

Because no one paused to complete the record.

The trusted advisor's first discipline is therefore simple.

Never allow important facts to remain only in memory.

A serious advisory file should show what the client represented, what the advisor explained, what was qualified, what was pending, and where specialist confirmation was recommended.

The format may be a meeting note, email summary, client declaration, onboarding checklist or internal advisory record.

The format is secondary.

The discipline is primary.

Memory changes after outcomes.

Files do not.

9.3 THE SIX INSTINCTS OF A TRUSTED NRI ADVISOR

After completing this book, the advisor should carry six instincts into every NRI conversation.

These are not academic points.

They are the working habits that separate ordinary selling from serious advisory.

1. He identifies the person before discussing the product

The weakest NRI conversation begins with the product.

The strongest one begins with the person.

Who is this client in the cross-border sense?

Is he an Indian citizen living abroad, a foreign citizen of Indian origin, an OCI cardholder, a returning Indian, an RNOR candidate, a long-settled overseas Indian, or a globally mobile professional whose country may change again?

The advisor may not finally determine every legal status himself.

But he must know that status is not a decorative detail.

It drives eligibility, documentation, banking route, tax review, reporting expectations, claim mechanics and future planning.

A product or asset discussed without understanding the client's cross-border profile is like prescribing medicine without asking the patient's age, allergies or history.

It may still work.

But that would be luck, not advisory quality.

2. He traces the money before giving comfort

In NRI work, money has a route.

That route matters.

The same rupee may carry a different practical meaning depending on whether it enters as premium, subscription money, purchase consideration, portfolio funding, deposit funding, property sale proceeds, rent, inheritance, redemption proceeds, NRE funds, NRO balances, FCNR(B) funds, foreign inward remittance, resident Indian funds or money routed through a family member's account.

The same maturity, surrender, claim, redemption, dividend, interest, rent, sale proceeds or distribution may create different questions depending on where the recipient lives, where the funds are credited, what the original source was, and whether repatriation is expected.

The trusted advisor does not stop at "premium paid," "subscription done," "redemption processed," "claim payable" or "sale completed."

He asks: where did the money come from, through which account did it move, whose money was it, and where may it need to go later?

That one habit prevents many future problems.

Because in NRI advisory, the route is often as important as the result.

3. He separates permission, taxation and documentation

A disciplined advisor does not mix every law into one fog.

He separates three questions.

Is it permitted?

Is it taxable?

Can it be documented?

These are not the same question.

A transaction may be permitted but taxable.

It may be tax-efficient but poorly documented.

It may be operationally possible but unsuitable for the client's family, remittance objective or foreign-country position.

This is where ordinary advisory conversations start bending.

The client asks about tax, but the real issue may be whether the route is permitted.

The client asks about the product, but the real issue may be whether the family can receive, redeem, transmit, repatriate or explain the money smoothly.

The client asks about remittance, but the real issue may be whether the source of funds can be proved.

The trusted advisor does not rush to answer the visible question.

He first identifies the hidden question.

That is what makes the conversation clean.

4. He qualifies comfort before it becomes a promise

Words like "tax-free", "DTAA", "NRI", "nominee", "NRE" and "repatriable" are useful only when used carefully.

Used loosely, they are dangerous.

"Tax-free" must be qualified by country, law, year, conditions and client status.

"DTAA" must be supported by facts, treaty article, TRC, prescribed declarations and professional review where required.

"NRE" does not mean every future transaction is automatically free from every question.

"Nominee" does not automatically mean final owner.

"Repatriable" does not mean the bank will move funds without documentation.

The trained advisor therefore does not create false comfort.

He creates informed comfort.

He says enough to guide the client, but not so much that he crosses into a technical conclusion beyond his role.

That balance is not weakness.

It is credibility.

5. He brings the family into the file before the family enters the crisis

In insurance, the family enters the file through nomination, beneficiary records, claim documents and succession questions.

In investments and assets, the family may enter through joint holding, mode of operation, transmission, nominee records, legal heirs, mandate holders, executors, trustees, guardianship, bank accounts and remittance routes.

Either way, the family should enter the file before the family enters the crisis.

For NRI families, this can become difficult quickly.

The nominee may live in another country.

The spouse may not understand Indian documentation.

The children may be minors.

The parents may be dependent in India.

The family may be divided across jurisdictions.

The client may have remarried.

A will may not exist.

The insurer's, bank's, AMC's, broker's, depository's, portfolio manager's or product provider's record may not match the family's present reality.

The trusted advisor does not wait for the claim, redemption, transmission, sale or succession event to discover these facts.

He asks the family questions while the client is alive.

That is not negative thinking.

That is responsible advisory.

A policy, investment or asset may look complete on paper.

But the claim, redemption, transmission, sale, remittance or succession file is the road through which value actually reaches the family.

If the road is blocked, the money is delayed.

6. He reviews because the NRI's life does not stand still

A domestic client's facts may remain stable for years.

An NRI client's facts can change with one relocation, one visa decision, one citizenship change, one family event, one inheritance, one return-to-India plan or one banking change.

The country of residence may change.

Tax residency may change.

Citizenship may change.

OCI status may become relevant.

Funding source may change.

Nomination, joint holding, beneficiary records, bank mandate or transmission instructions may need review.

A child may move abroad.

The client may decide to retire in India.

Foreign assets may enter the picture.

In transition years, this review habit matters most. A client leaving India, returning to India, or moving from one foreign country to another is not read by every system on the same date. The country of residence may read him one way, FEMA another, and Indian income tax differently for the same year. That is the NRI Kaalchakra™ at work.

The advisor need not resolve every clock himself. He must remember that the clocks exist, and ask the one question that protects the conversation before he offers comfort: which clock is reading this client as what, and from when?

The advisor need not conduct a legal audit every year.

But he must develop a review habit.

A simple periodic review can prevent the product, asset or file from becoming disconnected from the client's real life.

That is how an advisor remains relevant after the transaction.

9.4 THE SENTENCES A TRUSTED ADVISOR LEAVES BEHIND

A professional standard is built not only by what the advisor says. It is also built by what he stops saying.

He should stop saying, "You are NRI, so Indian tax will not apply."

He should say, "Let us first examine the Indian tax position based on residential status, source of income, nature of receipt and applicable law."

He should stop saying, "This is tax-free."

He should say, "This may be favourably treated in India subject to conditions, but the foreign-country position must be checked separately."

He should stop saying, "DTAA will solve it."

He should say, "Treaty relief depends on facts, treaty article, documentation and professional confirmation."

He should stop saying, "NRE money means no issue."

He should say, "NRE funds have a specific banking and FEMA character, but the transaction and future use still need to be understood."

He should stop saying, "The investment is fully clear because the money came through NRE."

He should say, "NRE funding may support the route, but the product, exit, tax, withholding, repatriation and foreign-country treatment must still be checked."

He should stop saying, "Nominee means the money belongs to that person."

He should say, "Nomination helps claim processing, but succession consequences must be reviewed separately."

He should stop saying, "Joint holder, nominee or family member means the matter is settled."

He should say, "Operational access, transmission, claim processing and final legal ownership are separate questions."

He should stop saying, "We will manage documentation later."

He should say, "Let us document the basis now."

This is not wordplay.

This is risk management.

In NRI advisory, one loose sentence can live longer than the meeting in which it was spoken.

9.5 WHEN REFERRAL BECOMES PART OF THE ADVICE

Some advisors fear referral because they think it reduces their authority.

In NRI work, the opposite is true.

Referral, done at the right time, increases trust.

A client does not expect one advisor to be the Income Tax Department, RBI, SEBI, IRDAI, IFSCA, probate court, banker, foreign tax office, insurer, AMC, broker, portfolio manager and lawyer in one person.

The client expects him not to bluff.

The advisor should therefore know the referral triggers.

Residential status, ITR filing, DTAA claims, TDS, foreign tax credit, foreign-asset disclosure and Indian tax treatment of insurance receipts, interest, dividends, capital gains, rent, redemption proceeds, sale proceeds or other India-linked income require Indian tax review.

Account redesignation, NRO remittance, repatriation, inheritance-related remittance, source-of-funds issues and unusual banking routes require FEMA or banking review.

Wills, succession, probate, guardianship, second-family issues, minor beneficiaries, MWPA structuring, trusts and property disputes require legal review.

Taxability, reporting, accrual, estate exposure or classification of the Indian policy, fund, portfolio, deposit, property, bond, IFSC product or other Indian asset in the client's country of residence requires foreign-country tax review.

Operational credit, remittance formats, bank documentation and timing require banker coordination.

Where the product falls outside the advisor's licence, registration, employment role or institutional mandate, the advisor should not pretend to recommend it. His role is to identify the cross-border question, document the concern and bring the right professional into the room.

The advisor's sentence should be calm and clear:

"This point is outside product advice. It needs specialist confirmation before we proceed."

That sentence does not weaken the advisor.

It separates him from the advisor who guesses.

9.6 THE ADVISOR'S OWN FILE

So far, the focus has been on the client's documents. The advisor also needs his own record.

Not to create fear.

Not to turn every meeting into a legal proceeding.

Simply to show professional discipline.

A good advisory note should capture the essentials.

Who was the client?

What was his country of residence?

What status did he represent?

What was the purpose of the policy, investment, asset or financial arrangement?

Which account, source and route were proposed for premium, subscription, investment, purchase, funding or remittance?

Was foreign-country tax exposure flagged?

Was nomination, joint holding, beneficiary designation, mandate, guardianship, will, transmission or succession discussed?

Was return-to-India planning relevant?

Was any specialist referral suggested?

Was the advisor's role limited by licence, registration, employment role or institutional mandate?

Was the product provider, platform or intermediary identified?

Was the relevant regulator or framework identified where necessary—IRDAI, SEBI, RBI, IFSCA, depository, bank or product provider?

Was country-of-residence reporting exposure flagged?

What documents were requested or pending?

What assumptions were made?

These notes do not need literary polish.

They need existence.

An advisor who leaves no trace of his process is asking to be judged by hindsight.

Hindsight is always unfair because it knows the ending.

The file must show what was reasonable when the advice was given.

That is the advisor's protection.

It is also the client's protection.

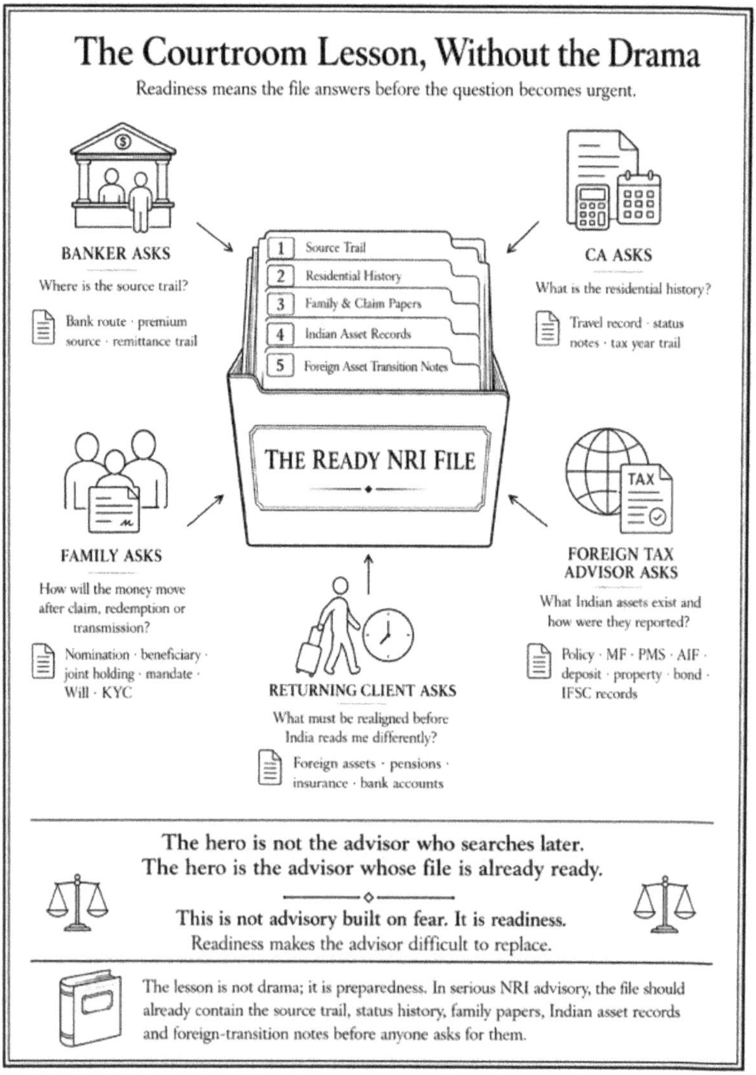

9.7 THE PROFESSIONAL STANDARD IN ONE FLOW

A credible NRI advisory conversation whether for insurance, investments, banking, property, IFSC products or legacy planning should follow a clean sequence.

First, understand the client.

Then understand the objective.

Then understand the money route.

Then identify the India-side tax and FEMA touchpoints.

Then flag foreign-country exposure where relevant.

Then connect the product or asset to the family outcome, exit route, redemption, claim, transmission, repatriation or succession consequence.

Then record assumptions.

Then refer specialist issues.

Then preserve documents.

Then review when life changes.

This sequence is not bureaucracy.

It is order.

It allows the advisor to sit across from an NRI family and bring structure to a conversation that may otherwise be scattered across relatives, bankers, CAs, lawyers, insurers, AMCs, brokers, portfolio managers, IFSC intermediaries and overseas advisors.

That is where the advisor's real value emerges.

Not in knowing every answer.

In creating a reliable pathway.

The client may not remember the technical terminology.

But he will remember that the advisor asked the question no one else asked.

He will remember that the advisor did not rush into comfort.

He will remember that the advisor connected the product or asset to the family, the money trail, the country of residence, the tax file, the exit route and the eventual claim, redemption, transmission or repatriation.

That is not ordinary selling.

That is advisory credibility.

9.8 THE COURTROOM LESSON, WITHOUT THE DRAMA

The old courtroom scene may be exaggerated, but it leaves one useful lesson.

The hero is not the person who begins searching for the document after the judge asks for it.

The hero is the person who already has the document in the file.

In NRI advisory, that is the standard.

When the banker asks for the source trail, it should exist.

When the CA asks for residential history, the travel record should exist.

When the family asks how the claim, redemption, transmission, sale or transfer will be processed, the nomination, beneficiary, joint holding, mandate, will, KYC and bank-route details should exist.

When the foreign tax advisor asks about the Indian policy, mutual fund, PMS, AIF, deposit, property, bond, IFSC product or other Indian asset, the product papers, transaction trail, tax notes and reporting history should exist.

When the client returns to India, foreign assets, pensions, insurance policies and bank accounts should not arrive as surprises.

This is not advisory built on fear.

It is readiness.

The advisor who creates readiness becomes difficult to replace.

Because he is not merely helping the client buy a policy, subscribe to a product, hold an asset or complete a transaction.

He is helping the client avoid future confusion.

9.9 BEFORE THE LABEL IS TESTED

This book began with one central idea.

An NRI is not just a customer living abroad.

He is a cross-border financial person.

His identity may be Indian.

His citizenship may be foreign.

His assets may sit in more than one country.

His family may be scattered.

His bank accounts may decide what can move and how.

His tax exposure may not follow his emotions.

His insurance, investments, deposits, property and India-linked assets may affect a family that does not live under one roof, one law or one tax system.

That is why ordinary product knowledge is not enough.

The advisor who has reached this point has moved beyond the question, "Which product should I suggest?" That question is not wrong. It is simply too early.

He now asks better questions.

Who is the client?

Where does the money sit?

Which route will it take?

What does India say?

What might the foreign country say?

Who receives the benefit?

What happens if the client returns?

What happens if the client does not return?

What happens on redemption, maturity, sale, claim, transmission or death?

What should be documented today?

These are the questions that separate an ordinary product seller from a trusted NRI advisor.

Not sounding knowledgeable.

Being useful when the matter becomes serious.

Not saying yes quickly.

Knowing which question must be answered first.

Not pretending to be every professional in the room.

Knowing which professional must enter the room.

Not leaving the client impressed for one meeting.

Leaving the client protected for the future.

Before any label is tested in law, the advisor must first understand the life behind it.

Only then should he test the identity, the status, the money route, the product route, the tax position, the family position, the foreign-country exposure and the evidence on which assurance will rest.

Where the discussion involves investments, securities, deposits, property, PMS, AIF, mutual funds, bonds, demat holdings, GIFT IFSC products or other financial arrangements, the applicable SEBI, RBI, IFSCA, depository, bank, product-provider, KYC, FATCA/CRS, tax-withholding, reporting and succession rules must be reviewed separately.

Because in NRI advisory, credibility does not begin when the advisor answers.

It begins in the pause before the answer, when he decides to understand properly.

Nothing in this chapter should be read as authorising an advisor to provide regulated investment, tax, legal, FEMA, securities or foreign-

country advice beyond his licence, registration, employment role or professional competence.

Technical Source Note —

This chapter should be read with reference to the Foreign Exchange Management Act, 1999 and applicable RBI directions, Master Directions and authorised-dealer bank processes governing residential status, account operation, remittance and repatriation; the Income-tax Act applicable to the relevant tax year, payment, transaction or filing period—including the Income-tax Act, 1961 for earlier years and the Income-tax Act, 2025 for tax years beginning on or after 1 April 2026, as applicable—including the life-insurance exemption (Section 10(10D) of the 1961 Act, now Section 11 read with Schedule II, Sr. No. 2 of the 2025 Act) and the provisions on payments to non-residents, including Section 195 of the 1961 Act and the relevant non-resident payment / withholding provisions under Section 393 of the 2025 Act, where applicable; applicable Double Taxation Avoidance Agreement provisions, the Tax Residency Certificate and the prescribed declaration in force, including Form 10F / Form 41, as applicable under the law and rules governing the relevant tax year; Indian succession, personal-law and Married Women's Property Act, 1874 principles where relevant; and the tax, reporting, estate and succession rules of the client's country of residence. Positions are fact-specific and must be confirmed against the law in force and the client's documents.

End of Chapter 9

PART V

THE OPERATING STANDARD

CHAPTER 10

THE NRI INDIA MANTRA™

Before You Advise an NRI on India, Apply INDIA

The most dangerous advisor in the NRI market is not always the advisor who knows too little.

Very often, it is the advisor who knows just enough to sound confident.

He has heard the product explanation. He remembers the tax benefit. He has seen a few similar cases. He knows that NRIs can buy Indian policies, enter Indian investment routes, hold Indian bank accounts, receive Indian income, deal with Indian property, use IFSC channels where eligible, and name nominees. He also knows that NRE money may carry a cleaner repatriable trail, that Indian law may give favourable treatment to certain life insurance receipts subject to conditions, that treaties can relieve double taxation in defined cases, and that nomination helps operationally at the time of a claim or transmission.

None of that knowledge is useless. In fact, it is necessary.

The problem begins when necessary knowledge is mistaken for complete advice.

The call comes late in the evening. Nikhil is in Toronto. The advisor is in Mumbai. Outside Nikhil's window, snow is settling on parked cars. Inside, the apartment is quiet—the children asleep, his wife somewhere in the next room. On the dining table sits an old folder, slightly bent at the edges, still carrying the smell of paper, ink and a life that began somewhere else. The Indian policy file.

In this story, the doorway is insurance. In another NRI file, the doorway may be a mutual fund redemption, sale of property, rent credit, dividend, deposit maturity, IFSC investment, inheritance, return to India review or remittance request. The product changes. The discipline does not.

The policy has matured.

The amount is meaningful. Not life-changing, perhaps. But large enough to matter. Large enough to plan around. Large enough for Nikhil to feel quietly proud that he continued paying for twenty years.

Most premiums came from his NRE account. One or two came from his NRO account. In one difficult year, when he was between jobs, his brother in Baroda paid from India and the family adjusted it later.

Nothing was hidden.

Nothing was designed to defeat the law.

It was simply life. A busy NRI life.

Now the maturity letter is open on the screen, and Nikhil asks the question every advisor recognises.

"Sir, this policy maturity is tax-free, right?"

It sounds like a small question.

The advisor knows the product. He remembers the brochure. The client sounds tired. There are other calls waiting. The answer is almost ready before the client has finished the sentence.

"Yes, sir. Tax-free."

That is the ordinary answer.

It may even be partly correct.

But in NRI advisory, a partly correct answer can still become a dangerous answer—because Nikhil did not ask one question. He asked many, and folded them into one.

Is the receipt exempt in India?

Were the premiums within the conditions that exemption depends on?

Does the mixed premium route change anything?

Can the maturity reach the account he has in mind?

Can the money move to Canada at all?

Will Canada tax it, or merely want it reported?

Has his status changed since the policy began?

If someone asks his family to explain this trail in ten years, can they?

And the question underneath all of them:

What evidence supports the comfort being offered tonight?

Nikhil asked a small question because clients usually do. They do not speak in FEMA categories, treaty articles, TDS provisions, policy conditions, banking routes, foreign-reporting rules and succession principles. They speak like human beings. They compress a year of quiet worry into ordinary words.

"Tax-free, right?"

"Repatriable, right?"

"Nominee will get it, right?"

These are not simple questions.

They are simple sentences.

A good advisor must know the difference.

The ordinary advisor hears the sentence and answers it.

The trusted advisor hears the concern and diagnoses it.

That is the purpose of this final chapter. Not to frighten the advisor. Not to make every answer sound complicated. Not to turn every client conversation into a legal opinion. The purpose is to give the advisor one disciplined way to think before answering an NRI client.

The ordinary advisor answers quickly.

The trusted advisor pauses.

And inside that pause, he applies INDIA.

A note on the word before we begin. Mantra is used here in its professional sense—a principle repeated until it becomes instinct. Not religious. Not devotional. A working memory tool: simple enough for a live call, serious enough for compliance, and strong enough to become a common language across an institution.

NRI advisory is not a race to answer first.

It is the discipline of understanding before assuring.

10.1 THE BOARDROOM PROBLEM BEHIND THE CLIENT QUESTION

For the advisor, Nikhil's question is a client-service moment.

For the institution, it is something larger.

It is a governance moment.

The NRI segment is attractive because it carries scale, ticket size, family loyalty, India affinity and long-term planning potential. That is the visible opportunity. But every visible opportunity in the NRI segment carries a hidden question:

Can the institution service tomorrow what the advisor promises today?

That is where many NRI strategies become fragile.

At onboarding stage, everything looks clean. The client signs. Money moves. The policy, investment, deposit, account, property instruction or IFSC transaction is completed. The advisor celebrates. The branch reports business. The regional team sees momentum. The leadership team sees a promising segment.

The real test rarely appears on day one.

It appears years later.

At maturity.

At surrender.

At repatriation.

At claim.

At return to India.

At foreign tax filing.

At a family dispute.

At a compliance desk.

And then the question travels upward through the system:

"Who told the client this?"

That is the boardroom question.

Not "Was the brochure correct?"

Not "Was the product approved?"

Not "Was the advisor enthusiastic?"

The real question is: was the advisor trained to understand the NRI life into which the product was being placed?

A domestic financial decision for a domestic client usually moves through one primary legal environment. An Indian product, asset, account or receipt placed into an NRI life moves across identity, citizenship, FEMA residence, tax residence, account route, foreign reporting, repatriation, family structure, succession, return planning and sometimes a second country's tax code.

The proposal form does not always show that complexity.

The client's smallest questions do.

"Tax-free, right?"

"Repatriable, right?"

"Nominee will get it, right?"

"If I return, everything becomes simple, right?"

Each of these sentences can become either a trust-building moment or a future institutional risk. The difference is not intention. Most advisors are well-intentioned. The difference is discipline.

Product training teaches the advisor what the product does.

NRI advisory training must teach him where the client sits.

That distinction is the distance between sales capability and advisory maturity.

This is why the final chapter of this book cannot be another technical summary. You have already walked through the NRI's emotional world, FEMA and tax distinctions, banking routes, claim-credit issues, insurance taxation, return-to-India traps, investment comparisons, GIFT City, inheritance risks and documentation discipline.

The remaining question is operational:

When all this knowledge meets a live client question, how should the advisor think before he answers?

The answer is The NRI INDIA Mantra™.

Before you advise an NRI on India, apply INDIA.

10.2 THE QUESTION BENEATH THE QUESTION

A client rarely begins with his real question.

Not because he is hiding anything.

Because he is living the problem, not drafting the file note.

A software engineer in Seattle may understand stock options better than most people in the room, then fall silent when asked whether his Indian policy must be disclosed in the United States. A nurse in Melbourne may know her pension contributions and mortgage schedule precisely, yet be unsure whether the policy she bought in India before migration needs review. A business owner in Muscat may manage suppliers, staff, visas and receivables every day, but hesitate when the bank asks whether his Indian account should be NRE, NRO or resident.

The client is not careless.

He is cross-border.

That is the whole difference.

He has one life.

The law reads it in parts.

So he asks in shorthand, and the shorthand hides a map.

"Can I enter this product or asset?" The visible question is eligibility. The hidden one may run through citizenship, FEMA residence, KYC, FATCA and CRS, payment route, foreign reporting, and whether the arrangement will still work if he returns to India.

"Can the maturity go back abroad?" The visible question is repatriation. The hidden one may involve source of funds, account character, tax-paid status, bank documentation, and whether a premium trail from fifteen years ago can be reconstructed at all.

"Is nomination enough?" The visible question is a form. The hidden one may involve a spouse, minor children, parents in India, a foreign-resident son, a will never signed, and a family that may discover the difference between nominee and legal heir only after the client is gone.

This is why the resident client and the NRI client are not the same client with a different postal address. A resident usually asks within one map—he earns, banks, files and plans largely in India. The NRI asks across maps. He may earn in dollars, pay school fees in pounds, hold a policy in rupees, support parents in Bhopal, and plan retirement with one eye on Bengaluru and the other on his children's lives abroad.

Emotionally, he may say, "India is home."

Legally, that sentence solves nothing.

Life insurance is the cruellest place to forget this because a policy outlives facts. At proposal, the client may be in Singapore. During the premium years, he may move to Dubai. At maturity, he may be in Canada. At claim, the nominee may be in India. A twenty-year policy does not merely travel through time. It travels through statuses, countries, accounts, tax systems and family changes.

So when the answer comes too fast, the danger is rarely that it is wholly wrong. More often, it is incomplete.

"Tax-free" may be right in India and incomplete for Canada.

"NRE is repatriable" may be broadly true and incomplete without source and documentation.

"Nominee will get it" may be operationally true at claim and incomplete as estate planning.

Short answers travel fast. They move from a client call to a WhatsApp message, from a WhatsApp message to a family discussion, and from a family discussion to a formal escalation—until the matter arrives at the one question no advisor wants to hear:

"Who told the client this?"

The trained advisor does not answer to sound impressive. He answers to be right. And to be right, he first places the question.

Which part is Indian tax?

Which part is FEMA?

Which part is banking?

Which part is foreign law?

Which part is succession?

Which part is not his to answer at all?

He is not expected to be a chartered accountant, lawyer, banker and foreign-tax preparer in every jurisdiction. That is not the standard. The standard is more practical, and more powerful:

Know enough not to overstate.

Know which system is speaking.

Ask for evidence before giving comfort.

Bring in the right professional when the question leaves your lane.

A weak advisor says, "No issue," because he wants the client to feel comfortable.

A trained advisor says, "There may well be no issue—but let us place the facts correctly first."

The first answer gives comfort.

The second builds credibility.

Speed wins the moment.

Diagnosis protects the relationship.

A hurried answer can close a call.

A diagnosed answer can protect a decade.

10.3 THE NRI INDIA MANTRA™

This chapter does not add a new topic to the book.

It assembles the whole book into a single habit.

Everything you have read converges here. The human being behind the label. FEMA that is not Income-tax, and citizenship that is not residence. Banking that is route, not storage. The danger of translating "tax-free in India" into "tax-free in the world." Insurance placed inside a wider investment reality. GIFT City as a gateway, not a magic word. Return treated as financial migration. Nomination separated from succession. Documentation discipline that turns memory into evidence.

Nine chapters of knowledge.

One operating discipline.

Before you advise an NRI on India, apply INDIA.

I—Identify the Person

Who is the client in law, for this transaction, on this date?

N—Navigate the Money Route

Where is the money coming from, where will it go, and what character will it carry?

D—Define the Purpose

What is the client really trying to protect, build, fund, transfer, access or compare?

I—Isolate the Systems

Which legal, tax, banking, insurance, succession or foreign-reporting systems are being mixed?

A—Anchor the Assurance

What evidence supports the comfort?

Not a script.

Not a pitch.

Not objection handling.

A thinking discipline.

Simple enough for a new advisor to remember. Deep enough for a senior leader to respect. Repeatable enough to train. Careful enough for compliance. Human enough for the client across the table.

Five questions, in order, before the answer.

10.4 I—IDENTIFY THE PERSON

No NRI answer begins properly until the person is legally placed. The advisor hears, "I am an NRI."

The law asks, "For which purpose?"

"NRI" is a convenient social word. It is not a complete legal answer. The same person may be an Indian citizen abroad, an OCI cardholder, or a foreign citizen of Indian origin. Under FEMA, he may be a person resident outside India. Under the Income-tax Act, he may be a Non-Resident, Resident but Not Ordinarily Resident (RNOR), or Resident and Ordinarily Resident (ROR). Within a policy, he may be the proposer, life assured, nominee, assignee, beneficiary or legal heir. Within another product or asset, he may be the account holder, investor, joint holder, authorised signatory, claimant, transferee, executor, legal heir or beneficial owner.

He may be asking for himself, but the real issue may sit with a spouse in Dubai, a daughter in London, a mother in Indore, or a nominee whose address was never updated.

That is why the first INDIA question carries three deliberate words at the end:

Who is the client in law—for this transaction—on this date?

A client may have bought the policy as a resident, paid premiums as an NRI, and receive maturity after returning to India. He may have been an Indian citizen at proposal and a foreign citizen at claim. A returning NRI may still call himself "NRI" because that is how his relatives, banker and old advisor know him—but the law may have already moved him.

Here, the two systems move on different clocks. Under FEMA, residential status can change when the person leaves India with the intention of staying abroad, or returns with the intention of staying in India. Under the Income-tax Act, residential status is tested year-wise, by day-count and other statutory conditions, after the financial year closes.

Identity is not memory.

Identity is status.

And status must be tested.

This is where the Compliance Highway Rule™ returns quietly. The first checkpoint is Papers because papers tell the law who the client is—not emotionally, but legally.

The stage of the question matters as much as the person. At purchase, identity affects eligibility, KYC, insurer process and payment route. During the holding years, it affects premium continuation, foreign reporting and status updates. At maturity, it affects tax, withholding, account credit and repatriation. At claim, it affects nominee, beneficiary location and documents. After death, it may stop being only an insurance question and become an estate and family-law question.

The ordinary advisor begins with the product.

The serious advisor begins with the person.

Because a policy is never sold to a label.

It is placed into a life.

And life changes faster than forms.

10.5 N—NAVIGATE THE MONEY ROUTE

Money remembers its route.

The client may not. The advisor may not. The bank relationship manager may change three times over the life of the policy. But the route stays in the story.

A premium paid from an NRE account does not carry the same history as one paid from an NRO account. A premium paid from foreign earnings does not raise the same questions as one paid by a resident father from his savings account. A maturity meant to travel back to Canada cannot be analysed as loosely as a maturity meant to be spent in Chennai. A claim payable to a spouse in Kochi is not operationally the same as a claim payable to a foreign-resident child in Vancouver.

In NRI advisory, the bank account is not a container.

It is a rail.

The rail chosen at payment or funding stage shapes the rail available at redemption, maturity, surrender, sale, transmission, claim and repatriation. The first payment is the seed. The account is the soil. Sow in one soil and you cannot demand a different harvest later without explaining the trail.

So Navigate the Money Route means asking early what would otherwise be discovered late.

Where is the money coming from?

From whose account?

Is it NRE, NRO, FCNR(B), a resident account, a foreign account, or a mix?

Is the payment a gift, loan, reimbursement or family support?

Where will maturity, surrender value or claim proceeds land?

Is the money meant for use in India or repatriation abroad?

Will the bank ask for documents?

Can the route be explained after ten years?

Consider the client in Singapore who says, "Can my brother in Surat pay this year's premium? I will settle with him later." The answer is not a casual yes or no. The advisor must first ask whether FEMA permits the arrangement, then understand who owns the policy, why the brother is paying, from which account, whether it is a gift, loan or reimbursement, how it will be recorded, and whether a future maturity trail will remain readable.

Or take the client in London asking, "Will maturity come to my NRE account?" That cannot be answered from NRI status alone. It turns on how the premiums were funded, whether the proceeds retain repatriable character, the insurer's process and the bank's reading of the trail.

The client sees money.

The bank sees route.

The tax law sees a receipt.

FEMA sees a movement.

The family sees a need.

The advisor must see all five.

That is why N is not a minor limb. It is the rail on which the whole transaction travels—and when the rail is wrong, even a good product arrives at a difficult destination.

10.6 D—DEFINE THE PURPOSE

A product cannot be suitable until the purpose is clear.

This sounds obvious.

It is ignored every day.

The NRI asks, "Why Indian insurance?"

The weak advisor rushes to compare returns.

The stronger one asks a single, disarming question:

"For what?"

Protection?

Rupee liquidity for parents in India?

A child abroad who may one day need to access something here?

A return to India being planned quietly?

Retirement income?

Estate liquidity so a family is not forced to sell property in a hurry?

Disciplined saving?

Currency diversification?

A liability sitting in rupees?

The same policy can be suitable for one purpose and unsuitable for another. The comparisons clients reach for often collapse when purpose enters the room.

A term policy is not an investment.

An endowment is not a fixed deposit.

A unit-linked plan is not a mutual fund merely because it holds units.

An NRE deposit is not life cover.

Real estate is not liquidity.

GIFT City is not an answer to a question nobody has asked yet.

This is where the advisor must resist defending the product before understanding the client. If the client wants foreign-currency preservation, a foreign-currency deposit may deserve the discussion. If he wants market-linked growth, funds or global portfolios may be relevant, subject to jurisdiction and onboarding. If he wants physical Indian assets, property may appeal—though title, liquidity, maintenance, tax, repatriation and succession all sit inside that choice. If he wants India-linked family protection, rupee liquidity or claim certainty, insurance may have a role.

But the role must be earned.

Not assumed.

The serious advisor does not say, "Insurance is better."

He says, "Better for what?"

Better for liquidity?

For protection?

For repatriation?

For parents?

For the simplicity the family will need on the worst day of their lives?

Until the purpose is defined, comparison is noise.

With purpose, the conversation becomes advice.

A product should never be made to carry a responsibility it was never designed to carry. That is how unsuitable advice begins—and Define the Purpose is the limb that prevents it.

A product without a purpose is a pitch.

A product with a purpose can become advice.

10.7 I—ISOLATE THE SYSTEMS

This is the intellectual heart of the Mantra.

Most NRI mistakes are not made because the advisor knew nothing. They are made because two systems were mixed and no one noticed.

In practice, the error is rarely visible as one large mistake. It appears as a series of quiet substitutions. FEMA is treated as if it were Income-tax. A banking route is mistaken for a tax conclusion. An insurance nomination is treated as succession planning. A treaty is invoked as if it were an exemption. An Indian answer is allowed to stand in for a foreign-country answer. GIFT City is casually equated with tax freedom. Residence in Dubai is converted into a universal "no issue" conclusion.

That is how confusion quietly becomes advice.

A trained advisor separates the systems before he answers.

FEMA is not Income-tax.

Income-tax is not banking.

Banking is not insurance regulation.

Insurance regulation is not succession law.

Nomination is not a will.

Claim access is not inheritance.

A treaty is not an automatic exemption.

Reporting is not the same as tax.

Repatriability is not a word that permanently lives on an account.

Take the phrase "tax-free." In India, a policy receipt must be tested against the life-insurance exclusion applicable to the relevant tax year, by reference to product type, premium thresholds, dates, exclusions and conditions. That Indian answer does not decide the foreign one. A Canadian resident may need Canadian review. A UK resident may face a different chargeable-event analysis. A US taxpayer may face classification and reporting questions. A New Zealand resident may have its own foreign-investment regime to consider.

The point is not to frighten the client.

The point is not to mislead him.

Indian exemption is an Indian answer.

It is not a passport.

It does not cross the border on its own.

Precision cuts both ways. A UAE-resident client is not in the same residence-tax position as a client in Canada, the UK or the US. An advisor who applies high-tax-country assumptions to a low-tax jurisdiction without checking the client's actual residence-country position is neither technically precise nor commercially balanced. But "Dubai means no issue" is the opposite error. The Indian tax position still has to be tested. The FEMA route still matters. The account still matters. The premium-source trail still matters. CRS and bank documentation may matter. A future move to a higher-tax country before maturity may matter most of all.

The correct advisor does not exaggerate risk.

He does not flatter it away.

He locates it.

The same discipline applies to a DTAA. A DTAA is not a magic eraser. It may allocate taxing rights, reduce withholding, or support a credit depending on the article, the facts, the residential status and the documents, including the Tax Residency Certificate and the prescribed treaty-relief declaration, including Form 10F / Form 41, as applicable under the law and rules governing the relevant tax year or event. It does not generally export an Indian domestic exemption into a foreign tax code. A treaty must be applied. It cannot be invoked like a slogan.

And the same discipline applies to return. Returning to India is not one legal switch. Under FEMA, residence may change by intent and circumstances. Under the Income-tax Act, residence is tested by statutory day-count and related conditions, after the year, looking backward. RNOR may offer a transition window before full resident status pulls foreign income and assets into deeper Indian reporting. NRE accounts may need redesignation. Foreign pensions, brokerage accounts and policies may need review.

The emotional return happens at the airport.

The legal return happens across documents, over months.

The advisor who isolates systems may sound slower.

He is not slower.

He is safer.

The serious advisor never makes one law answer another law's question.

That is the discipline.

10.8 A—ANCHOR THE ASSURANCE

No assurance should travel farther than the evidence supporting it.

That sentence belongs on every NRI advisor's desk.

Words are light when spoken and heavy when questioned. The client will remember the comfort. A bank may later ask for the trail. A foreign preparer may ask for classification. A family may ask for nomination papers. A compliance team may ask why a particular sentence was ever said.

This is where file discipline becomes live advisory discipline.

Before giving comfort, the advisor should ask five quiet questions:

What do we have?

What do we only believe?

What must be verified?

What must be documented?

What must be referred?

A cautious statement without evidence is still weak.

A confident statement without evidence is worse.

Even a careful sentence—"this maturity should be exempt in India"—needs facts beneath it: policy type, issue date, premium history, applicable thresholds, recipient, tax residence, account route, and documents.

The sentence "fully tax-free" should almost never be spoken casually to an NRI. If the advisor means "generally exempt in India, subject to Indian conditions," he should say exactly that. If foreign tax has not been reviewed, he should say so. If repatriation depends on bank documents, he should say so.

Compare two answers to Nikhil's question.

The first:

"Yes, tax-free."

The second:

"Based on Indian law, this may well be exempt if the policy meets the applicable conditions. Let us confirm the premium history and plan type. Separately, because you are tax-resident in Canada, the Canadian treatment must be checked locally before we call it tax-free in a complete sense. And before maturity, let us align the account route and premium-source documents."

The second answer is longer, but that is not why it is better.

It is better because it is honest.

It gives comfort where comfort is available. It draws the boundary where India's answer ends. It protects the client from a false global conclusion and protects the advisor from his own confidence.

Evidence is not bureaucracy.

It is the advisor's memory when people change, years pass and the original conversation can no longer be reconstructed.

When memory becomes uncertain, evidence becomes the only voice left in the room.

A good advisor does not merely comfort the client today.

He protects the client's future file—and sometimes, the family's future peace.

10.9 INDIA IN ONE VIEW

Limb	Core question	What it prevents
I—Identify the Person	Who is the client in law, for this transaction, on this date?	Treating "NRI" as one universal answer
N—Navigate the Money Route	Where is the money from, where will it go, and what character will it carry?	Treating bank accounts as clerical containers
D—Define the Purpose	What is the client really trying to protect, access, compare or solve?	Product pushing and false comparison
I—Isolate the Systems	Which systems are being mixed?	Confusing FEMA, tax, banking, insurance, succession and foreign law
A—Anchor the Assurance	What evidence supports the comfort?	Verbal assurance without defensible records

This table is not meant to close a conversation. It is the lens for the next one.

It is the advisor's operating lens for every NRI conversation.

Every NRI question can be placed somewhere inside it. "I am OCI. Can I enter this?" begins with Identify. "Can the money go abroad?" begins with Navigate. "Why this route instead of another?" begins with Define. "Is this favourable in India and also clean abroad?" begins with Isolate. "What documents support this comfort?" begins with Anchor.

The framework is simple.

The discipline is not.

That is why it must be practised until it becomes instinct—and why it can travel with the advisor into a call, a branch meeting, a training room, a compliance review and a boardroom.

10.10 WATCH INDIA WORK: ONE CLIENT, ONE QUESTION

Return to that evening in Toronto.

Nikhil has asked, "Sir, this policy maturity is tax-free, right?" The ordinary answer is already forming. Watch what happens instead when the advisor takes the professional pause and runs the five letters in his head before speaking.

Identify. Who is Nikhil in law tonight? Indian citizen or Canadian citizen? OCI? Person resident outside India under FEMA? Non-resident under the Income-tax Act for this year, by day-count? Is he the policyholder and life assured? Has his status changed since the policy began?

Navigate. The premiums came mostly from NRE, some from NRO, and one from his brother's resident account in Baroda. The maturity is meant eventually to reach Canada. So the route is mixed at the source and repatriation-bound at the destination. The trail must be reconstructed now, with statements, before the bank reconstructs it for him at the counter.

Define. What is this money for? Is Nikhil repatriating it to settle into Canadian life, parking it in India for parents, or keeping it as a rupee reserve for a possible return he has not yet admitted he is planning? The purpose decides what comfort he actually needs.

Isolate. There are at least three systems in his four-word question: Indian tax, banking/FEMA and Canadian law. Indian tax asks whether the receipt fits the life-insurance exclusion applicable to the tax year, and whether any withholding or reporting consequence remains. Banking and FEMA ask whether proceeds retain the right character and reach the right account. Canadian law may ask its own tax and reporting questions. Three systems. One sentence. They must not be merged.

Anchor. What does the advisor actually have tonight? A client's recollection, a brochure and a maturity letter. What must he verify? Premium trail, plan type, dates and thresholds. What must he refer? Canadian treatment, to someone qualified there.

And so the advisor does not say, "Yes, tax-free."

He says the longer, honest sentence: the Indian position must be tested, the Canadian boundary must be drawn, and the route must be aligned before maturity.

Nikhil does not applaud.

He simply feels, perhaps for the first time in twenty years of paying premiums, that someone has finally understood that his policy lives in two countries at once.

That feeling is the beginning of trust.

10.11 HOW AN INSTITUTION CAN IMPLEMENT INDIA

A framework becomes valuable to leadership only when it can be trained, measured and repeated.

The NRI INDIA Mantra™ is not meant to remain a clever final chapter line. It can become an institutional operating standard for NRI conversations.

For a training head, INDIA becomes a curriculum spine.

Every NRI module can be mapped to one of the five limbs: identity, money route, purpose, systems and evidence. Instead of training advisors through disconnected technical lectures, the institution can train them through one repeatable decision process. The advisor may forget a section number under pressure. He is less likely to forget the five checks before assurance.

For a sales leader, INDIA becomes a quality filter.

It does not slow sales. It improves the quality of sales. It helps an advisor move from "I have a product" to "I understand the client's cross-border life." In the NRI segment, that movement is not philosophical. It is commercial. Trust is what converts. Loose comfort may win the first sale; defensible trust earns every one after it.

For a compliance leader, INDIA becomes a risk-control language.

It reduces dangerous phrases before they leave the advisor's mouth: "fully tax-free," "DTAA will take care," "nominee means owner," "Dubai means no issue," "NRI money is always repatriable," "foreign citizens are no problem," "returning to India makes everything simple." The issue is not that every such phrase is always false. The issue is that each is incomplete unless facts, systems and documents support it.

For a branch manager, INDIA becomes a coaching tool.

After a client call, the manager does not need to ask only, "Did the client agree?" He can ask better questions. Did you identify the person correctly? Did you trace the money route? Did you define the purpose? Did you isolate tax, FEMA, banking, succession and foreign issues? Did you anchor your comfort in documents?

For a service team, INDIA becomes a future-file discipline.

The best NRI service process is built before the problem arrives. Premium-source records, account routes, status updates, nominee details, tax documents, family contact points and claim pathways are not clerical debris. They are the institutional memory that protects the client when the original advisor has moved branches, changed roles or left the business.

For leadership, INDIA creates four institutional advantages.

First, it creates language discipline. Advisors stop using attractive but dangerous shortcuts without qualification. Small words create large liabilities. Discipline removes risk at its source.

Second, it creates diagnostic consistency. Whether the advisor sits in Kochi, Delhi, Ahmedabad, Bengaluru, Singapore or Dubai, every NRI conversation begins with the same five checks—person, route, purpose, systems and evidence. Consistency is what lets quality scale across geographies and teams.

Third, it creates defensible conduct. If a question is raised later, the institution can show that its advisors were trained to identify status, trace money, define purpose, separate systems and anchor comfort in evidence before assuring anything.

Fourth, it creates trust-based differentiation. In this segment, the winning advisor is not the one who speaks fastest. It is the one who leaves the client feeling that a cross-border life has been understood.

For institutional leadership—a board, MD, compliance head or training leader—the question is not merely whether the NRI segment can produce more business.

It is whether that business can be sourced, explained, documented, serviced and defended with institutional confidence.

In the NRI segment, quality is not business volume alone. Quality is clean status identification, proper money routing, honest purpose mapping, tax caution, succession clarity, documentation discipline, and an advisor who knows when to say, "This one is not mine to answer."

A product, asset or route handled without diagnosis can become future friction.

The same decision handled with discipline becomes part of a defensible relationship.

That is why this is not a slogan.

It is an operating standard.

Do not train advisors merely to sell to NRIs.

Train them to think across borders.

Remember Ramakrishnan on the Indian road.

His issue was not that he had lived in America. His issue was that he carried the American lane into Indian traffic.

That is the exact mistake the trusted advisor must prevent.

An NRI client may carry memories from India, earnings from Dubai, tax residence from Canada, a rupee policy, children in the UK, parents in Pune and a retirement plan that has changed shape more than once.

To the client, it is one life.

To the law, it may be many systems reading the same life differently.

The advisor's job is not to panic.

It is not to answer quickly merely because the client is waiting.

It is to apply the hierarchy of this book.

The Compliance Highway Rule™ gives the map.

The NRI Kaalchakra™ gives the timing lens.

The NRI INDIA Mantra™ gives the operating discipline.

Synchronise the clocks, separate the systems, and only then offer comfort.

Identify the person.

Navigate the route.

Define the purpose.

Isolate the systems.

Anchor the assurance.

The trusted advisor does not stop at:

"Where has this client come from?"

He asks:

Where is he standing now, which road is he on, which clock is reading him, and which rulebook applies before I answer?

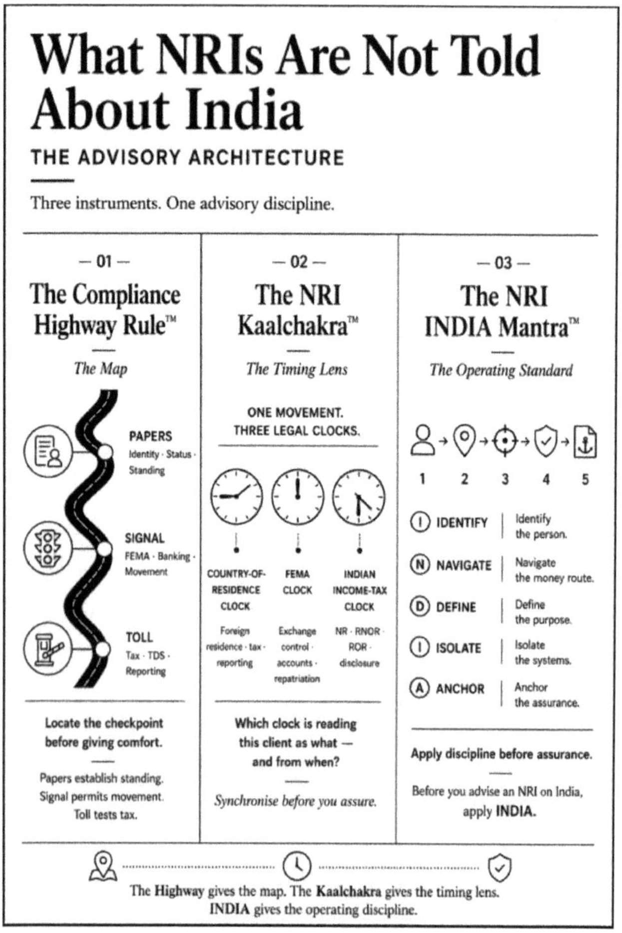

10.12 THIRTY QUESTIONS, THIRTY DOORS

A framework earns leadership attention only when it survives field reality.

The real test is not whether the idea sounds elegant in a chapter or impressive in a training room. The real test is whether it helps advisors handle the messy questions that arrive every day—in branches, airport lounges, family WhatsApp groups, NRI webinars, bank referrals, video calls and late-night client conversations.

The thirty questions that follow are insurance led because insurance is often the first practical doorway through which the advisor meets the NRI family. They should not be read as the boundary of INDIA. The same diagnostic method applies when the receipt is rent, interest, dividend, redemption, sale proceeds, inheritance, deposit maturity, IFSC distribution or remittance. Read the questions as drills in thinking, not as the outer limit of the framework.

The thirty questions below are therefore not a decorative FAQ. They are field tests of the INDIA Mantra.

What follows are not scripts. They are not objection-handling templates designed to "win" a conversation. They are diagnostic drills. Each common question is placed through INDIA, so that when it arrives, the advisor does not go silent because the question is complex. He becomes accurate because it is complex.

A trained advisor does not pretend to know everything. He knows how to place the question, state the boundary, and bring the right professional into the room when the answer leaves his lane. What he carries is not omniscience. It is the discipline to recognise what each question is really asking.

That is the distance between product familiarity and advisory maturity.

Before the thirty questions begin, one clarification matters. The INDIA Mantra is ordered: **Identify, Navigate, Define, Isolate, Anchor**. In practice, not every client question needs all five steps. The advisor applies only the relevant steps, but where multiple steps appear, they follow the logic of the mnemonic. This keeps the method disciplined without making every answer mechanical.

A. Identity and Status

1. "I am an NRI. Can I buy this policy?"

Four ordinary words, and to the client an anxious one. He is not only asking about a product. He is asking whether the life he built abroad has quietly placed him outside India's financial system.

The instant answer: "Yes, NRIs can buy." True enough to feel safe, yet incomplete enough to create confusion later.

The same enquiry, worked through The NRI INDIA Mantra™:

Identify. The advisor places the person before the product. Indian citizen abroad, OCI cardholder, or person of Indian origin resident outside India. The FEMA starting point is generally permissive for these profiles, provided the premium route and insurer process are correct. Paying a life insurance premium is generally treated as a permitted current account transaction when routed through the proper banking channel. The client's Income tax residence runs on a separate clock under section 6 and does not decide insurance eligibility today.

Isolate. FEMA permissibility, Income tax residence and insurer underwriting are different questions. What remains after the FEMA starting point is factual: the insurer's appetite for the country of residence, KYC, FATCA and CRS, product eligibility and payment route.

Anchor. He gathers the documents that turn permission into an issued policy: passport, overseas address proof, OCI card where held, PAN where required, KYC, FATCA and CRS declaration, and the proposed premium route.

The informed answer: "Yes, in most cases this is possible, whether you are an Indian citizen abroad, an OCI, or a person of Indian origin resident outside India, subject to the insurer accepting your country of residence, your documents and the premium route. Send me your passport, residence proof and KYC, and I will confirm the right insurer and route before we proceed."

The instant answer gives comfort. The informed answer converts comfort into an issued policy and a defensible file.

2. "I am OCI. Am I treated exactly like an NRI?"

He took the OCI card believing it made him Indian enough for everything. Now he wants to know whether that belief holds for insurance.

The instant answer: "Yes, OCI is the same." Reassuring, but too broad to be safe across every transaction.

The same enquiry, worked through The NRI INDIA Mantra™:

Identify. An OCI is a foreign citizen with broad economic parity in India, though not identical to an Indian citizen for every purpose. For buying and holding Indian life insurance, that parity is usually enough, subject to the insurer's process, country of residence rules and documents.

Isolate. OCI differences may matter in voting, constitutional rights, agricultural land and certain capital account matters. They do not usually disturb the life insurance purchase question. The advisor answers the transaction in front of him and does not let one reassuring generalisation cover six different questions.

The informed answer: "For Indian life insurance, OCI status usually gives you the eligibility we need, subject to the insurer accepting your country of residence and documents. It is not identical to Indian citizenship for every purpose in life, but for this conversation it is generally workable. Tell me what you would like to put in place and I will confirm it against the insurer's rules."

3. "What if I change citizenship after buying?"

He may be years from a new passport, but he is already wondering whether becoming Canadian, British, Australian or Singaporean will disturb the Indian policy he has funded faithfully for years.

The instant answer: "No issue, it will continue." Broadly comforting, and incomplete, because it treats a change of legal identity as if nothing around the policy moves with it.

The same enquiry, worked through The NRI INDIA Mantra™:

Identify. A validly issued policy does not usually collapse merely because the policyholder later changes citizenship. The contract generally continues, subject to its terms. What moves is the person across the three checkpoints. Papers, who he now is. Signal, what FEMA permits a foreign national or person resident outside India to do. Toll, how his tax residence reads.

Anchor. Citizenship change is a review trigger. On the day the passport changes, KYC, FATCA and CRS status, country of tax residence, premium route and claim documentation are refreshed and recorded, so the file still tells the truth ten years on.

The informed answer: "Your policy should generally continue. The change does not by itself undo it. What we update is the record around it: your KYC, FATCA and CRS status, country of tax residence, premium route and claim documents. When your citizenship changes, tell me, and I will refresh the file with you."

4. **"My spouse and children are foreign citizens. Can they be nominees?"**

This is not a form filling question. It is a family protection question, and he is asking it while looking at his sleeping children.

The instant answer: "Yes, just put their names." Correct on the narrow point, and silent on everything that decides whether the money actually reaches them.

The same enquiry, worked through The NRI INDIA Mantra™:

Identify. Foreign citizenship by itself does not normally prevent a spouse or child from being named as nominee, subject to the insurer's process and documents.

Isolate. Nomination, beneficial entitlement, succession and claim routing are different things. Under section 39 of the Insurance Act, 1938, a spouse, child or parent nominated under a life policy may hold as a beneficial nominee, subject to the section's qualifications. Even so, nomination is not a complete estate plan where the family, assets or heirs sit across countries.

Where the objective is to protect proceeds for a wife and children, section 6 of the Married Women's Property Act, 1874 may be relevant. Properly used, it places the policy proceeds in trust for them, generally outside the estate and outside the husband's creditor reach, subject to valid structuring and the fraud on creditors exception.

Anchor. The advisor aligns nomination, will, guardian details for any minor, the MWPA route where relevant, the bank route and the claim documents.

The informed answer: "Yes, their foreign citizenship is not the barrier. But let us not stop at naming them. We should align the nomination with your will, guardianship if any child is a minor, and consider an MWPA structure where the aim is to protect your wife and children. That is how we move from a name on a form to real protection."

B. Banking and the Money Route

5. "Can I pay the premium from any Indian account?"

He is thinking of convenience. Which account has money, which login works, which bank is easier.

The instant answer: "Any account is fine." Easy to say, and unsafe, because it forfeits a choice that decides what the client can do with the money later.

The same enquiry, worked through The NRI INDIA Mantra™:

Navigate. The first check is not whether the account is Indian, but what kind of Indian account it is. NRE, NRO and FCNR(B) each carry different consequences, and an old resident savings account should not be casually used by a person who is non resident under FEMA, since it may require redesignation. The premium is the seed and the account is the soil. NRE soil gives the cleanest repatriable trail. NRO soil gives a restricted, document driven exit.

Define. If the client may want the maturity abroad, NRE funding gives the cleanest trail. If the policy is for India based use, NRO may be acceptable. The choice should be made consciously, not by default.

Anchor. The premium source must be preserved from the first payment, because the maturity and repatriation discussion will depend on it.

The informed answer: "Not from any account. First we check whether the account is NRE, NRO, FCNR(B), or an old resident account that should have been redesignated. If you may want the maturity abroad, we use the NRE route where possible. If it is for use in India, NRO may work. Let us choose the route before the first premium."

6. "Can my father in India pay the premium?"

A practical family question. Dad has the money this year. The client will adjust later. Everyone sees it as help, not structure.

The instant answer: "Yes, family can pay." Correct, and not complete.

The real question is not only whether the premium can be paid. The real question is what character that payment gives to the money trail.

The same enquiry, worked through The NRI INDIA Mantra™:

Navigate. A resident family member may pay the premium, subject to the insurer's acceptance and proper documentation. But the route must be understood clearly. If the premium is paid from an Indian resident account, an NRO account, or any other non repatriable source, that part of the funding does not become NRE funded merely because the policyholder is an NRI. The money has entered through a different rail, and that rail can affect the treatment of the corresponding proceeds at maturity, surrender, claim or repatriation stage.

Isolate. The character of the payment must be clear: gift, loan, reimbursement or family support. It must also be separated from the client's own NRE funded trail. If part of the policy has been funded from repatriable money and part from resident side or non repatriable money, the file should not later describe the entire policy as NRE funded or fully repatriable. The comfort must be limited to the facts.

Anchor. A simple record now prevents confusion later. Preserve the father's bank proof, the policyholder's explanation, the nature of the family arrangement, and the year in which the payment was made. If the proceeds are questioned at maturity, surrender, claim or remittance stage, the file should be able to show which part came through which route.

The informed answer: "Yes, your father may pay, subject to the insurer's acceptance and proper documentation. But we should not treat that payment as if it came from your NRE account. If the premium is paid from an Indian resident account or another non repatriable source, that portion of the funding may carry a non repatriable character. So we should record whether the payment is a gift, loan, reimbursement or family support, preserve the bank trail, and keep the policy file clear."

This small note today can decide whether the money is explained properly years later.

7. "Will the maturity proceeds go back abroad?"

He assumes that because he is an NRI, the money is automatically free to leave India.

The instant answer: "Yes, NRI money is repatriable." Too loose, because repatriation is not a property of the person.

The same enquiry, worked through The NRI INDIA Mantra™:

Navigate. Repatriation is a property of the route and the documentation. NRE funded proceeds generally carry a cleaner repatriable trail. NRO funded proceeds may move under the remittance of assets framework, broadly up to USD 1 million in a financial year, subject to tax compliance and bank documentation.

Anchor. Where premiums are old or mixed, the advisor reconstructs the premium trail well before maturity, with statements, rather than letting the client discover at the counter that the paper does not support the wish.

The informed answer: "It can, but not merely because you are an NRI. It depends on how the premiums were funded and what documents support that route. If you may need the maturity abroad, we use the NRE route where possible and preserve the trail from now, so it moves cleanly when you need it."

8. "Can the maturity be credited to my NRE account?"

He has an NRE account ready and assumes the money can simply land there.

The instant answer: "Yes, you are NRI, so NRE is fine." Plausible, and it skips the one thing the credit actually turns on.

The same enquiry, worked through The NRI INDIA Mantra™:

Navigate. NRE is repatriable by design, but money reaches it on the strength of its source, not the holder's label. NRE funding gives the strongest basis for repatriable treatment and an NRE credit, subject to the insurer's process and bank documentation.

Isolate. If past premiums were partly NRO funded, or funded by a resident relative, the credit route may need a split, an explanation or different treatment.

The informed answer: "We make the NRE credit possible by keeping the funding route clean. If premiums are paid from NRE, we have the strongest basis to support NRE credit or repatriable treatment, subject to the insurer and the bank. If past premiums were mixed, we sort that trail before maturity."

9. "Premiums were paid partly from NRE and partly from NRO. Is that a problem?"

Life was untidy. A job change, a tight year, a switched account. Now the client wants to know whether the old mix will hurt him.

The instant answer: "No issue, both are NRI accounts." Too casual.

The same enquiry, worked through The NRI INDIA Mantra™:

Navigate. Mixed funding is usually not a disaster, it is a documentation job. The NRE funded part and the NRO funded part may carry different repatriation consequences. The NRE funded part generally carries a cleaner repatriable trail. The NRO funded part moves through its own restricted, document driven route.

Anchor. The advisor captures the account wise split while statements are still available, turning an untidy history into a clean, bankable record.

The informed answer: "Not a disaster, but we should not ignore it. The NRE funded part and the NRO funded part may have different repatriation treatment. Let us capture the premium wise split now, with bank statements, so the maturity can be routed correctly when it comes."

C. Currency and Comparison

10. "Why invest in India when the rupee keeps depreciating?"

He is not asking for a lecture on India. He is asking whether his foreign currency earnings will quietly lose strength when converted into rupees.

The instant answer: "Rupee depreciation does not matter, India grows faster." A slogan rarely defeats lived experience.

The better answer begins by asking where the money is coming from and where the money is finally meant to be used.

The same enquiry, worked through The NRI INDIA Mantra™:

Navigate. First trace the funding route. If the client is converting fresh dollars, pounds, dirhams or Canadian dollars into rupees to pay today, currency risk is a real entry question. But if the client already has rupee income in India, such as rent, interest or other recurring Indian income, or if he wants to use rupee balances already lying in permitted Indian accounts, the question changes. He is not suffering a fresh conversion from foreign currency into rupees at that moment. The money is already in rupees. The issue then is not entry conversion loss. The issue is whether that rupee money is being used for the right rupee linked purpose, through the right account route, with the right repatriation character preserved.

Define. The first question is purpose. If the money is for parents, property, a future return, retirement in India or family liquidity in India, the rupee is not merely an investment currency. It is the spending currency. A rupee linked goal is affected differently from a dollar measured outcome. If the client measures success in dollars, pounds, dirhams or Canadian dollars, the currency concern remains valid. But if the income is earned in India and the goal is also in India, rupee depreciation against a foreign currency may not be the central risk.

Isolate. Do not mix three different cases. Fresh foreign currency converted into rupees is one case. Indian rupee income used for an Indian goal is another. Existing rupee balances in NRE, NRO or other permitted accounts are a third. Each has a different currency question and a different route question. NRE balances may have a cleaner repatriable character. NRO or other non repatriable balances may not. Using rupee money already available in India may reduce the entry currency concern, but it does not automatically solve tax, FEMA, account route, documentation or future repatriation questions.

For India linked planning in foreign currency, the answer is to reduce the mismatch rather than argue it away. There are two separate routes to examine. One is the domestic Indian insurer route, under the insurance regulatory framework read with the Foreign Exchange Management (Insurance) Regulations, 2015, where foreign currency denominated policies may be issued to persons resident outside India with premiums collected in foreign currency from abroad or from NRE or FCNR accounts. The other is the GIFT IFSC route, regulated by IFSCA. Each route must be tested for insurer, product, eligibility, tax treatment and residence country consequences.

The informed answer: "Your currency concern is valid if you are converting fresh foreign earnings into rupees and later measuring the outcome in foreign currency. But if the premium is being paid from rent, interest or other rupee income already arising in India, or from rupee balances already lying in permitted Indian accounts, then the entry currency risk is different. The money is already in rupees. We should then ask a sharper question: is this rupee money meant for a rupee goal, and what is its account route and repatriation character? NRE funded money, NRO money and resident side Indian income cannot be treated as the same rail. If you want the outcome measured in dollars, we should not dismiss currency risk. We can also examine foreign currency options where available, through the domestic Indian insurer route or through GIFT IFSC, subject to eligibility and tax review."

11. "What if rupee depreciation wipes out my returns?"

He does not trust the projection sheet. He wants to know the real result in his own currency.

The instant answer: "India's growth will compensate." That is hope, not advice.

The same enquiry, worked through The NRI INDIA Mantra™:

Define. For a foreign currency earner, a rupee return must be judged after currency movement, tax, cost and exit friction. The brochure return is not the client's real return. If the goal itself is rupee linked, currency movement does not affect it in the same way it affects a foreign currency measured outcome.

Isolate. If currency mismatch is the real concern, it should not be wished away. A foreign currency policy may reduce the rupee mismatch where available. The domestic Indian insurer route and the GIFT IFSC route are separate, and both require product, cost, surrender value, reporting, tax and residence country review.

The informed answer: "If you will spend in dollars, we judge the rupee return after currency, tax and cost, not by the headline number. If currency risk is the main concern, we can examine foreign currency options, through a domestic Indian insurer route or through GIFT IFSC. That may reduce the mismatch, and we still review product terms, tax and exit before recommending it."

12. "Why not just keep the money in FCNR(B)?"

He trusts foreign currency. FCNR(B) feels familiar, clean and safe, and the real question is quieter. Why accept rupee risk at all?

The instant answer: "Insurance gives better returns." That is the wrong comparison.

The same enquiry, worked through The NRI INDIA Mantra™:

Navigate. FCNR(B) is a foreign currency deposit route. It is useful for parking capital, preserving foreign currency exposure and maintaining deposit style certainty. If the money is only to be parked, FCNR(B) may be the better answer, and the advisor should say so.

Define. Insurance enters only if the client wants something beyond parking: protection, family security, a structured payout or long term planning. If those needs exist in foreign currency, the domestic Indian insurer route and the GIFT IFSC route can be examined separately for eligibility, product terms, tax and reporting.

The informed answer: "FCNR(B) is a sound way to hold capital in foreign currency. If your only goal is parking and preservation, I will not move you away from it. Insurance comes into the discussion only if you want protection, family security or a longer planned payout, and then we can examine whether a foreign currency route is available and suitable. We compare both on purpose, not on return."

13. "Why not an NRE fixed deposit?"

He wants simplicity, liquidity and repatriability.

The instant answer: "Insurance is better than an FD." Too blunt, and usually unhelpful.

The better answer gives the deposit its rightful place, and then shows where its job ends.

The same enquiry, worked through The NRI INDIA Mantra™:

Navigate. An NRE fixed deposit is a clean repatriable rupee deposit route. It is useful for money the client may need in the near term and for liquidity that should remain easy to move abroad. But it should not be described as if it has no time condition at all. It is still a fixed deposit. It has a deposit tenure, and premature withdrawal may affect interest, bank treatment and the client's expected return. Clean repatriability does not mean there is no product discipline.

Define. The comparison must be made by purpose, not by headline rate. An NRE fixed deposit is suitable for parking money, preserving liquidity and keeping funds on a repatriable rupee rail. Insurance belongs to a different purpose: life cover, family protection, estate liquidity, disciplined long term allocation or a planned payout. A policy may carry lock in, surrender terms and product conditions. The deposit also carries tenure conditions and reinvestment risk. When the NRE deposit matures, the client must reinvest only at the rate available at that time. If interest rates fall, the next deposit may not carry the same return. A long term insurance product, where suitable and properly understood, may lock the benefit structure for a longer period with guaranteed returns, subject to the policy terms.

Isolate. Do not compare an NRE fixed deposit and insurance as if both are doing the same job. The NRE deposit answers liquidity, repatriability and short to medium term parking. Insurance answers protection, family continuity, long term certainty or structured payout. The deposit may win on flexibility. The policy may win on tenure discipline and protection design. The right answer may be both, but not with the same rupee.

The informed answer: "An NRE fixed deposit is a good route for money you may need soon, especially where you want the balance to remain on a clean repatriable rupee rail. But it is still a fixed deposit. It has a tenure, premature withdrawal can affect interest, and when it matures you face reinvestment risk because the next rate may not be the same. Insurance is not a replacement for that liquidity. It solves a different job: protection, family continuity, disciplined long term allocation or a planned payout. So we should not ask which is better in isolation. We should ask which money needs liquidity, which money needs protection, and which money needs longer term certainty."

14. "Why not invest in mutual funds instead?"

He follows markets and suspects insurance is the slower, lower return cousin.

The instant answer: "Insurance is safer." That ducks the real comparison.

The better answer does not defend insurance blindly. It separates the job of a mutual fund, the job of a traditional insurance policy, and the job of a ULIP.

The same enquiry, worked through The NRI INDIA Mantra™:

Define. Mutual funds are primarily market linked investment products. Traditional insurance is generally used for protection, certainty, family financial planning or a structured long term payout. ULIPs sit in a different space. They are insurance contracts with life cover and unit linked value. They may offer market participation, fund switching and long term allocation, but they also carry policy charges, lock in, surrender rules, mortality cost, product conditions and insurance law treatment. A ULIP should not be described as a mutual fund with insurance added. It is a policy first, with an investment component inside it.

Isolate. If pure market growth is the only goal, the question may belong to an appropriately authorised investment professional, and the advisor should not force an insurance answer into it. If the client wants market linked participation along with life cover, family continuity, disciplined holding or policy based structuring, then a ULIP may be examined on its own terms. For some NRIs, especially those resident in the United States or Canada, Indian mutual funds, ULIPs and other market linked Indian products may each raise different onboarding, tax reporting, foreign asset disclosure and residence country classification questions. That does not make one automatically better than the other. It means the comparison must include regulation, charges, liquidity, lock in, tax treatment, reporting friction and the client's actual purpose.

The informed answer: "If your only goal is pure market growth, a mutual fund or another investment product may need review by the appropriately authorised investment professional, and I should not force insurance into that question. But we should also not treat every insurance product as if it is only a guaranteed product. A ULIP is a policy with life cover and a unit linked value, so it must be compared differently from a traditional plan and differently from a mutual fund. The right comparison is not insurance versus mutual fund as a slogan. The right comparison is purpose, cost, liquidity, lock in, tax treatment, reporting, residence country impact and family outcome. Let us first decide what job this money is meant to do."

15. "Real estate feels safer. Why insurance?"

Property feels safe because it can be seen. It has a door, a name plate, a location and a family story attached to it. For many NRIs, a flat in India is not only an asset. It is proof that the India connection is still alive.

The instant answer: "Insurance is better than property." That argues with emotion and loses.

The same enquiry, worked through The NRI INDIA Mantra™:

Define. Property has its place. It may give use, emotional comfort, rental income, long term asset value and a future base in India. But property is wealth in a heavy form. It is not instant money. It is not automatically repatriable money. It is not always easy money for the family.

Navigate. Real estate has its own full route. The money used to buy it must be explained. The title must be clean. The tenant must deduct TDS correctly where the law requires it. Rent may need to be credited through the right account and reported correctly. Property tax, society dues, repairs, maintenance, possession, tenancy papers and local follow up must all be managed from another country. When the NRI sells, the buyer may deduct TDS at non resident rates unless the lower tax order or process is followed. The sale proceeds may come into NRO. Repatriation may need tax compliance, bank documents and the applicable FEMA route. Finding a buyer, negotiating from abroad, collecting papers, clearing dues and closing the sale can take months.

Isolate. Insurance does not replace property. It answers a different weakness in the property plan. Property may create value, but it may not create timely liquidity. A family cannot pay hospital bills, education fees, debt pressure or living expenses with a flat unless someone can sell it, rent it, mortgage it, transfer it or manage it properly. A properly documented policy can create a defined claim amount without forcing the family to search for title papers, deal with tenants, negotiate with brokers, accept a distress price or discover tax and repatriation rules after the emergency has already arrived.

Anchor. If the client chooses property, the file should still carry title papers, source of funds, rent records, tenant TDS records, tax filings, loan papers, nomination or succession notes, will reference and expected exit route. If the client chooses insurance, the file should carry the policy papers, premium source trail, nominee details, claim route and family instructions. The advisor's job is not to insult property. It is to prevent the family from mistaking an asset for available money.

The informed answer: "Property has a real place, especially where India remains emotionally and practically important. But property is slow money. It needs a buyer, clean title, tenant compliance, tax handling, maintenance, sale timing and repatriation paperwork. Insurance is readiness money. It gives your family a defined liquidity route if something happens to you, so they are not forced to sell a flat in distress or learn property compliance during a crisis.

Property may build wealth. Insurance protects the family's time, dignity and choices. In a strong NRI plan, they are not rivals. They do different jobs."

16. "Global products are better. Why Indian insurance?"

He has seen international plans and assumes global means superior. There is a quiet status question inside the financial question.

The instant answer: "Indian products are always best." A loyalty claim is not an argument.

The same enquiry, worked through The NRI INDIA Mantra™:

Define. Global products may suit global goals. If the need is foreign currency retirement, children's education abroad, overseas estate planning or a goal that will be spent outside India, the foreign product universe may deserve proper review. Indian insurance earns its place when the responsibility is India linked: parents in India, spouse or children who may need India side access, rupee needs, claim servicing in India, planned return, Indian estate liquidity or dependants living in India.

Navigate. The route must be separated from the label. A domestic Indian policy, a foreign currency policy issued through a permitted Indian insurance route, and an IFSC product are not the same thing. Currency, regulator, issuer, claim process, tax treatment, account route and family usability must each be read separately.

Isolate. Global is not automatically better. Indian is not automatically better. The better product is the one that fits the place where the responsibility lives. A foreign product may look elegant on a statement, but if the family problem is in India, the advisor must ask whether the money can reach the family, in the right currency, through the right process, at the right time.

The informed answer: "Global products may be right for global goals. Indian insurance earns its place where the responsibility is India linked, family here, claim access here, rupee liquidity here, a planned return here, or estate continuity here. If what attracts you is foreign currency, we should examine the domestic Indian insurer route and the GIFT IFSC route separately through the proper process. The question is not Indian versus global. The question is where the risk sits, where the family will need money, and which route will serve them cleanly."

17. "I can get India exposure through an overseas fund. Why come directly to India?"

He is not wrong. An overseas platform may give him India exposure without Indian onboarding friction. What he cannot yet name is the difference between exposure and access.

The instant answer: "Direct India is always better." Too dismissive.

The same enquiry, worked through The NRI INDIA Mantra™:

Define. An overseas India fund may be a fair way to participate in India's market story. It may sit comfortably inside the client's foreign brokerage account, foreign tax system and foreign currency balance sheet. For pure portfolio exposure, that question may belong to an appropriately authorised investment professional.

Navigate. Direct India is different. It creates an India side financial arrangement. Money may enter Indian accounts, Indian products, Indian property, Indian insurance, Indian deposits or IFSC channels. That brings route, KYC, tax, repatriation, nomination, transmission and family access into the decision.

Isolate. Exposure is not access. A fund may give market participation. It does not automatically give India side family liquidity, domestic banking usability, a claim process in India, rupee support for dependants, property linked planning or succession readiness around Indian responsibilities.

The informed answer: "An overseas India fund may be a good way to get market exposure to India. But exposure and access are not the same. If you only want portfolio participation, that is an investment allocation question. If you need India side liquidity, family usability, rupee support, claim access, succession readiness or a route connected to Indian responsibilities, direct India may have a different role. First tell me what problem you are solving: exposure to India, or an India ready financial arrangement."

D. Tax, Treaty and Foreign Reporting

18. "Is the maturity tax-free?"

This is one of the most dangerous small questions in NRI advisory. Twenty years of premium, product design, tax law, residence change and family expectation are folded into four words.

The instant answer: "Yes, fully tax free." Comforting, and often reckless.

The same enquiry, worked through The NRI INDIA Mantra™:

Identify. First identify the policyholder, life assured, payee, country of residence, tax year, product type and year of receipt. A maturity question is not answered from the brochure. It is answered from facts.

Isolate. India must be answered first, and India is not the world. The Indian life insurance exclusion may apply only if the conditions under the law applicable to that year are satisfied. Issue date, premium history, sum assured relationship, product type, ULIP or non ULIP classification, aggregate premium thresholds, multiple policy aggregation and death versus maturity treatment must be checked. If the receipt is chargeable in India and paid to a non resident, withholding may also need review.

The foreign country is a separate system. It may classify, tax, defer, exempt or require disclosure differently. An Indian exemption is an Indian answer. It is not a passport that travels automatically.

Anchor. The file should hold the policy schedule, issue date, premium history, sum assured, maturity statement, payment trail, TDS position and Indian tax note. The foreign country position must be confirmed separately.

The informed answer: "In India, it may be exempt if the policy satisfies the applicable conditions. But I will not call it tax free until I check the policy type, issue date, premium history, sum assured, thresholds, aggregation and maturity papers. And I will not call it tax free in your country of residence. India answers Indian tax. Your country of residence must be checked separately."

19. "Will the DTAA make it tax-free?"

He has heard DTAA used like a magic word. He wants the treaty to do what domestic law may not do.

The instant answer: "The DTAA will take care of it." That is not how treaties work.

The same enquiry, worked through The NRI INDIA Mantra™:

Isolate. A treaty does not erase tax automatically. It may allocate taxing rights, reduce withholding in defined cases, or support credit relief where both countries tax the same income. It does not export India's domestic exemption into another country's tax law.

Define. The income character must be identified first. Interest, dividend, pension, annuity, capital gain, insurance receipt, salary, rent and other income may not sit in the same treaty article. A treaty is applied article by article, not by slogan.

Anchor. Where treaty relief is claimed, the file must hold the Tax Residency Certificate, prescribed declaration, PAN where required, beneficial ownership position, income characterisation, withholding record and supporting documents.

The informed answer: "A DTAA can help, but it does not make a receipt tax free by magic. It may reduce withholding or support credit relief depending on the article, the country and the facts. First we identify the income correctly. Then we apply the treaty with the right documents. We do not use the word DTAA as a shortcut for comfort."

20. "I live in Dubai, so there is no tax issue, right?"

He has moved to a low or no personal tax environment and wants that comfort confirmed. The advisor must not import unnecessary fear. He must also not create false safety.

The instant answer: "Yes, Dubai means no issue." Too easy.

The same enquiry, worked through The NRI INDIA Mantra™:

Isolate. UAE residence may make the foreign personal tax side simpler today than residence in countries such as the United States, Canada, the United Kingdom, Australia or New Zealand. That comfort should not be denied. But it does not remove Indian tax, FEMA, banking route, policy conditions, withholding, CRS records, source trail or future relocation risk.

Identify. The client's present country is only one clock. The advisor must also ask whether the client may move later, return to India, take another passport, shift tax residence, or hold the policy until a year when his status is different.

Anchor. Give comfort only for today's facts. Keep the file ready for tomorrow's movement.

The informed answer: "Your UAE residence may make the foreign personal tax side simpler today, and I will not import US or Canada concerns onto your file unnecessarily. But we still keep the Indian side clean: tax position, account route, premium trail, documentation and reporting records. Also, if you may later move to a higher tax country or return to India before maturity, we should not wait until that year to think about it."

21. "Will the US, UK or Canada tax this Indian policy?"

He wants foreign certainty on an Indian policy. The temptation is to extend Indian comfort across the border.

The instant answer: "No, it is tax free in India." A true statement about the wrong country.

The same enquiry, worked through The NRI INDIA Mantra™:

Isolate. The Indian exemption answers Indian law only. The United States, the United Kingdom, Canada and other countries may apply their own rules on classification, timing, cash value, surrender, maturity, death benefit, estate treatment, foreign asset disclosure and reporting. The Indian commercial label is useful evidence. It is not always conclusive abroad.

Define. Product type matters. A pure term policy, traditional endowment, money back policy, whole life policy, annuity, pension product or ULIP may not receive the same foreign treatment. A policy that looks simple in India may become a reporting or classification question abroad.

Anchor. The advisor prepares a clean Indian summary: policy type, owner, life assured, issue date, premium history, sum assured, surrender value, maturity value, account route and Indian tax position. The client takes that to the foreign tax advisor.

The informed answer: "India can tell us the Indian tax position. It cannot decide how your country of residence will classify the policy. The US, UK, Canada or any other country may look at cash value, surrender value, product type, reporting thresholds and estate rules differently. I will give you a clear Indian policy summary. Please have the foreign tax treatment confirmed locally before we assume the answer."

22. "Do I even need to disclose this policy abroad?"

He assumes no tax means no reporting. That is one of the most expensive misunderstandings in cross border life.

The instant answer: "If there is no tax, there is no disclosure." Wrong principle.

The same enquiry, worked through The NRI INDIA Mantra™:

Isolate. Tax and reporting are different obligations. A country may require disclosure even where no tax is payable. The trigger may depend on ownership, surrender value, cash value, account value, premium paid, beneficiary interest, foreign financial asset thresholds or local classification rules. FATCA and CRS may also bring the policy or account trail into the information system.

Define. The question is not only, "Is it taxable?" The sharper question is, "Is it reportable, by whom, in which country, for which year, and at what value?"

Anchor. The advisor does not answer foreign reporting law casually. He gives the client the Indian facts in a format the foreign tax advisor can use.

The informed answer: "Do not connect tax and disclosure too quickly. You may owe no tax and still have a reporting obligation abroad, depending on your country, thresholds, policy value and local rules. I will give you the policy details, Indian tax position and value information clearly. Before assuming silence is safe, please confirm the reporting position in your country of residence."

E. Return to India

23. "What if I return to India later?"

He sees a flight ticket. The advisor must see a migration of status. The instant answer: "Nothing changes." Kind, and wrong.

The same enquiry, worked through The NRI INDIA Mantra™:

Identify. Return changes status, but not on one clock. FEMA may read the person differently when he returns to India with an intention to stay for an uncertain period. Indian income tax residence is tested separately under the applicable day count and residence rules for the financial year. The country he leaves may also have exit, reporting or continuing residence rules.

Isolate. RNOR, where available under the applicable Indian income tax law, can be a valuable transition window. But it is not the same as being non resident forever. During that window, certain foreign income may remain outside Indian tax unless received in India or connected with a business controlled from India or profession set up in India. As full resident status approaches, foreign income, foreign assets and disclosures may come into deeper Indian scope.

Anchor. The advisor maps three stages: before return, transition year and full resident phase. Bank accounts, insurance, foreign investments, pensions, property, wills, nominations and reporting records should be reviewed before the return becomes operational.

The informed answer: "More changes than most people realise, but it can be managed if we plan before you return. FEMA residence, Indian tax residence and your foreign country position do not always move on the same day. There may be an RNOR window depending on your past stay pattern, but it is a transition window, not a permanent shelter. Before you fly, we should map your accounts, policies, foreign assets, pensions, income flows and reporting duties with a qualified CA."

24. "Can I continue my NRE account after I return?"

He is back in India, but emotionally he may not feel fully settled. The law does not work by mood.

The instant answer: "Yes, until you feel settled." Comfortable, and wrong.

The same enquiry, worked through The NRI INDIA Mantra™:

Identify. NRE is for a person resident outside India under FEMA. Once the person returns to India with the intention to stay for an uncertain period, the basis for holding the NRE account changes, even if the client still feels like an NRI in his mind.

Navigate. The NRE account should not continue by habit after the FEMA residence trigger is crossed. It should be redesignated as a resident account, or the funds may be moved to an RFC account where eligible. That preserves account discipline instead of forcing an old NRI label into a new resident life.

Isolate. Income tax residence does not decide NRE eligibility. FEMA answers the account question. Income tax answers the tax question. The Kaalchakra discipline is to synchronise the clocks before giving comfort.

The informed answer: "Once you return with the intention to stay, the NRE account should not simply continue because it is convenient. It should be redesignated, or the eligible balance should move to an RFC account where that route is available. We must not confuse your tax status with your FEMA account status. The bank account must match the legal clock that governs it."

25. "Should I surrender the policy before returning?"

He wants a clean slate before coming home. But clean may become costly.

The instant answer: "Yes, surrender before you return." Too mechanical.

The same enquiry, worked through The NRI INDIA Mantra™:

Define. What is he really seeking: liquidity, simplicity, tax efficiency, reduced reporting, relief from premium commitment, family protection or emotional closure? Surrender is only one possible answer, and often not the best one.

Isolate. The decision touches surrender value, loss of cover, Indian tax treatment, foreign tax treatment, residence timing, RNOR possibility, premium history, future reporting, family protection and whether the policy still has a useful role after return. A policy taken for family continuity should not be surrendered merely because the client is changing countries.

Anchor. Compare three options: continue, surrender before return, or surrender after return. Map the dates, tax year, residence year, value, cover need and documents before deciding.

The informed answer: "Do not surrender just to feel tidy. That may cost you value, cover and future family protection. Let us compare three options: continue, surrender before return, or surrender after return. The right answer depends on surrender value, tax treatment in both countries, your return year, RNOR possibility, reporting impact and whether your family still needs the protection."

F. Legacy, Claim and Family Access

26. "Is nomination enough?"

He wants to believe one form has protected his family. The form matters. But it is not the whole family plan.

The instant answer: "Yes, the nominee gets everything." Too simplistic.

The same enquiry, worked through The NRI INDIA Mantra™:

Identify. Who is the nominee: spouse, child, parent, sibling, minor, foreign citizen, OCI holder, resident abroad, second spouse or someone outside the immediate family? The legal and practical answer changes with the person.

Isolate. Nomination has legal force, especially where the law gives a stronger position to certain close family nominees. But nomination should not be treated as a complete estate plan. Succession law, will, beneficial entitlement, guardianship, MWPA, creditors, family disputes, second families, foreign residence and country of claim receipt can still matter.

Anchor. Align nomination, will, guardian details, beneficiary intention, bank route, claim documents and MWPA where suitable. The family file should say not only who is named, but why the structure was chosen.

The informed answer: "Nomination is important, but I would not treat it as the whole estate plan. The nominee position may be strong in certain close family cases, but we should still align it with your will, guardian details if minors are involved, bank route, claim documents and MWPA where protection for wife and children is intended. The claim route and the entitlement story should not fight each other later."

27. "Will insurance avoid inheritance disputes?"

He wants insurance to become the peace his family may otherwise not have.

The instant answer: "Yes, insurance avoids disputes." Too absolute.

The same enquiry, worked through The NRI INDIA Mantra™:

Define. Insurance can reduce friction because it creates a defined claim amount, a named claim route and a document-based process. But no product can correct an unclear family structure by itself.

Isolate. Disputes arise from outdated nominees, second marriages, minor children, informal separations, inherited assets, dependent parents, creditors, unclear wills, cross border heirs, personal law conflicts, missing documents and assets spread across countries. MWPA may strengthen protection for wife and children where suitable, but it is not a substitute for complete estate planning.

Anchor. The file must connect the policy to the family structure. Nomination, MWPA, will, guardian details, beneficiary intention, claim route and bank details should not sit in separate drawers.

The informed answer: "Insurance can reduce inheritance friction, but only if it is structured properly. A clear nomination helps the claim move. A will clarifies the estate. MWPA may protect the proceeds for wife and children where suitable. But the product alone does not create peace. Peace comes when the product, papers, family intention and legal structure tell the same story."

28. "Will my children abroad get the claim smoothly?"

He is imagining his family dealing with an Indian process on the hardest day of their lives.

The instant answer: "Yes, claim settlement is easy." Only if it is prepared.

The same enquiry, worked through The NRI INDIA Mantra™:

Identify. Are the children adults or minors? Indian citizens, OCI holders or foreign citizens? Where do they live? Who will sign? Who will act for a minor? Who will coordinate from India if documents are needed here?

Navigate. The claim is not only a form. It is a money route. Where should the money be credited: Indian account, NRO, NRE where permitted, resident account of a claimant, foreign account through remittance, or another route permitted by the process? The answer depends on claimant status, account eligibility, insurer process, bank documentation and FEMA rules.

Anchor. Build the claim ready file now: policy copies, nominee details, identity proof, address proof, citizenship or OCI documents where relevant, bank details, guardian papers, will reference, death claim process, advisor contact, insurer contact and simple family instructions.

The informed answer: "We make it smooth by preparing it before the family needs it. I need to know whether your children are adults or minors, where they live, what citizenship they hold, who can sign, and which bank route the claim should follow. The best claim process is not the one we explain after death. It is the one your family can follow because the file already speaks."

29. "Can my foreign-citizen spouse be the nominee?"

He wants to know whether the person closest to him will be recognised.

The instant answer: "Yes, no problem." Correct direction, but too thin.

The same enquiry, worked through The NRI INDIA Mantra™:

Identify. A foreign citizen spouse can generally be named as nominee, subject to the insurer's documents, KYC and process. Her citizenship is not the real difficulty. The real question is whether the claim, entitlement, tax, bank route and family file are ready for a cross border spouse.

Isolate. Her protection should not stop at the nomination form. The nomination should align with the will, marriage documents, tax residence, address proof, bank route, claim documents, possible remittance needs and any foreign country consequence. If the intention is to protect proceeds specifically for her and the children, MWPA may be examined through proper legal review.

Anchor. Keep her identity, address, citizenship, tax residence, bank details, marriage evidence, nominee record, will reference and claim instructions in the file.

The informed answer: "Yes, her foreign citizenship by itself should not be treated as the obstacle, subject to the insurer's documentation. But we should not stop at naming her. We should align the nomination with your will, marriage records, bank route, tax residence and claim documents. If the intention is to protect the proceeds for her and the children, MWPA should also be examined properly. The goal is not only to name her. The goal is to make sure the file can serve her."

30. "Will my family even know what to do if something happens to me?"

The simplest question in the chapter, and perhaps the most important. There is no jargon in it at all.

The instant answer: "The insurer will guide them." That hands away the one duty the advisor is best placed to discharge.

The same enquiry, worked through The NRI INDIA Mantra™:

Anchor. The whole answer is the family ready file. Not a pile of documents. A usable map. The file should tell the family what exists, who to contact, which document to use, which bank route to follow, what not to assume, and where professional help is needed.

The file should hold policy details, nominee records, KYC, citizenship and residence details, premium source trail, account route, claim forms, insurer contact, advisor contact, will reference, guardian information where relevant, tax records, repatriation notes and simple instructions written for the family, not for the advisor.

Isolate. The family must not be left to discover the difference between nominee and heir, NRE and NRO, claim and remittance, Indian tax and foreign tax, or policy record and succession record on the worst day of their lives.

The informed answer: "Let us make sure they know. We will build a family ready file with the policy details, nominee records, KYC, bank route, premium trail, claim documents, contacts, will reference, guardian details where relevant, tax notes and simple instructions. The best claim process is the one your family can follow calmly when you are not sitting beside them."

The instant answer trusts the system to carry the family. The informed answer gives the family a map.

The Point of the Thirty

These are not thirty answers.

They are thirty doors.

Behind every one of them is the same discipline:

Do not answer from memory.

Do not answer from the brochure.

Do not answer from one law when five systems are in the room.

Do not answer from confidence when the documents are missing.

Apply INDIA.

Identify the person.

Navigate the money route.

Define the purpose.

Isolate the systems.

Anchor the assurance.

That is how an advisor moves from being responsive to being reliable.

And reliability is where serious NRI advisory begins.

10.13 THE DISCIPLINE OF TRUST

The NRI client carries more than a passport.

He carries unfinished decisions.

Where will I finally retire?

Will my children understand India?

Will my parents be secure?

Will my spouse know what to do if I am not around?

Will my money move cleanly when it is needed?

Will two countries ask two different questions about the same policy, asset or account?

Will the advice I receive today survive the facts of tomorrow?

These questions almost never arrive in formal language.

They arrive as small lines on a phone call, late in the evening, with snow settling on parked cars somewhere far from home.

"Tax-free, right?"

"Repatriable, right?"

"Nominee will get it, right?"

"If I come back, everything becomes simple, right?"

An ordinary advisor hears a question.

A serious advisor hears the weight behind it.

Because in NRI advisory, the client is rarely asking only what the words appear to ask. He is asking whether India will remain orderly when he is not physically present to explain himself. He is asking whether his family, his money, his documents and his future will stand together when two systems, two clocks and two sets of rules begin reading the same life differently.

That is why this work cannot be reduced to product knowledge.

Product knowledge tells the advisor what can be offered.

Cross-border discipline tells him what must be checked before it is offered.

The Compliance Highway Rule™ gave the advisor the map.

The NRI Kaalchakra™ gave him the timing lens.

The NRI INDIA Mantra™ gives him the operating discipline.

Identify the Person.

Navigate the Money Route.

Define the Purpose.

Isolate the Systems.

Anchor the Assurance.

Before you advise an NRI on India, apply INDIA.

For an individual advisor, this is the difference between sounding informed and becoming dependable.

For an institution, this is the difference between having an NRI business and building NRI advisory capability.

That difference matters.

Because NRI trust does not break only when a product fails. It breaks when a family discovers that the account route was not understood, the foreign question was never asked, the tax answer was too casually given, the nominee was mistaken for a successor, the return to India was treated as simple, or the file cannot explain what the advisor once promised.

A quick answer can win a conversation.

A disciplined answer can protect a family, a claim, a remittance, a tax position, a relationship, a trainer's curriculum, a compliance desk and an institution's reputation.

That is the standard this book has been building towards.

Not louder selling.

Not larger promises.

Not the confidence of knowing one product deeply.

The discipline of reading the person, the papers, the route, the timing, the tax, the family, the foreign overlay and the evidence—before comfort is given.

This is where serious NRI advisory begins.

And this is where credibility stops being a line in an advisor's introduction and becomes something far stronger.

A standard.

A culture.

A habit that the client can feel, the family can rely on, the institution can train, and the market can trust.

End of Chapter 10

ACKNOWLEDGEMENTS

A book may carry one author's name, but it is rarely written from one person's life alone.

This book has come from more than two decades of conversations, across countries, time zones, professions, families and stages of life. I have had the privilege of speaking to NRIs and Indian-origin families from more than twenty-five countries: business owners, doctors, technology leaders, consultants, seafarers, senior executives, fund professionals, entrepreneurs, investors, returning Indians and families who have built remarkable lives far away from India.

Many of them are stalwarts in their own fields. They lead teams, build businesses, manage capital, serve institutions, create employment, solve difficult problems and carry the Indian name with quiet strength across the world.

Every such conversation has taught me something.

Sometimes I learnt about money. Sometimes about law. Sometimes about tax, remittance, return, inheritance or documentation. But very often, I learnt something deeper: how Indians carry India even after building successful lives elsewhere.

That has been one of the greatest privileges of my professional journey.

To be associated with the NRI community is to witness India in motion. India in boardrooms. India in clinics. India on ships. India in technology companies. India in family businesses. India in global finance. India in homes where children may speak a different accent but still hear stories of a village, a city, a festival, a parent, a house, a responsibility waiting back home.

This book owes a great deal to that community.

I am deeply grateful to every NRI, returning Indian and Indian-origin family who trusted me with their questions. Some questions were technical. Some were emotional. Some were urgent. Some were postponed for years. But each one helped me understand the NRI life better, not as a market, not as a segment, but as a human journey across countries, duties, laws, memories and unfinished decisions.

I am equally grateful to my clients, whose trust has allowed me to see real situations closely and responsibly. Their confidence gave me the opportunity to understand not only what the law says, but how the law enters a family's life, a bank file, a return-to-India plan, a succession concern, an investment decision or a late-night call from another time zone.

No confidential client information has been used in this book. But the learning that comes from years of trust has shaped its spirit.

I place on record my deep gratitude to **The Institute of Chartered Accountants of India**. ICAI did not merely give me a professional qualification. It gave me a way of thinking. It taught discipline, independence, documentation, professional scepticism, responsibility and respect for public trust. The values that ICAI inculcates in professionals rank among the finest traditions of professional discipline anywhere in the world. Whatever professional care this book carries, it owes much to that foundation.

I am also grateful to the financial institutions, insurance companies, banks, fund platforms, GIFT IFSC focused funds, fintech companies, training teams, compliance professionals and industry leaders with whom I have interacted over the years. These conversations helped me see the institutional side of NRI advisory. They showed me that the NRI opportunity is large, but the responsibility is larger.

NRI business cannot be built only on enthusiasm. It cannot be built only on product knowledge. It needs structure, documentation, professional boundaries and a common language. Many of the ideas in this book became sharper because of these industry interactions.

A special acknowledgement is due to **HDFC Life** for the opportunity to train more than 200 senior NRI-facing professionals as part of the NRI Wealth Specialist learning journey. Those training rooms strengthened my belief that advisors are willing to learn deeply when they are given the right framework. They also confirmed that NRI advisory must move beyond scattered rules and comfort sentences. It needs disciplined thinking.

In that journey, one person deserves a very special mention: **Kapil Pratap Singh**.

Kapil Singh, a seasoned life insurance professional and corporate sales trainer, was my co-trainer during the HDFC Life training sessions. My interactions with him opened a new window for me into the world of teaching, training and structured communication for financial professionals. He helped me understand how knowledge must travel from the expert's mind to the advisor's field reality.

Most importantly, the idea of putting this learning into the form of a book came from him.

He did not merely suggest it once and move on. He pushed me, reminded me, challenged me and encouraged me until the idea became a manuscript. Sometimes he did this as a professional colleague. Sometimes as a friend. Sometimes as an elder brother. Sometimes simply as a person who believed that this work should reach more people.

Without his encouragement, persistence and emotional support, this book may have remained only a set of training notes, conversations and unfinished thoughts. I am deeply grateful to him for seeing the book before I had fully seen it myself.

I am grateful to the professionals and teams working around GIFT City and GIFT IFSC. The evolution of GIFT IFSC is one of the most significant developments in India's cross-border financial architecture. It has opened a new way to think about India, not only as a domestic market, but as an international financial gateway within India. My conversations with fund professionals, fintech founders and GIFT oriented platforms helped me understand this shift with greater clarity.

In this context, I would like to specially thank **Ankur Choudhary**, CEO and co-founder of Belong. His inputs and discussions were particularly helpful while shaping the GIFT City chapter. Ankur has been closely engaged with the emerging NRI investment and GIFT City ecosystem, and his perspective helped me appreciate how new-age fintech platforms are trying to simplify access, understanding and execution for NRIs in a space that is still evolving.

I am also grateful to **CA Anjani Ladia**, Chairman and Founding Chairman of the ICAI Luxembourg Chapter, who has been a mentor and a steady source of professional encouragement in my journey. His support, guidance and faith have meant a great deal to me. In a profession where one often learns through seniors, colleagues and well-wishers, I have been fortunate to receive his advice and goodwill over the years.

A very special mention must be made of **Shailesh Gadre**. From the early stages of my career, he has been associated with me professionally in one way or another. More importantly, he has been a guide, sounding board and elder-brother figure. At different turning points, his direction, advice and steady presence helped me think more clearly. Some people support you by giving answers. Some support you by helping you ask better questions. I am grateful to him for both.

I thank my colleagues, professional friends, Chartered Accountant peers, lawyers, tax professionals, FEMA and banking professionals, insurance professionals, trainers, researchers and well-wishers who have contributed directly or indirectly to my understanding of this subject. Cross-border work teaches humility very quickly. No one professional can know everything. The better professional learns to separate systems, respect boundaries and bring the right person into the room at the right time.

To my friends, thank you for your encouragement during the long process of writing this book. A manuscript does not get written only in writing hours. It follows the author everywhere, into weekends, travel, family time, late nights, early mornings and ordinary conversations. Your support made that journey lighter.

To my parents, thank you for the values, discipline and sense of responsibility that shaped me long before this book was imagined. Whatever professional work I do carries something of the foundation you gave me.

To my wonderful wife, thank you for being a constant source of inspiration, strength and support throughout this journey. For more than a year, this book travelled with us through writing, rewriting, thinking, doubting and refining. A book takes space: mental space, emotional space and family space. You gave me that space with patience, love and grace.

To my beautiful children, thank you for being the joy that brings me back from every intense working day. You may not fully know what this book demanded, but your presence gave me the energy to complete it.

I must also lovingly acknowledge my dear sister, my supportive brother-in-law, and my wonderful nephew and niece, whose own NRI and OCI journey has allowed me to see cross-border life from very close quarters. Through them, I have seen not only the financial questions, but also the emotional rollercoaster of an NRI family: distance, duties, return conversations, children growing across cultures, and the constant effort to remain connected with India. Their experiences, affection and support have quietly enriched this book.

Finally, to the reader, whether you are an advisor, trainer, compliance professional, institutional leader or NRI, thank you for entering this book seriously.

This book has been written with respect: respect for the NRI, respect for the advisor, respect for the law and respect for India's growing place in the world.

If it helps even one advisor pause before giving a casual answer, ask a better question, separate the systems, document the facts and guide an NRI family with greater responsibility, the effort behind these pages will have served its purpose.

ABOUT THE AUTHOR

CA **Sagar Soman** is a Chartered Accountant with more than two decades of experience in NRI and HNI personal finance, NRI taxation, cross border wealth structuring, FEMA, DTAA, repatriation, return to India planning, GIFT IFSC and India linked wealth decisions for global Indians.

Having lived outside India himself, he brings to his work a practical understanding of the NRI life from both sides of the table: first as a person carrying India from abroad, and later as a professional helping NRIs, OCIs, returning Indians and Indian origin families navigate India related financial, tax and regulatory decisions.

Over his professional journey, Sagar has interacted with NRIs, advisors, institutions and professional communities across more than twenty five countries. His work covers Indian tax residential status, FEMA residential status, NRE, NRO and FCNR banking, cross border wealth, repatriation of Indian assets, taxation of Indian income, DTAA relief, foreign tax credit awareness, Indian property exits, life insurance taxation, return to India transitions, GIFT IFSC opportunities, documentation discipline and succession related awareness for cross border families.

Sagar is known for explaining complex NRI issues in plain English, without making the subject casual. His teaching style combines first principles, practical examples, Indian context and field level clarity. This has made his work useful for NRI families as well as financial advisors, relationship managers, training teams, fintech platforms, compliance professionals and institutions serving the NRI community.

He has conducted NRI focused learning initiatives for financial professionals, institutions and professional forums. A significant part of this work includes course designing and training more than 200 senior NRI facing professionals at HDFC Life as part of the NRI Wealth Specialist learning journey.

His professional views and educational work have appeared across mainstream financial media, webinars, professional forums and NRI education platforms. He has been quoted in publications such as Mint & Financial Express on return to India, FEMA, banking, taxation and NRI compliance issues. He has also participated in NRI taxation and compliance education initiatives with platforms such as Groww, Belong, Desi Return and professional bodies including the International Chapters of ICAI. His work has further extended to fintech led NRI education and compliance resources, including advisory and content support for NRI focused platforms such as Belong.

Sagar's work also includes backend research, advisory inputs and educational structuring for fintech companies, NRI platforms and India linked financial services businesses that serve global Indians. This gives him a practical view of how NRI compliance, product access, onboarding, documentation, tax awareness and client education operate beyond individual advisory conversations.

In **What NRIs Are Not Told About India**, Sagar introduces three teaching frameworks created from his professional experience: **The Compliance Highway Rule™**, **The NRI Kaalchakra™** and **The NRI INDIA Mantra™**. These frameworks are designed to help advisors, institutions and serious NRI readers bring structure, timing discipline and responsible conduct into NRI financial conversations.

As a Chartered Accountant, Sagar's work is guided by professional independence, documentation discipline, regulatory respect and the values inculcated by The Institute of Chartered Accountants of India. He believes NRI advisory must be simple enough to understand, serious enough to respect the law, and structured enough to protect the client, the advisor and the institution.

What NRIs Are Not Told About India is his attempt to bring that discipline into one place for NRIs, advisors and institutions that want to understand India linked cross border decisions with greater clarity.

Connect

For institutional training, professional education, speaking engagements, media requests or select NRI advisory conversations, CA Sagar Soman may be contacted through:

Email: sagar@nrifinancetax.com

Phone: +91 7350223366

Location: Nagpur, India

www.ingramcontent.com/pod-product-compliance
Lightning Source LLC
LaVergne TN
LVHW050927210926
848482LV00013B/558
9798905408717